The Legacy of Crimes and Crises

STUDIES IN POLITICAL TRANSITION

Edited by Klaus Bachmann

VOLUME 5

PETER LANG
EDITION

Klaus Bachmann / Dorota Heidrich (eds.)

The Legacy of Crimes and Crises

Transitional Justice, Domestic Change and the Role of the International Community

PETER LANG
EDITION

Bibliographic Information published by the Deutsche Nationalbibliothek
The Deutsche Nationalbibliothek lists this publication in the Deutsche Nationalbibliografie; detailed bibliographic data is available in the internet at http://dnb.d-nb.de.

Library of Congress Cataloging-in-Publication Data
Names: Bachmann, Klaus, 1963- editor. | Heidrich, Dorota, 1977- editor.
Title: The legacy of crimes and crises : transitional justice, domestic change and the role of the international community / Klaus Bachmann, Dorota Heidrich (eds.).
Description: Frankfurt am Main ; New York Peter Lang GmbH, 2016. | Series: Studies in political transition ; volume 5 | Includes bibliographical references.
Identifiers: LCCN 2015036007 | ISBN 9783631661727
Subjects: LCSH: International criminal law. | Transitional justice. | International courts. | International crimes.
Classification: LCC KZ7000 .L444 2016 | DDC 340/.115--dc23 LC record available at http://lccn.loc.gov/2015036007

The editors are grateful to the Polish National Research Center (Narodowe Centrum Nauki), which sponsored the research program "International Criminal Tribunals as Actors of Domestic Change" (grant no. 2012/06/A/HS5/00249, granted to SWPS University of Social Sciences and Humanities), in whose framework this book was published. They also express their gratitude to the Institute of International Relations of the University of Warsaw and the Ignacy Jan Paderewski Polish Institute of Diplomacy for having provided resources to organize the conference in commemoration of the 20th anniversary of genocide in Rwanda titled *Dealing with the legacy of crimes and crises – transitional justice, reconciliation and the challenges for the international community* (Warsaw, May 8, 2013) during which part of the contributions to the volume were presented in their initial version

Reviewer: Prof. Dr. hab. Marian Edward Haliżak, University of Warsaw

Cover photo courtesy of Klaus Bachmann.

ISSN 2191-3307
ISBN 978-3-631-66172-7 (Print)
E-ISBN 978-3-653-05805-5 (E-Book)
DOI 10.3726/978-3-653-05805-5

Peter Lang Edition is an Imprint of Peter Lang GmbH.

Peter Lang – Frankfurt am Main · Bern · Bruxelles · New York ·
Oxford · Warszawa · Wien

www.peterlang.com

Table of contents

List of tables and graphs

List of abbreviations

AIETD	All-Inclusive Intra-East Timor Dialogue
ANC	African National Congress (South Africa)
ASP	Assembly of State Parties (International Criminal Court)
AU	African Union
C/OSCE	Conference/Organization for Security and Cooperation in Europe
CAR	Central African Republic
CAVR	Comissão de Acolhimento, Verdade e Reconciliação (East Timor)
CIPEV	Commission of Inquiry into Post Election Violence (Kenya)
CNCDH	La Commission nationale consultative des droits de l'homme (France)
CNDP	Conseil national pour la défense du peuple (Democratic Republic of Congo)
CNDP-FDD	National Council for the Defence of Democracy-Forces for the Defence of Democracy (Burundi)
CORD	Coalition for Reforms and Democracy (Kenya)
CSVR	Centre for the Study of Violence and Reconciliation (South Africa)
CTF	Commission of Truth and Friendship (East Timor)
DDR	disarmament, demobilization, reintegration
DPP	Directorate of Public Prosecutions (Uganda)
DRC	Democratic Republic of Congo
ECOSOC	Economic and Social Council (United Nations)
EDPRS2	Second Economic Development and Poverty Reduction Strategy
EU	European Union
EULEX	European Union's Rule of Law Mission in Kosovo
FARDC	Forces Armées de la République Démocratique du Congo
FDLR	Forces démocratiques de libération du Rwanda
FORD-Kenya	Forum for the Restoration of Democracy-Kenya
FRETILIN	Frente Revolucionária de Timor-Leste Independente
FRPI	Forces de résistance patriotique pour l'Ituri (Democratic Republic of Congo)

FRY	Federal Republic of Yugoslavia (see also: SRJ)
GCG	Grand Coalition Government (Kenya)
GoU	Government of Uganda
HRC	Human Rights Council (of the United Nations)
HSM	Holy Spirit Movement (Uganda)
ICC	International Criminal Court
ICCPR	International Covenant on Civil and Political Rights
ICD	International Crimes Division of the Ugandan High Court
ICESCR	International Covenant on Economic, Social and Cultural Rights
ICISS	International Commission on Intervention and State Sovereignty
ICJ	International Court of Justice (United Nations)
ICRC	International Committee of the Red Cross
ICT(s)	international criminal tribunal(s)
ICTR	International Criminal Tribunal for Rwanda
ICTY	International Criminal Tribunal for the Former Yugoslavia
IDPs	internally displaced persons
IFP	Inkatha Freedom Party (South Africa)
IJR	Institute for Justice and Reconciliation (South Africa)
IRIN	Integrated Regional Information Networks
ISIS	Islamic State of Iraq and Sham
JCE	Joint Criminal Enterprise
JLOS	Justice Law and Order Sector (Uganda)
JNA	Jugoslavenska narodna armija (see also: YPA)
KFOR	Kosovo Force
KLA	Kosovo Liberation Army
KNDR	Kenya National Dialogue and Reconciliation
KWECC	Kosovo War and Ethnic Crimes Court
LRA	Lords Resistance Army
M 23	March 23 Movement (Democratic Republic of Congo)
MDGs	Millennium Development Goals
MICT	Mechanism for International Criminal Tribunals
MLC	Mouvement de libération congolais
MONUC	Mission de l'Organisation des Nations Unies en République Démocratique du Congo (until 2010)
MONUSCO	Mission de l'Organisation des Nations Unies en République Démocratique du Congo

MSF	Médecins sans frontières
NATO	North Atlantic Treaty Organization
NCTR	National Council of Timorese Resistance
NGOs	non-governmental organizations
NRA/M	National Resistance Army/Movement (Uganda)
NURC	National Unity and Reconciliation Commission (Rwanda)
OCHA/UN OCHA	United Nations Office for the Coordination of Humanitarian Affairs
ODM	Orange Democratic Movement (Kenya)
OSAPG	Office of the Special Advisor on the Prevention of Genocide (United Nations)
OTP ICC	Office of the Prosecutor of the International Criminal Court
PALIPEHUTU-FLN	Party for the Liberation of the Hutu People-Forces for National Liberation (Burundi)
PEV	post-election violence (Kenya)
PNU	Party of National Unity (Kenya)
R2P	Responsibility to Protect
RCD	Rassemblement Congolais pour la Démocratie
RNC	Rwanda National Congress
RPF	Rwandan Patriotic Front
SA	South Africa
SACP	South African Communist Party
SAO SBWA	Srpska autonomna oblast Slavonia, Baranja and Western Srem
SFRY	Socialist Federal Republic of Yugoslavia
SRJ	Savezna Republika Jugoslavija (see also: FRY)
SRSG	Special Representative of the Secretary-General (United Nations)
TJRC	Truth, Justice and Reconciliation Commission (Kenya)
TNA	The National Alliance Party (Kenya)
TO	Teritorijalna obrana (Territorial Defence)
TRC(s)	truth and reconciliation commission(s), specifically also the South African Truth and Reconciliation Commission
UK	United Kingdom
UN	United Nations
UNCHR	United Nations Commission on Human Rights
UNEPS	United Nations Emergency Peace Service

UNICEF	United Nations Children's Fund
UNLA	Uganda National Liberation Army
UNMIK	United Nations Mission in Kosovo
UNSC	United Nations Security Council
UNTAET	United Nations Transitional Administration in East Timor
UPDA	Uganda People's Democratic Army
UPDF	Ugandan People's Defence Force
URP	United Republican Party of Kenya
US	United States of America
USAID	United States Agency for International Development
YPA	Yugoslav People's Army (see also: JNA)

Introduction

In 2011 protesters, outraged by the suicide of a petty trader in Tunis, took to the streets of Tunisia and ousted Zine al-Abidine Ben Ali, who had run the country as a dictator. The protests opened the doors to the first and so far only success of the Arab Spring. After the formation of several interim governments and a number of violent incidents and political assassinations, the country held successful and peaceful elections, approved a new constitution and elected a president. By then, it had already come under the pressure of various groups, which lobbied for contradicting requests and demands. There were victims' organizations, which, as usual after a transition, demanded justice, understood as retribution against the perpetrators of past Human Rights abuses and compensation for themselves. There were groups urging for bringing to justice policemen, since the police were regarded as instrumental in carrying out the repressions against protesters prior to Zine al-Abidine Ben Ali's escape to Saudi Arabia. But there were also groups that deplored the dire state of public security under the conditions of a disorganized, widely despised and disoriented police force. Political parties linked to the (mostly exiled) opposition against Ben Ali urged for the screening and vetting of public employees, in order to cut off elite bonds between the *ancien regime* and the new order.

Looking for closer ties with Western democracies, the Tunisian government was encouraged by the European Union to ratify the Rome Statute of the International Criminal Court (ICC) (which it has done) and thus to join the global "fight against impunity", which, after the end of the cold war, had led to creation of the UN *ad hoc* tribunals and a number of internationalized jurisdictions, as well as the ICC itself. The calls for "punishing perpetrators" in Tunisia seemed to prevail, although the main culprit – Zine al-Abidine Ben Ali himself – was beyond their reach, because Saudi Arabia, never having ratified the Rome Statute, refused to extradite him. The further events of the Arab Spring raised doubts about the universal applicability of the fight against impunity and its potential consequences for a country like Tunisia.

In Libya, popular protests similar to the ones in Tunisia have not led to democratization, but to a cruel and protracted civil war, the intervention of foreign military forces (officially undertaken in order to protect civilians, but de facto with the aim of supporting the armed opposition against Muhammar Gaddafi and to overthrow him) and the division of the country among competing and fiercely fighting rival militias. At a relatively early stage of the conflict, the United Nation

Security Council (UNSC) decided to refer the situation in Libya to the ICC, which in consequence issued arrest warrants for several members of the Libyan leadership, including Muhammar Gaddafi. Soon afterwards, United States (US) diplomats found out that by supporting the ICC referral, they had closed a back door to transition, which would have enabled Gaddafi and his entourage to escape and therefore facilitate a peaceful transition of power. After the ICC referral, Gaddafi was forced to fight to the bitter end. Common criticism among the Arab League and the African Union states towards Gaddafi's policies that had been of primary importance for the foreign intervention authorized by UNSC resolution 1973 (2011) was paramount to the lack of asylum offers for the authoritarian Libyan leader. US attempts to find an acceptable shelter for Gaddafi failed, and, as we know, Gaddafi did decide to continue fighting, increasing the number of casualties, and devastating his country.[1] None of the three Libyan nationals whose cases were referred to the ICC have been surrendered to The Hague.[2] In July 2015, a court in Tripoli ruled against thirty former members of the Gaddafi regime, nine of whom, including Saif Al Islam Gaddafi and Adbullah Al Senussi (with whose cases the ICC has dealt), were sentenced to death by firing squad.[3]

UNSC ICC referral, thought of as a measure "to hold to account those responsible for attacks, including by forces under their control, on civilians"[4], spurred doubts among the ICC critics and hopes for the proponents of the idea of universal jurisdiction. The former ones advocated for holding the trials on national soil. But, as the former Justice Minister of Libya Salah al-Marghani (who still held his post when the trial was initiated) has put it after the verdict of the Tripoli court

---

1 Agnieszka Bieńczyk-Missala's and Dorota Heidrich's chapters in this book deal with the legal consequences of the events in Libya and their importance for the concept of "Responsibility to Protect" (R2P) and crime prevention at the UN.

2 The case against Muammar Gaddafi was formally terminated by the Court due to the death of the accused; the case against Abdullah Al-Senussi was declared "inadmissible before the ICC as it was currently subject to domestic proceedings conducted by the Libyan competent authorities and that Libya [was] willing and able genuinely to carry out such investigation" (See: 'Situation in Libya'. http://www.icc-cpi.int/en_menus/icc/situations%20and%20cases/Pages/situations%20and%20cases.aspx). The third case against Saif Al Islam Gaddafi, though challenged by Libyan government, is still pending, however Tripoli has been refusing to surrender the accused to the custody of the Court, claiming that the trial against him before national court makes the ICC's proceedings inadmissible.

3 'Libya death sentences cast long shadow over rule of law'. *BBC News*, online at: http://www.bbc.com/news/world-africa-33855860 (accessed August 12, 2015).

4 UNSC Resolution 1970 (2011), S/RES/1970 (2011).

was announced, the home trial was a "miscarriage of justice".[5] Not surprisingly, external observers have been critical of the trial, too. One of the defence lawyers in the trial has claimed that "the verdicts had been discussed and 'decided' on a senior level between two parliamentarians and a judicial official in Tripoli days before they had been made public."[6] Even though such allegations are impossible to prove, the way justice is conducted in Libya leaves serious doubts as to the fairness of such trials (no witnesses heard in front of the judges, no evidence discussed or presented to the court, defence lawyers faced with threats and obstacles in contacting their clients in detention). It seems that the judicial process has been highly politicized and may be an example of what Alexandra Barahona de Brito and Laurence Whitehead have called "a lesson of legalized revenge."[7] Despite the hopes for fair judicial proceedings, it is not particularly surprising that a politically unstable country with no post-conflict and post-gross Human Rights violations recovery mechanisms in place whatsoever, and – most importantly – torn apart by a brutal civil war, has not been able to conduct prosecutions and trials that would bring about justice, not vengeance.

The Libyan case shows that one of the mechanisms of transitional justice, namely criminal prosecutions for past Human Rights violations (whether at the domestic, foreign/transnational or international level[8]) against individuals, is by no means an easy task, just as transitional justice, also discussed in this volume, is not. It is difficult to prove beyond reasonable doubts (even though such voices are not rare[9]) that the Libyan experience prevented the UNSC from referring the

5 'Libya death sentences cast long shadow over rule of law', *BBC News,* online at: http://www.bbc.com/news/world-africa-33855860 (accessed August 12, 2015).

6 Ibid.

7 Barahona de Brito, A. and Whitehead, L. (2012). 'Transitional justice: Reframing the Debate.' In: Popovski, V. and Serrano, M. (eds) (2012). *Transitional Justice in Latin America and Eastern Europe.* New York: United Nations University Press, p. 446.

8 We are referring here to the differentiation made by Kathryn Sikkink: "domestic level involves trials for individual criminal accountability conducted in a single country for Human Rights abuses committed in *that* country. The foreign or transnational level has included trials conducted in a single country for Human Rights abuses committed in another country (…)". International trials are held before international jurisdictions. Sikkink, K. (2012). 'Models of accountability and effectiveness of transitional justice'. In: Popovski, V.; Serrano, M. (eds) (2012). *After Opression. Transitional Justice in Latin America and Eastern Europe.* New York: United Nations University Press, pp. 19–38.

9 Ulrich, S. (2013). 'Strafrechtler fordern Prozess gegen Assad in Den Haag'. *Süddeutsche Zeitung*, online at: http://www.sueddeutsche.de/politik/buergerkrieg-in-syrien-strafrechtler-wollen-assad-in-den-haag-den-prozess-machen-1.1759936

atrocities of the conflict in Syria to the ICC, however "the Libyan argument" has been appearing in Council debates on the situation in Syria. National prosecutions are a difficult task, as could be seen in post-Saddam Iraq and post-Mubarak Egypt. National tribunals were established in both countries to judge members of the former regime, but they were strongly criticized by Human Rights organizations as biased, flawed and lacking independence from the new leadership and external influences.

International scholarly debate on transitional justice shows little consensus as to its scope, effectiveness and even definition.[10] First seen as a filed purely for legal scholars, transitional justice has now been regarded as a concept which requires a much broader analysis by lawyers, political scientists, IR scholars but also such disciplines as anthropology, cultural studies, development studies, economics, education, ethics, history, philosophy, psychology, sociology and theology.[11] The gradual widening of the range of disciplines interested in transitional justice results from broadening of the concept itself; it has moved from merely dealing with past human rights abuses to the concept of mechanisms of transition understood in the broadest possible way. One may look at transitional justice as Ruti Teitel proposes it, saying that "[t]he problem of transitional justice arises within the distinctive context of transition – a shift in political orders".[12]

In this volume transitional justice is understood as a broad set of judicial and non-judicial measures implemented in a state (or towards a state) in order to redress the legacies of massive Human Rights abuses. These measures may include: criminal prosecutions, truth commissions, amnesty provisions, reparations and reconciliation programs, memorialization programs and processes and various kinds of institutional reforms. The aim of transitional justice is not only to deal with the past, but it can also be a way to contribute to social and political change and to address current and future political problems, particularly to developing a more just state and society, with legitimate laws and institutions. The final goal of

---

(accessed September 2, 2013); German foreign minister Guido Westerwelle had already earlier demanded to bring the Syrian president Bashar al-Assad before the ICC. 'Westerwelle fordert Prozess gegen Assad.' *Deutsche Welle,* online at: http://www.dw.com/de/westerwelle-fordert-prozess-gegen-assad/a-16226334 (accessed on September 7, 2012)

10 See for example Bell, Ch. (2009). 'Transitional Justice, Interdisciplinarity and the State of the "Field" or "Non-Field"'. International Journal of Transitional Justice, vol. 3, no. 1.

11 Bell, Ch. (2009), p. 9.

12 Teitel, R. G. (2000). Transitional Justice. Oxford: Oxford University Press, p. 5.

transitional justice is to build a political, social and institutional order that would preclude any future gross Human Rights violations.

The revolution of Human Rights that has been in place since the end of the Second World War, the process of globalization of Human Rights standards, and the debate on democratization and the rule of law together with the horrific Human Rights violations committed in the optimistic time of the 1990s after the fall of the Iron Curtain continue to make the discussion on the need of transitional justice mechanisms highly relevant, even though the roots of the concept may be traced back as far as the late 1960s and mid-1970s, when the first investigations into Human Rights mass violations in Greece, Portugal and, later on, in countries of Latin America were launched. Today transitional justice processes have been underway in virtually all regions of the world (Europe, Latin America, Asia, and Africa). The mechanisms are being rediscovered and structured to the local needs as states and their communities face new challenges of the past Human Rights abuses. Discussions erupt anew with "irruptions of memory"[13] that "have the power to destabilize the collective memories of a democratic society"[14] and once again open the discussion on what mechanisms should be implemented to effectively deal with past abuses[15].

This volume presents various aspects of the transitional justice debate, including case studies of countries undergoing political transition. The contributions prove that transitional justice measures are not universal: there is no universal "toolkit" for transitions, which could teach lessons about how to deal with past atrocities and perpetrators. Transitional justice mechanisms must be characterized by the principle of local ownership; they must be crafted to circumstances on the ground and the relative strength of key stakeholders, such as the army, the security sector, victims' organizations, networks of the old regime's supporters, the structure of the post-transitional party system and the power of the institutions, which every transition country inherits from the previous regime. Only then can they be effective,

---

13 The concept of "irruptions of memory" is explained in Barahona de Brito, A. and Whitehead, L. (2012). 'Transitional justice: Reframing the Debate'. In: Popovski, V. and Serrano, M. (2012) (eds), pp. 439–462.

14 Barahona de Brito & Whitehead (2012), 451.

15 An example of such "irruption" could be recent debates in Poland on the cases of complicity of the Poles in crimes of the Holocaust committed by the Nazi Germany. Hot debates erupt each time disturbing facts come to light, be it in films, books, or individuals' accounts. After seventy years from the end of Nazi occupation of Poland, such "irruptions" disturb the collective memory institutionalized and taught for decades in schools and at homes.

actually contributing to redressing past Human Rights violations. The effectiveness of the applied justice mechanisms also depends on their transparency.

Even under normative assumptions, a universal answer about how crimes from the past are to be addressed is not possible. Retributive justice and the fight against impunity are likely to sustain accountable governance and bolster awareness for Human Rights and the rule of law, as Kathryn Sikkink and her followers argued with regard to Latin American transitions.[16] However the fact that transitions in East and Central European, in 1990s did not rely on retribution against high-ranking perpetrators so much and still led to mostly stable and prosperous liberal democracies, tends to indicate that accountable governance and the rule of law can also be achieved without resorting to large-scale retribution for past crimes. It may be argued that less retribution is more favorable to creating unity, reintegrate supporters of the old regime and reconcile them with the new order. In this way, societies can avoid the formation of old boys' networks and revenge campaigns, which often threaten the stability of transitional countries.

Within the scope of debates on the effectiveness and goals of transitional justice, the problem of potential conflicting interests of justice and peace has frequently been on the table. Jack Snyder and Leslie Vinjamuri have questioned the idea of transitional justice judicial prosecutions, pointing especially to international (or internationalized) jurisdictions. The scholars allege that "decisions to prosecute should be taken by political authorities" and – in the case of international prosecutions – by the UNSC, and "not by judges who remain politically unaccountable".[17] A critical approach to international prosecutions was based on the belief that the harm they can cause triggers instability, reverses the march to peace and leads to future atrocities, instead of bringing redress.[18] Snyder and Vinjamuri are among the scholars who believe that amnesties or – put differently – the policy of forgetting, if implemented responsibly, may be more effective in some cases and that they should be respected if national policies of transitional

---

16 Sikkink, K. (2001). *The Justice Cascade. How Human Rights Prosecutions are Changing World Politics.* New York, London: W. W. Norton & Co.; Sikkink, K. and Lutz, E. L. (2001). 'The Justice Cascade. The Evolution and Impact of Foreign Human Rights Trials in Latin America.' *Chicago Journal of International Law* 1, pp. 1–34; Risse, T.; Ropp, S. C.; Sikkink, K. (2002) (eds). *The power of Human Rights. International Norms and Domestic Change.* Cambridge: Cambridge University Press.

17 Snyder, J., Vinjamuri, L. (2003/2004). 'Trials and Errors: principle and Pragmatism in Strategies of international Justice.' *International Security* 3, p. 44.

18 See: Sikkink, K. (2012).

justice entail their implementation.[19] Paul Ricoeur's idea of "happy forgetting" may be a way to understand how forgetting could be an effective transitional justice strategy.[20]

This book does not endeavour to give an authoritative answer to the question whether fighting against impunity is a better approach to past atrocities and the legacy of dictatorial regimes than concealing the past in the name of a brighter future. As previously stated, it claims that there is no single one-fits-all strategy and it even challenges some of the few preliminary conclusions which have been drawn in the most recent transitional justice literature. We try to show how transitional justice experiences influence domestic change and what the role of the international community in these processes is.

This volume has been divided into three parts. The first one presents regional and local transitional justice efforts, aiming to show different mechanisms implemented within transitional justice efforts. It allows us to see how political and social factors determine the final goals of transitional processes. The following part deals with the role and impact of international criminal tribunals (ICTs) set up to prosecute grave Human Rights abuses.[21] The third part deals with the approach of the international community to crimes prevention. Here we try to answer the question as to what extent the present international system can play a role in preventing future grave Human Rights abuses and what the role of international actors in this preventive machinery is.

In the first contribution, Patrick Wegner describes how judicial intervention by the ICC met resistance on the ground in Uganda and how local restorative traditions clashed with the ICC's punitive approach.

Allan Rutambo Ngari in turn presents challenges to reconciliation in the Great Lakes region. He paints a disruptively complex picture of the interdependencies

19 Snyder & Vinjamuri (2003/2004), 40–50.

20 As claimed in Barahona de Brito, A., Whitehead, L., *Transitional justice: Reframing the Debate.* In: Popovski, V., Serrano, M. (2012) (eds). *Transitional Justice in Latin America and Eastern Europe.* New York: United Nations University Press, where the authors refer to Ricoeur, P. (2006). *Memory, History, Forgetting.* Chicago: University of Chicago Press. The problem of potential contradictions between peace and justice are mentioned in Patrick Wegner's contribution to this volume.

21 In the title of that part, we apply the term 'mass atrocities' that derive from the notion of 'mass atrocity crimes' which are usually understood as genocide, crimes against humanity, war crimes (forming the material scope of jurisdiction of the International Criminal Court). If we draw on the definition and scope of the responsibility to protect concept (elaborated in Dorota Heidrich's contribution to this volume), we would need to separately mention ethnic cleansing.

in the region that impede the on-going transitional processes there through the presentation of case studies pertaining to Rwanda, Burundi and the Democratic Republic of Congo.

By and large the case studies in this volume describe the twofold dilemma which transition societies face, but often are unable to solve: the dilemma between restorative and retributive justice on one hand, and – if this dilemma is solved in favour of retribution – the dilemma between international and local justice. It is rare for transitional societies and governments to solve these dilemmas openly and justify their choice. Most frequently, the outcome (which is often somewhere half-way between retribution and restoration and – in the former case – a mix between international judicial intervention and the measures undertaken by local institutions) is the result of domestic power struggles between different stakeholders, important social and political groups and external pressure. Hardly ever do we have such clear-cut examples of political pragmatism as in the case of Lebanon after the end of the civil war, when all main conflict parties agreed not to punish anyone (in order to maintain the cohesion of their movements and to prevent another outbreak of sectarian violence)[22] or in the case East Timor, where most retributive and internationally supported approaches to justice failed and the president of the country bluntly declared that transitional justice had to step back in the name of stability, reconstruction, unity, nation building and development. Anna Grzywacz describes this in her chapter about transitional justice (and the lack thereof) in East Timor.

In such situations, the South African TRC is often invoked as an example on how to deal with atrocities in a transitional country that cannot afford to create new cleavages and divisions. The South African experience is often presented as a normative example of reconciliation, rather than a case of political pragmatism, but Jan Hofmeyr shows the limits of such an interpretation: the TRC managed to promote an inclusive narrative and sustain the South African nation-building process after apartheid, but it mostly failed with its more precise and far-reaching aims; its promise of compensation for victims remained an empty one. Recent developments in South Africa also call into question whether reconciliation is a notion that is endorsed by the generation born and socialized in post-apartheid South Africa and often rejects the TRC process as a tainted compromise between elites.

---

22 Szekely, O. (2014). *The Costs of Avoiding Transitional Justice: Lessons from Lebanon*. In: Fisher, K. J.; Stewart, R. (2014) (eds). *Transitional Justice and the Arab Spring*. London, New York: Routledge, pp. 94–111.

The first part of the book is closed by a case study on Kosovo by Gjylbehare Bella Murati who discusses the approach of "a surrogate state" (drawing on the analysis presented by the report of the Kosovo Ombunsperson of 2000). The analysis extensively presents the endeavours of the international community to transform the territory (and later state) of Kosovo to a functioning political organism. The chapter provides an insight into transitional processes that have been implemented under the supervision of the international territorial administration represented by a number of actors, the most significant being the United Nations and the European Union.

The second part of the volume on the role of ICTs in mass atrocity crimes prosecutions begins with a chapter by Klaus Bachmann, who shows how different the formal goals of international jurisdictions may be from their on-the-ground evaluation. The latter is, as Klaus Bachmann concedes, to a large extent influenced by ethnicity and local stereotypes.

Ana Ljubojević in her contribution claims that international jurisdiction (looking at the example of the International Criminal Tribunal for the Former Yugoslavia) may build a different memory of history of conflict from the one built by national courts. Her chapter presents an interesting phenomenon from the point of view of the Completion Strategy of the International Criminal Tribunal for the former Yugoslavia (ICTY) and International Criminal Tribunal for Rwanda (ICTR), namely the problem concerning what challenges must be faced by national jurisdictions that deal with cases referred from ICTs.

As we shall see in Allan Rutambo Ngari's chapter on foreign judicial intervention and the media, it would be premature to conclude that international judicial intervention is always doomed to fail. In Kenya, the ICC pressure led to the creation of an inter-ethnic and inter-party coalition government, which joined forces in order to fight back against the ICC and shelter high-ranking accused from the ICC's reach. His chapter also challenges the conclusions some experts of *ad hoc* criminal tribunals have drawn from the partial failure of the ICTR and the ICTY.

As Allan Rutambo Ngari shows the ICTs' case selection criteria may be deeply biased and that perhaps the ideal solution for international jurisdiction would be to choose an indictment strategy cutting across all conflict parties' interests, for example by indicting, prosecuting and judging high-ranking perpetrators from all ethnic communities first. In Kenya, as Ngari concedes, the ICC did so and targeted both conflict sides equally from the very beginning, attacking the highest echelons of power first. However, this did not prevent public opinion from rejecting its intervention as biased, mainly because the stronger side in the Kenyan conflict managed to outmanoeuvre the ICC better and in the end the ICC prosecutor was left with accused from one conflict side only. Patrycja Grzebyk's chapter in the volume in turn deals with the assessment of the ICTR and the ICC judiciary achievements and their impact on countries in Africa whose cases have so far been prosecuted before these Tribunals. Attention is drawn to challenges these two Tribunals face in fulfilling their mandates (resulting mostly from their character and the fact that they function within the international community and are governed by international law, with all its peculiar characteristics).

In its last part, this volume attempts to show what the international community has so far done to prevent the commission of grave Human Rights abuses in the future. The role of the United Nations in crimes prevention is discussed by Agnieszka Bieczyk-Missala. We have also tried to present a case study of a national policy towards one of the most significant instruments of crimes prosecution within transitional justice mechanisms – the ICC. Isabelle Tellec discusses what role the Court has played in French foreign policy.

The volume is closed by Dorota Heidrich's contribution with an analysis of the concept of R2P which, when it was endorsed by the 2005 UN Summit, seemed to be a promising idea on how to make the "never again" slogan a reality. The author claims that the process of operationalization of R2P has been a step in the right direction, however the concept's significance is owed more to the discussions it has provoked than its actual endorsement.

Acknowledgements

This book is the result of several workshops and conferences, whose contributors agreed to deliver and adapt their papers accordingly. Some of the chapters stem from a joint workshop session of the European Consortium for Political Research in Antwerp 2012, coordinated by Adam Czarnota and Klaus Bachmann and dedicated to Transitional Justice. Some others are the result of a conference jointly organized and co-financed by the University of Social Sciences and Humanities, the Institute of International Relations of the University of Warsaw and the Ignacy Jan Paderewski Polish Institute of Diplomacy, titled *Dealing with the legacy of crimes and crises – transitional justice, reconciliation and the challenges for the international community. Conference organized in commemoration of the 20th anniversary of genocide in Rwanda* (Warsaw, May 8, 2013). The remaining contributions were initially presented at a workshop organized in the framework of a larger project on Transitional Justice and International Criminal Tribunals at the University of Social Sciences and Humanities and present preliminary results of some of this project's field research. The editors of the book would like to thank the University of Social Sciences and Humanities, the Institute of International Relations of the University of Warsaw and the Ignacy Jan Paderewski Polish Institute of Diplomacy for having provided the financial resources to organize the above mentioned events. They are particularly grateful to the Polish National Research Center (Narodowe Centrum Nauki) for sponsoring the research program, in framework of which this book could be published.[1]

1 The project is titled "International Criminal Tribunals as Actors of Domestic Change" (grant no. 2012/06/A/HS5/00249.)

Part I:
Regional and Local Transitional Justice Efforts

Patrick Wegner[1]

Regional and Local Perceptions of Justice and Their Impact on ICC Investigations – The Case of Uganda

Based on a literature overview of transitional justice research and case studies of the *Lord's Resistance Army* conflict in Central Africa, this chapter argues that the current research on transitional justice has a tendency to neglect some contextual variables important to assess the impact of transitional justice in areas like democratization, protection of Human Rights, and its impact on conflict dynamics. This is particularly true for the quantitative research. The chapter starts with a short overview of the current stage of transitional justice research to illustrate how most of the research neglects context variables. It then moves on to the case study of the International Criminal Court (ICC) investigations in Uganda to show how one of these context variables, namely justice perceptions, influences both the effects of international investigations as well as local concepts of transitional justice. This chapter is based on research conducted on the impact of ICC investigations in conflict contexts in the scope of a PhD project. The chapter will thus focus on international investigations and trials, specifically those undertaken by the ICC. Nevertheless, the chapter also discusses the implications of the findings for transitional justice research in general.[2]

---

1 This article contains excerpts of the upcoming book "The International Criminal Court in Intrastate Conflicts" of the author to be published by Cambridge University Press in autumn 2015.

2 The findings of the case studies are based on expert interviews conducted both in Europe and in Uganda. The sampling of the interviews followed the 'purposeful sampling methodology', choosing sources with a direct stake in the conflicts, in peace negotiations, or the ICC investigations. Other interview partners were chosen for being in a unique position to relate the events (mostly direct personal involvement), or because of their general knowledge about the situation countries. 39 interviews on the Ugandan case could be conducted during field research in Uganda. Due to reasons of confidentiality, interviews can only be quoted anonymously in this chapter and no verbatim excerpts from the recordings are used. The results of the interviews were complemented through the findings of an analysis of news sources with the LexisNexis database. The news sources were used to follow the developments of the conflicts and the ICC investigations on a day-to-day basis.

The State of the Art

In the last decades and years, transitional justice has increasingly become a field of interest for political science. Questions the literature grapples with include, for example, the impact of different justice mechanisms on transitions from authoritarianism or conflicts, the reasons why different approaches of transitional justice are adopted in different states, and the role of transitional justice in international relations and conflict resolution.

Despite a growing body of literature authored by jurists, historians, ethnologists, and political scientists, the research on transitional justice is still in its early phases. The current stage of research has in particular been criticized by many authors for its lack of empirical foundations.[3] Additionally, some level of polarization between the supporters of restorative and retributive justice measures can be found in the literature. Both sides make claims insufficiently based on data to advance their line of argument. Some have claimed in different contexts that it is necessary to tackle justice in order to ensure sustainable peace.[4] Others claim that pacifying measures at the cost of justice may be preferable.[5] Ramesh Thakur has claimed that restorative justice has a better track record than retributive justice, while Kingsley Moghalu claims that forms of legal accountability have a better

---

3 Akhavan, P. (2009). 'Are International Criminal Tribunals a Disincentive to Peace?: Reconciling Judicial Romanticism with Political Realism.' *Human Rights Quarterly* 31, p. 627; Hazan, P. (2006). 'Measuring the Impact of Punishment and Forgiveness: A Framework for Evaluating Transitional Justice.' *International Review of the Red Cross* 88, no. 861, p. 19; Thomas, O. N. T.; Ron, J. & Paris, R. (2008). *The Effects of Transitional Justice Mechanisms: A Summary of Empirical Research Findings and Implications for Analysts and Practitioners.* Ottawa: University of Ottawa Center for International Policy Studies.

4 Du Plessis, M. & Ford, J. (2008). 'Executive Summary.' In: Du Plessis, M. and Ford, J. (Eds.) (2008). *Unable or Unwilling? Studies on Domestic Implementation of the ICC Statute in Selected African Countries.* Pretoria: Institute for Security Studies, pp. 1–7; Lederach, J. P. (1995). *Preparing for Peace: Conflict Transformation across Cultures.* Syracuse, N.Y: Syracuse University Press; Van Acker, F. (2004). 'Uganda and the Lord's Resistance Army, the New Order no One Ordered.' *African Affairs* 103, no. 412, pp. 335–357.

5 Kritz, N. (2009). 'Policy Implications of Empirical Research on Transitional Justice.' In: Van Der Merwe, H. and Chapman, A. R. (Eds.) (2009). *Assessing the Impact of Transitional Justice: Challenges for Empirical Research.* Washington DC: United States Institute of Peace Press; Snyder, J. & Vinjamuri, L. (2003). 'Trials and Errors: Principles and Pragmatism in Strategies of International Justice.' *International Security* 28, pp. 5–44.

track record than other measures.[6] Those are but a few examples for the wealth of contradicting claims brought forward in the literature.

Reacting to the criticism of lacking empirical data, some authors have increasingly started to produce quantitative studies on the impact of transitional justice. The findings have unfortunately again been inconclusive or based on shaky foundations. Many cross-case studies have achieved the necessary numbers for obtaining results by lumping together different transitional justice measures or different transitional contexts. On this basis, Hunjoon Kim and Kathryn Sikkink could prove a correlation between trials and the reduction of Human Rights abuses, both in civil wars as well as in democratic transitions.[7] Another recent quantitative study applying the same approach of grouping cases found positive long-term impacts of trials in combination with amnesties and truth commissions on democracy and Human Rights.[8]

Even though this grouping of cases allows for the necessary numbers to use quantitative approaches, it can be problematic. For example, many studies do not distinguish between national and international trials. Yet, there might be significant differences between the two. Whether national trials are conducted in a country depends on the local context and willingness. International trials on the other hand have been started in cases in which credible national trials would arguably not have been possible for a long time (e.g., former Yugoslavia and Sudan). The impacts will therefore obviously differ depending on whether a trial is imported from the outside, or emerges out of a national context.

In other cases, transitional justice institutions with vastly different mandates, or even cases of transitional justice conducted in conflicts and those conducted in democratic transitions are lumped together. The lack of distinction between conflict and regime change contexts is inherent to the whole field of study. Most

---

6 Thakur, R. (2006). *The United Nations, Peace and Security: From Collective Security to the Responsibility to Protect.* Cambridge: Cambridge University Press p. 127; Moghalu, K. C. (2009). Prosecute or Pardon? Between Truth Commission and War Crimes Trials. In: Sriram, C. L. and Pillay, S. (Eds.), *Peace Versus Justice? The Dilemmas of Transitional Justice in Africa*. Scottsville: University of KwaZulu-Natal Press, p. 70.

7 Kim, H. & Sikkink, K. (2010). Explaining the Deterrence Effect of Human Rights Prosecutions for Transitional Countries. *International Studies Quarterly* 54, no. 4, pp. 939–963.

8 Olsen, T. D., Payne, L. A. and Reiter, A. (2010). *Transitional Justice in Balance: Comparing Processes, Weighing Efficacy.* Washington DC: US Institute of Peace Press; Olsen, T. D., Payne, L. A. and Reiter, A. G. (2010). The Justice Balance: When Transitional Justice Improves Human Rights and Democracy. *Human Rights Quarterly* 32, pp. 980–1007.

transitional justice advocates do not have any qualms when suggesting the same 'toolkit' of transitional justice measures for conflict and transition contexts.

This admittedly brief and selective critique of the research is supposed to emphasise two main points. First, research findings seem to be contradictory. Second, contextual factors like the cultural setting, the transitional context, and the institutional design of the transitional justice mechanisms are often neglected.

On this basis I argue that it is important to focus on specific contexts of transitional justice at this stage of the research, instead of lumping together different contexts and approaches that have been united under the rubric 'Transitional Justice'. The chapter will therefore focus on a specific context of transitional justice, namely that of ongoing conflicts. Within this context the chapter will focus on international trials, to be more precise, on investigations of the International Criminal Court (ICC) carried out in an ongoing conflict in Uganda. By focusing on a clearly defined subset of cases, it should be possible to shed some light on the contextual factors that influence transitional justice and have so far been neglected in the literature.

The ICC in Ongoing Conflicts

The ICC arguably stands for a new trend in transitional justice, namely prosecuting crimes in ongoing conflicts. This is illustrated by a remark of the ICC's outgoing Chief Prosecutor, Louis Moreno Ocampo:

> "[t]he ICC's mandate to select the most serious crimes committed after July 1, 2002, requires that we engage in judicial proceedings in relation to conflicts even before they have ended. [...] My Office is part of a new system dealing with a complex new reality: transitional justice during ongoing conflicts."[9]

Both the numbers as well as recent events seem to confirm that there is a trend towards prosecutions in conflicts. The ICC started new investigations in two conflicts subsequent to United Nations Security Council (UNSC) referrals of the situation in Sudan and Libya, and by converting preliminary investigations into full investigations in the context of the civil strife ensuing after the contested presidential election in Côte d'Ivoire.

The literature is divided between supporters and critics of this development. The supporters claim that justice and accountability are needed for successful conflict resolution.[10] ICC Chief Prosecutor Luis Moreno Ocampo has claimed

---

9 Moreno Ocampo, L. (2007). 'Transitional Justice in Ongoing Conflicts.' *The International Journal of Transitional Justice* 1, no. 1, p. 9.

10 Du Plessis & Ford (2008); Lederach (1995); Van Acker (2004), 356.

that the Court brings warlords to the negotiation table, focuses the debates surrounding the conflict on accountability issues, helps reduce crimes, weakens the support for spoilers by de-legitimisation, and ensures harmony in post-conflict situations through dealing with past atrocities.[11]

Critics of international trials in conflicts on the other hand suggest that investigations and prosecutions in conflicts could lead to an impasse in peace negotiations and other forms of peaceful conflict resolution and management efforts. The main worry is that parties might reject a compromise out of fear of being tried after the conflict.[12] The debate goes back to the 1980s, when the first transitions in Latin America took place and triggered first a debate about the legitimacy, efficiency, and morality of the amnesties, which accompanied gradual democratization in Chile and Argentina. Later, when the amnesties were formally or indirectly revoked (or disrespected by the judiciary), a discussion about their potentially destabilizing consequences ensued.[13]

Research conducted by the author on the impact of international trials in conflict contexts has shown that the findings in the literature are based on relatively few cases, that the claims brought forward in the literature are contested, and that many claims directly contradict each other. The situation is therefore similar to the current stage of research in the field of transitional justice as a whole. This opens up an important question for future research, namely how is it possible that the literature is so fundamentally divided about the impacts of international trials and investigations in conflicts across a large number of cases? There is no consensus about the impact of international criminal justice interventions in most of the cases included in the overview. In 14 of the 19 cases of international or hybrid trials addressed in the literature, both positive and negative impacts of trials on the conflict have been claimed, and in 12 of the 19 cases even directly contradicting effects were claimed. It is not plausible that errors of judgment and measurement are the main reason for this confusing picture. The most probable

---

11 Moreno Ocampo, L. (2008). 'Building a Future on Peace and Justice: The International Criminal Court.' In: Ambos, K. Large, J. & Wierda, M. (Eds.) (2008), *Building a Future on Peace and Justice: Studies on Transitional Justice, Peace and Development.* Heidelberg: Springer, p. 18.

12 Akhavan (2009), 625; Sriram, C. L. (2008). 'Conflict Mediation and the ICC: Challenges and Options for Pursuing Peace with Justice at the Regional Level.' In: Ambos, K. Large, J. & Wierda, M. (Eds.) (2008), p. 306.

13 The debates are summarized by, among others, Sikkink, K. (2012). *The Justice Cascade: How Human Rights Prosecutions Are Changing World Politics.* Norton Series in World Politics, pp. 1–35.

explanation is that international criminal justice may indeed have contradicting effects in conflict situations and that these effects depend highly on context. The lack of accounting for important contextual factors, or third variables, could be a logical explanation for the contradictory findings in both the literature and the quantitative studies.

Case studies are the method of choice for shedding light on the influence of these third variables and contextual factors. This chapter will introduce perceptions of justice on the local, regional and international level as an important third variable that has an influence on how transitional justice is implemented in a conflict situation. With perceptions of justice I mean the views and opinions of stakeholders and actors about what kind of justice should be implemented, and how it should be implemented. The chapter will show how both international trials as well as national concepts for transitional justice are influenced when local and international notions of justice meet. The findings are based on a case study of ICC investigations in Uganda. The case study will start with a brief introduction of the conflict context. Subsequently, relevant perceptions of justice will be presented in order to analyse their impact in a final step.

The Case: Uganda

The conflict between the Government of Uganda (GoU) and the Lord's Resistance Army (LRA) has been devastating East and Central Africa for 25 years by now. While the conflict emerged in northern Uganda, it has since spread beyond the borders of the country, gradually encompassing parts of South Sudan, the Democratic Republic of Congo (DRC) and the Central African Republic (CAR). Northern Uganda saw its last major LRA attacks in late May 2005 when a total of 62 people were killed in separate incidents near Lakale and Pagak.[14] Since the Juba talks between the GoU and the LRA started in 2006, peace has returned to northern Uganda. Yet the failure of the LRA to sign the final agreement produced during the Juba talks and the subsequent attack by the Ugandan People's Defence Forces (UPDF) on the LRA headquarters in Garamba National Park, DRC, put an end to the efforts to solve the conflict peacefully in December 2008. Even though northern Uganda remains calm, the LRA is still killing and abducting civilians

---

14 Allen, T. (2010). 'Bitter Roots: The "Invention" of Acholi Traditional Justice.' In: Allen, T. & Vlassenroot, K. (eds) (2010). *The Lord's Resistance Army: Myth and Reality.* London/New York: Zed Books, pp. 242–261. Rodriguez, C. (2009). *Tall Grass: Stories of Peace and Suffering in Northern Uganda.* Kampala: Fountain Publishers, p. 224.

in parts of the DRC, CAR and South Sudan. The conflict can thus be considered as ongoing to date.

Even though the conflict has been pushed out of northern Uganda during the last six years, the root causes for the conflict are to be found in Uganda's history of tribal divisions. A short overview of these root causes is provided to facilitate the understanding of the context of this chapter.

Until its independence in 1962, Uganda was a British colony. The British colonial administration took advantage of the tribes from the north as a recruitment reservoir for their King's African Rifles, while the southern tribes became the economic backbone of the country, with all cash crops being planted in their territories.[15] The British colonial administration thereby laid the foundation for a north-south divide that has never been completely overcome in Uganda. The country's history after independence is marked by a series of coups and counter-coups after which the respective leaders always based their power on the preferential treatment of their tribes and regions of origin. The last of these coups took place in 1986, when the National Resistance Army/Movement (NRA/M) took Kampala from the transitional government of Tito Okello, making its leader Yoweri Museveni the new president.

While the NRA/M managed to bring the southern and western parts of Uganda under its control rather quickly, the army of the ousted regime, the Uganda National Liberation Army (UNLA) retreated to the northern areas, where a majority of their rank and file, the Acholi and Langi, hailed from. Since the UNLA moved with considerable arms stockpiles, the NRA/M interpreted them as a threat and continued to advance north.[16]

Many people in the northern regions, on the other hand, felt marginalized after the government of their tribesman Okello had been ousted. They also feared retaliation by the NRA for massacres committed by the UNLA in the Luwero Triangle while fighting the NRA. The NRA then again perceived the north as a natural support base and recruitment reservoir for the UNLA and thus applied a brutal counter-insurgency strategy. In reaction, several rebel groups emerged out of the UNLA, including the Uganda People's Democratic Army (UPDA), the Holy Spirit

---

15 Apuuli, K. P. (2008). 'The International Criminal Court and the Lord's Resistance Army Insurgency in Northern Uganda.' In: Nhema, A. & Zezela, P. T. (eds) (2008). *The Resolution of African Conflicts: The Management of Conflict Resolution and Post-Conflict Reconstruction.* Addis Ababa: Ossrea, p. 53; Dolan, C. (2009). *Social Torture: The Case of Northern Uganda, 1986–2006.* New York/Oxford: Berghahn Books, pp. 41–42.

16 Eichstaedt, P. (2009). *First Kill Your Family: Child Soldiers of Uganda and the Lord's Resistance Army*, Chicago: Lawrence Hill Books, p. 151.

Movement (HSM), and finally the Lord's Resistance Army. While most of these rebellions had ended by 1988, the LRA prevailed. Due to the atrocities attributed to the NRA in the north and allegations of large scale cattle rustling, some Acholi saw the NRA offensive as an attempt to permanently marginalise them. As the last remaining rebel group, the LRA therefore received some local support in the beginning.[17] Yet the LRA soon started to attack Acholi civilians in the north, abducting, killing and maiming their own kin. As a result, neither the NRA nor the LRA were able to secure popular support in the north and the conflict reached a stalemate. When the NRA realized that it was not able to defeat the LRA militarily, it resorted to a strategy of isolating the LRA from the civilian population, which it still saw as the LRA's support base. The NRA implemented this strategy by forcing the Acholi population into 'protected villages' from 1996 onwards.[18] It did so by issuing ultimatums, followed by shelling and bombing to force the villagers into the camps.[19] Once forced into the camps, the Acholi population was subjected to harassment by the UPDF garrisons as well as ongoing LRA attacks.[20] Chris Dolan has analysed this camp system in depth and summed up that it violated the rights of these Internally Displaced Persons (IDPs) to health and education as well as their economic rights without providing adequate protection in return.[21] Over 90 per cent of the population in Acholiland had to live in these camps at the height of the conflict, while up to 40,000 children commuted from the camps to the urban centres of northern Uganda every night to avoid abduction by the LRA.[22]

Since then the GoU has tried to wipe out the LRA in northern Uganda in various military offensives, including Operation North (Operation Simsim) in 1991, Operation Iron Fist in 2002, Operation Iron Fist II in 2004 as well as Operation Lightning Thunder in 2008. Alternating between a military approach and the attempt to negotiate a surrender of the LRA, the GoU also engaged in peace talks

---

17 Finnström, S. (2010). 'Reconciliation Grown Bitter?: War, Retribution, and Ritual Action in Northern Uganda.' In: Shaw, R. & Waldorf, L. (Eds.), *Localizing Transitional Justice: Interventions and Priorities after Mass Violence,* Stanford: Stanford University Press, pp. 135–156.

18 Allen & Vlassenroot (2010), 14.

19 Dolan (2009), 110.

20 International Crisis Group (2005). *Building a Comprehensive Peace Strategy for Northern Uganda*. Nairobi/Brussels: International Crisis Group, p. 7.

21 Dolan (2009), 151.

22 Latigo, J. O. (2008). 'Northern Uganda: Tradition-Based Practices in the Acholi Region.' In: (2008), L. & Salter, M. (Eds.). *Traditional Justice and Reconciliation after Violent Conflict: Learning from African Experiences.* Stockholm: IDEA, pp. 85–120.

with the LRA in 1994, 2004–2005, and 2006–2008. In 2000, the Government also passed an Amnesty Act under heavy civil society pressure from the north, providing amnesty to all rebels who were willing to lay down their arms. It is against this background that the GoU referred the crimes committed by the LRA during the conflict in northern Uganda to the ICC in 2004.

Ugandan President Yoweri Museveni and ICC Chief Prosecutor Luís Moreno Ocampo announced the referral of Uganda as a situation country to the ICC at a joint press conference in London in January 2004. In July 2004, the ICC decided to open investigations in Uganda. Warrants of arrest against LRA Chairman Joseph Kony and four of his top commanders were unsealed in October 2005.

Perceptions of Justice in Uganda

From the very beginning of the investigations, the ICC met strong scepticism among the population in the conflict affected areas in northern Uganda and the Ugandan civil society more broadly. One of the reasons for this scepticism was the way the investigations were initiated. As described above, Chief Prosecutor Moreno Ocampo decided to announce investigations by the side of President Museveni even though the Government of Uganda was a party to the conflict and many people in the north felt that the government army was responsible for grave Human Rights violations. This created the impression that the ICC was biased from the beginning, being just a tool of the government to tackle the LRA conflict with different means.[23] Even though the ICC Chief Prosecutor soon made clear that he would conduct independent investigations of both sides of the conflict, the initial impression of the joint declaration with President Museveni was not easy to revoke. Additionally, there had been no prior warnings or consultations with those affected by the conflict and the civil society, which created the impression that local voices had been ignored by the ICC.[24]

Apart from the allegation of bias mentioned above, the criticism brought forward by the local civil society and shared by many people in northern Uganda followed two main lines of argument. On the one hand, the local population was disappointed when it learned that the ICC would rely on state parties to arrest the indicted LRA leaders.[25] After all, the UPDF and other armies in the region had tried in vain to stop the LRA threat for decades. Secondly, parts of the population and many

23 Dolan (2009), 100.

24 Hovil, L. (2012). *A Poisoned Chalice? Local Civil Society and the International Criminal Court's Engagement*. Kampala: International Refugee Rights Initiative, p. 7.

25 Hovil (2012), 10.

civil society organisations believed the ICC would hinder a peace process with the LRA.[26] They also feared prosecutions would disrupt attempts to reconcile through an amnesty offer in force since 2000 and the use of traditional rituals of the Acholi people.[27] These three points of criticism essentially stem from a different perception of justice and will be introduced in more detail in the following paragraphs.

Many local civil society organisations and authors claim a general cultural preference for reconciliation among the people living in the war affected areas, especially the Acholi.[28] To be more precise, the claim is that the people in northern Uganda prefer to deal with the LRA with an amnesty and the use of traditional justice rituals. Indeed, the Parliament of Uganda passed the Amnesty Act in 2000, which allowed all rebels who laid down arms and renounced rebellion to receive amnesty, basically amounting to a blanket amnesty. It is also true that politicians and traditional as well as religious authorities from the north had lobbied for the Amnesty Act for a long time, playing an important role in ensuring that the act was passed. According to recent figures, 22,520 rebels have accepted the amnesty offer since the act was passed, approximately 48 per cent of them being LRA members. Local support for the amnesty law also remains high, with 98 per cent in Acholiland thinking that the amnesty is relevant and should not be abolished in December 2011.[29]

Apart from the amnesty approach, traditional leaders and some local nongovernmental organizations (NGOs) promote the Acholi reconciliation ritual, known as *mato oput,* as an alternative to ICC trials or retributive justice in general. The ritual is designed to cope with murder on an individual level. It involves asking for

---

26 International Center for Transitional Justice (2005). *Forgotten Voices: A Population-Based Survey on Attitudes about Peace and Justice in Northern Uganda.* New York: International Center for Transitional Justice, p. 34; Pham, P., Vinck, P., Stover, E., Moss, A., Wierda, M. & Bailey, R. (eds)(2007). *When the War Ends: A Population-Based Survey on Attitudes about Peace, Justice, and Social Reconstruction in Northern Uganda.* Berkeley: Human Rights Center University of California, p. 5.

27 Allen (2006), 85–86; Wyrzykowski, P. and Kasozi, B. O. (2010). *Why Being Able to Return Home Should be Part of Transitional Justice: Urban IDPs in Kampala and their quest for a Durable Solution.* Kampala: Refugee Law Project, p. 7.

28 Hovil, L. & Lomo, Z. (2005). *Whose Justice? Perceptions of Uganda's Amnesty Act 2000: The Potential for Conflict Resolution and long-term Reconciliation.* Kampala: Refugee Law Project, p. 10.

29 Otwili, E. A., Schulz, P., Lonergan, K. & Ogora, L. O. (2011). *To Pardon or to Punish? Current Perceptions and Opinions on Uganda's Amnesty in Acholi-land,* online at: http://justiceandreconciliation.com/wp-content/uploads/2011/12/JRP_Brief_Amnesty-Dec-2011.pdf.

forgiveness by the perpetrator, complex compensation negotiations between the clans of the victim and the perpetrator, and a final reconciliation ritual in which a goat is slaughtered and the perpetrator and a representative of the victim's clan drink a brew mixed from goat blood and the bitter juice of the eponymous *oput* root. After the ceremony the clans share food and drinks together as a symbol of their reconciliation. The most detailed descriptions of a *mato oput* ceremony can be found in reports by Erin Baines and Stephen Lamony.[30] The involved clans will act as if the crime had not occurred after a *mato oput* ritual which allows them to cooperate and live together in the future. The compensation is traditionally used to pay the bride price for a new marriage to ensure that children born into the clan replace the dead member.[31] Between 2004 and 2006 alone USAID has funded 54 of these ceremonies.[32] Ugandan researchers claim that the local population wants their reconciliation values to be reflected in the national transitional justice policy, even though the population does reportedly not insist on particular rituals.[33]

It is undeniable that the amnesty and the use of reconciliation rituals are of importance for the people in northern Uganda, and that they represent a local restorative approach to justice to some degree. Still, it is important to acknowledge some limitations of this 'restorative justice' culture. While the amnesty was and is still widely supported in the north, it is done so in the hope that it will lead to peace while retributive justice measures might undermine it.[34] Additionally, there is a lot of cultural pressure among northern Ugandans to support the amnesty.[35] Some persons, particularly direct victims of the LRA, are extremely opposed to the amnesty and see it as a scandal that some former LRA commanders are now

30 Lamony, S. A. (2007). *Approaching National Reconciliation in Uganda: Perspectives on Applicable Justice Systems*. Kampala: Uganda Coalition for the International Criminal Court, pp. 11–15; Baines, E. (2005). *Pursuing Peace and Justice: International and Local Initiatives*. Liu Institute for Global Issues Conflict and Development Programme, pp. 57–63.

31 Latigo (2008), 104.

32 Latigo (2008), 105.

33 Komakech, L. & Sheff, A. (2009). *Tradition in Transition: Drawing on The Old to Develop a New Jurisprudence for Dealing with Uganda's Legacy of Violence*. Kampala: Refugee Law Project, pp. 39, 43.

34 Hovil & Quinn (2005), 34.

35 Allen (2006), 85–86; Oxfam International (2007). 'The Building Blocks of Sustainable Peace: The Views of Internally Displaced People in Northern Uganda.' *Oxfam Briefing Paper 106*, Oxfam International, p. 16.

allowed to live in relative luxury.[36] Still, most of these critics would not openly voice this opinion.[37] Public opinion on these issues also seems to change according to the situation. When there are negotiations, people want the ICC to lay low. After negotiations failed, calls were made for the ICC to arrest the LRA already.[38] Accordingly, many more recent reports claim that there is a majority in northern Uganda for trying those most responsible for the crimes committed.[39]

In the case of the *mato oput* rituals, a number of problems regarding their legitimacy and effectiveness remain. First of all, the ritual was designed for individual reconciliation on a clan level, not to deal with war crimes and atrocities on a large scale and in a context where perpetrators and victims can seldom be identified.[40] Second, youths and women have no real role in the rituals.[41] Third, the cultural knowledge to perform these rituals has been partly lost during the civil war and many young people and born-again Christians no longer accept the traditions.[42] Fourth, some of the rituals that have been performed no longer meet the traditional criteria and authors have suggested they are mainly performed to get access to funding.[43] Finally, the rituals are impractical in the context of a regional war that has meanwhile spread over the territory of four states and has even led to intertribal animosity.[44] Research suggests that the local population is seeing the role of traditional justice mainly in reintegrating LRA returnees.[45]

---

36 Hovil & Quinn (2005), 34; Clarke, K. M. (2009). *Fictions of Justice: The International Criminal Court and the Challenge of Legal Pluralism in Sub-Saharan Africa.* Cambridge: Cambridge University Press, p. 31.

37 There are some exceptions, like a number of politicians from northern Uganda who were openly against dropping the ICC warrants as Kony had not made use of past opportunities to make peace.

38 Glasius, M. (2009). 'What is Global Justice and Who Decides? Civil Society and Victim Responses to the International Criminal Court's First Investigations.' *Human Rights Quarterly* 31, pp. 497–520.

39 OHCHR (2007). *Making Peace our Own: Victims' Perceptions of Accountability, Reconciliation and Transitional Justice in Northern Uganda.* Geneva: United Nations, pp. 30, 54.

40 Finnström, S. (2008). *Living With Bad Surroundings.* Durham/London: Duke University Press, pp. 201–209.

41 Komakech & Sheff (2009), 33.

42 Baines (2005), 107; Latigo (2008), 109.

43 Allen (2010), 250; Baines (2005), 95.

44 Allen (2010), 258–259.

45 International Center for Transitional Justice and Human Rights Center of the University of Berkeley (2005). *Forgotten Voices: A Population-Based Survey on Attitudes about Peace and Justice in Northern Uganda.* New York: International Center for Transitional Justice, pp. 32, 40.

The final argument of locals and the civil society brought up against the ICC investigations is the alleged bias of the ICC. The court is seen as not having investigated the government side in order to not endanger the cooperation of the GoU. This criticism of the court's work is not connected to different notions of justice, it is rather a criticism of *how* justice is being applied by the ICC. Some victim groups, many northerners, and some Ugandan politicians want to see the government side investigated, too.[46] The foundations for this criticism are clear and simple. The Office of the Tribunal Prosecutor (OTP) announced its investigations side by side with President Musveni, to date no warrants against government soldiers or officials have been issued, the ICC has made barely any information on its investigation of the government side public, and the ICC depends on the Ugandan Army to provide security during the investigations.[47] The lack of public information on the ICC investigations into alleged government crimes even led to a Ugandan newspaper wrongly declaring that the UPDF and the government had been 'cleared' by the ICC.[48] It is beyond the scope of this chapter to give an estimation of whether prosecution of government crimes by the ICC are called for from a legal perspective. Yet, as described in the historical overview, it is clear that the government side has committed numerous crimes and atrocities during the LRA conflict. Admittedly, most of them were committed long before the Rome Statute came into force in 2002.[49] It is fair to say that reports of wide-spread rape and torture by UPDF soldiers and the displacement of nearly the entire population of northern Uganda as a counter-insurgency strategy do indeed warrant investigations. Since the ICC has not published any details on its findings, it remains unclear whether these allegations have been investigated. The argument of the ICC Prosecutor has always been that the gravity of crimes committed by the UPDF was not even close to that of the LRA, and that investigations into UPDF crimes were still ongoing.[50] It is hard to deny that the main motivation of President Museveni and the government of Uganda in referring the case to the ICC was to use it in

46 ICTJ & Human Rights Center of the University of Berkeley (2005), 3, 5.

47 Unger, T. and Wierda, M. (2008). 'Pursuing Justice in Ongoing Conflict. A Discussion of Current Practice'. In: Ambos, Large & Wierda (2008), 277.

48 Nouwen, S. & Werner, W. (2010). 'Doing Justice to the Political: The International Criminal Court in Uganda and Sudan.' *European Journal of International Law 21*, p. 951.

49 Latigo (2008), 94.

50 ICC (2010). *Report of the International Criminal Court.* A/65/31. New York: United Nations.

order to mobilise world opinion against the LRA.[51] The army has also made clear that it wants to avoid ICC investigations of UPDF crimes in a Daily Monitor article on August 16, 2004: 'Our position is if they come across any allegations against government officials, they should let them be tried by the government'.[52]

There were several reasons why these disagreements escalated in the early phase of the ICC investigations. Firstly, people had very little knowledge and very high expectations of the court and its work.[53] This led to rumours and misinformation that further strengthened the criticism of the ICC. There were, for example, rumours that the ICC was using government infrastructure in its investigations when it was in reality supported by the United Nations Office for the Coordination of Humanitarian Aid (UN OCHA).[54] There were also other false reports about the ICC investigations, culminating in the claim that the ICC had already issued warrants for the LRA in late 2004.[55] Secondly, the ICC and its international supporters from Human Rights NGOs tried to suppress the criticism from the Ugandan civil society which led to a confrontational stance between the two sides for the first two years or so of the investigations.[56] The fact that the Chief Prosecutor implied on several occasions that he saw Acholi critics of the investigations siding with the LRA did not help.[57] Soon, a majority of the Ugandan civil society was flat out against any ICC involvement.[58] Some northern politicians, traditional authorities and members of the clergy were particularly vocal in their criticism.[59]

Both the lack of information as well as the controversy arising within the Ugandan civil society organisations was due to an initial failure of the ICC to engage in meaningful outreach in northern Uganda.[60] The court had focused on contacting and informing stakeholders (like journalists, lawyers, and members of the judiciary) in the early phases of its investigation, but failed to inform the population

51 Branch, A. (2007). *The Political Dilemmas of Global Justice: Anti-Civilian Violence and the Violence of Humanitarianism, the Case of Northern Uganda*. PhD Thesis. Columbia University. p. 488.

52 Finnström (2010), 138.

53 ICTJ & Human Rights Center of the University of Berkeley (2005), 5.

54 Allen (2006), 97.

55 Human Rights Watch (2005). *Uprooted and Forgotten Impunity and Human Rights Abuses in Northern Uganda*. New York: Human Rights Watch, pp. 56–57.

56 Hovil (2012), 4–7.

57 Marion, S. & Paschyn, C. M. (2010) *Luis Moreno-Ocampo on Darfur, the LRA*. Online at: http://pulitzercenter.org/blog/news-points/luis-moreno-ocampo-darfur-lra.

58 Glasius (2009), 507.

59 Baines (2007), 96.

60 Glasius (2009), 510.

and the civil society at large.[61] The ICC initially also failed to use radio stations for outreach, the communication medium that arguably reached the most people in the conflict affected areas, thus leaving the airwaves to LRA representatives who were spreading misperceptions about the court.[62] But in 2006/2007, the outreach activity of the ICC slowly started gaining pace. Awareness of the ICC in northern Uganda rose from 25 per cent in 2005 to 60 per cent in 2007.[63] The ICC started communicating with its critics, most importantly the traditional leaders.[64] In 2006, Moreno Ocampo invited delegations from the northern civil society organisations to The Hague to discuss the investigations.[65] The civil society organisations and the Prosecution even published a joint statement to the Government of Sudan, asking it to cooperate further with the ICC and not to support the LRA.[66] The OTP also conducted field missions and workshops to better understand the needs of victims.

The outreach efforts of the ICC have succeeded in winning at least some of its critics over, and handle some of the misperceptions that had emerged concerning the court's work.[67] For example, 68 per cent of northern Ugandans considered the ICC to be neutral and 69 per cent saw it as independent from the GoU in a 2007 survey.[68] An ICC Outreach report even claimed that a staggering 98 per cent of people were happy with the ICC presence.[69]

Still, some problems remain. The lack of ICC investigations on the government side is still consistently being put forward by civil society members on the ground that the author interviewed during field research in late 2011. Also, people in the affected areas are increasingly disappointed by the ICC because arrests are not forthcoming more than six years after the warrants were issued.[70] The court is also still perceived as removed from the realities on the ground since it is located in The Hague and has no offices in the war-affected areas.[71] Factual knowledge of the court and its rules also remains weak, and the ICC has failed to understand

61 ICG (2006), 9.

62 Human Rights Watch (2010), 61.

63 Pham & others (2007), 35–39.

64 Unger & Wierda (2008), 277.

65 Allen (2006), 178–179.

66 Office of the Prosecutor (2006). *Report on the Activities Performed During the First Three Years*. The Hague, p. 17.

67 Hovil (2012), 14.

68 Pham & others (2007), 37.

69 Registry Of The ICC (2010). *Outreach Report 2010*. The Hague: ICC, pp. 20–21.

70 OHCHR (2007), 50.

71 Hurinet, UCICC & No Peace Without Justice. (2010). *Visits by ICC States Parties Delegates to Uganda*. Kampala, pp. 8, 46.

some community issues and to respond adequately to them, for example the alleged lack of investigations into UPDF crimes.[72] It also has to be said that the ICC investigations have lost a lot of relevancy for the people in northern Uganda as new issues emerge six years after peace has returned to the once affected areas. According to a survey, priorities in 2010 had shifted from peace and security to fulfilment of basic needs like access to food, healthcare, education and seeds for agriculture.[73] Important topics that repeatedly came up during field research were land issues as well as the mysterious nodding disease that is affecting a high number of children in the area.

After this overview of local perceptions concerning justice and the ICC investigations in particular, the next section will analyse in how far the discourse between global and local notions of justice influenced transitional justice in Uganda in general, and the ICC's work in particular.

The Impact in Uganda

On a national level the ICC investigations, the outreach and advocacy connected to it as well as the reactions among the population in Uganda, and the north in particular, have shaped the transitional justice agenda in Uganda. The ICC investigations and the international advocacy efforts to guarantee accountability led to extensive discussions about the issue during the Juba peace talks between the GoU and the LRA between 2006 and 2008. The discussion culminated in an Agreement on Accountability and Reconciliation that became agenda item 3 of the Juba Agreement. Even though the LRA never signed the final agreement, the GoU started implementing some of its provisions. The agreement tried to formulate a compromise between western notions of retributive justice and criminal accountability on the one hand, and northern Ugandan values of reconciliation and the use of traditional justice on the other. It was the first attempt to negotiate a peace agreement with accountability measures designed to fulfil the Rome Statute's complementarity principle. The final compromise was a result of the international pressure for accountability that was met with the LRA delegation's and the local civil society's calls for reconciliation. Even though the insistence of the local civil society and the LRA's position in the talks foreclosed a solution that would have given full precedence to accountability, its role was a lot stronger than it had been in previous peace talks and the issue was higher on the public agenda than in the past. The creation of the International Crimes Division (ICD) of the Ugandan High Court, a division able to try war crimes

72 Pham & Vinck (2010), 5, 43; Finnström (2010), 155.

73 Pham & Vinck (2010), 2.

and crimes against humanity as well as the domestication of the Rome Statute in Uganda are examples of how the accountability trend influenced the national transitional justice agenda. A local transitional justice expert concluded that all local justice alternatives were now being constructed to pass complementarity, which has led to a funding bias in favour of retributive, prosecutorial alternatives.[74] Interviewees working in the field of transitional justice or directly involved in the work of the ICD in Uganda consistently emphasized that the founding of the ICD was a result of the debates surrounding the ICC investigations during the peace talks.

At the moment, Uganda has not yet found a long-term compromise between (mostly) international calls for accountability and (mostly) local calls for reconciliation. As a result, there is currently no clear consensus on the way forward for transitional justice in Uganda. Even the legal situation in Uganda demonstrates this. On the one hand, there is a court division capable of trying war crimes and crimes against humanity under the ICC Act, while on the other hand a blanket amnesty for all rebels is still in place. Inevitably, this situation led to conflicts during the first war crimes trial of the ICD during which a former mid-level LRA commander was charged with war crimes under the Geneva Conventions Act.[75] Several courts have judged that the defendant, Thomas Kwoyelo, should be freed as there is no way to legally bar him from receiving amnesty. Until today, the Ugandan Directorate of Public Prosecutions (DPP) has defied these rulings and is holding Kwoyelo in prison, arguing that amnesties for war crimes are not permissible. The DPP has also expressed its desire to prosecute more similar cases in the future. At the same time, the Justice Law and Order Sector (JLOS) of the Ugandan government is working on an integrated transitional justice agenda that is supposed to include elements of truth commissions and traditional justice.

Apart from the effects on the national agenda for transitional justice, local and international views on justice have also had an impact on the effects of the ICC investigations. One of the most common claims in the literature is that trials further reconciliation in war-affected areas.[76] Yet reconciliation is impossible without

---

74 Oola, S. (2011). *The Coalition for Reconciliation in Uganda: Important Lessons for Proactive Civil Society Engagement in Catalysing Transitional Justice Discourse.* Johannesburg: African Transitional Justice Research Network Workshop: Advocating Justice: Civil Society and Transitional Justice in Africa, p. 11.

75 Uganda ratified the Geneva Conventions in 1964 through national legislation. The respective law is known as the Geneva Conventions Act.

76 Stromseth, J. E. (2003). 'Introduction: Goals and Challenges in the Oursuit of Accountability.' In: Stromseth, J. E. (Ed.) (203). *Accountability for Atrocities: National and International Responses,* New York: Transnational Publishers, p. 8.

victims buying into the process. According to surveys conducted in northern Uganda as well as interviews with victims' organisations, the direct victims of the LRA are mostly interested in receiving support with immediate livelihood needs and compensation for the crimes committed against them.[77] The ICC on the other hand focuses on the accountability of the perpetrators and is not able to meet the material needs of victim communities. The Victim Trust Fund of the ICC is conducting some projects that directly benefit victims, but the fund is financed by voluntary state contributions and has limited resources.

Combined with the initial lack of responsiveness by the ICC and its supporters vis à vis local criticism, and the fact that arrests have so far not been forthcoming, many victims feel that the ICC is not reacting to their needs. This is a typical example of how different expectations towards justice can lead to a disconnect between the court and the victims that in turn undermines the expected effects of trials. The perception that the ICC came into the conflict as an external force trying to impose its approach of guaranteeing accountability, while not heeding the views of the affected population, has according to some researchers even fostered dissent in the northern areas and has thus become an obstacle to reconciliation.[78]

Many authors also claim that trials can help boost the respect for laws, strengthen the rule of law, and help further national legal reforms.[79] Arguably, this public education function of trials can also only work if this message reaches the general population. A clash between international efforts to prosecute and local efforts to reconcile will undermine these effects. Indeed, if local stakeholders feel that their approach to transitional justice is not taken into account by the ICC, they might very well become passive in the whole process of seeking justice and accountability. Various authors have criticized the ICC along these lines, stating it disempowers the Acholi people.[80] As a matter of fact, a number of interviewees stated that they had the impression the ICC staff did not understand traditional justice mechanisms in northern Uganda and did not even bother trying to understand them.

---

77 ICTJ & Human Rights Center of the University of Berkeley (2005), 25. The interviewees cannot be named openly in this chapter as permission was only obtained to quote the data in the PhD thesis. The information is from an interview with staff members of an organization that works with victims of the LRA conflict and another organization that works with LRA returnees.

78 Dolan (2009), 244.

79 Stromseth (2003), 11.

80 Branch (2007), 480, 508.

In how far international trials can lead to the deterrence of further crimes and the strengthening of accountability on a national level also highly depends on the perception of the prosecutions on a national level. If the court is seen as ineffective in obtaining arrests, it will be difficult to deter potential war criminals from committing new crimes. The literature on deterrence has in fact found that potential war criminals have to perceive a high probability of being arrested for deterrence to kick in (Rothe, 2010, p. 10, 102). The indictees can potentially even use local perceptions of bias to undermine the legitimacy of the ICC investigations. LRA representatives at the Juba talks, for example, said that they did not condemn the ICC investigations and warrants as such, but rather the bias of the ICC by not investigating any GoU crimes in order to rally local support (Finnström, 2010, p. 152). If individuals indicted by the ICC are able to tap into popular criticism of the court, they might be able to undermine the local support for investigations and trials which in turn makes it harder for the ICC to secure arrests.

The strengthening of accountability is another effect often attributed to international trials (Olsen, Payne, Reiter, 2010, p. 997). In the case of northern Uganda, many of those living in the war-affected areas called for accountability for crimes committed by the UPDF and the government more broadly. The fact that the ICC cooperated with the GoU and has so far not published any detailed information on its investigations of the UPDF contributed to the perception that the UPDF has nothing to fear from the ICC. As described above, there have even been counterfactual newspaper reports that the ICC had cleared the UPDF.[81] Additionally, government officials have repeatedly stated that they do not expect the ICC to prosecute members of the army. These developments have a tendency to undermine local calls for accountability. As an interviewee working with victims of Human Rights violations put it: If an international court deems the army to be innocent, who am I as a victim to challenge such a finding?

There is verbal compliance with accountability principles on the part of the Ugandan army, both in interviews with the author as well as with newspapers, but in practice the Human Rights record of the UPDF remains problematic. This has emerged from interviews with local Human Rights organisations but can also be established from newspaper sources and reports of think tanks.[82] In the last months reports of misconduct of Ugandan troops in the Central African Republic have been increasing. The accusations are similar to those brought forward a

81 Even an interviewee working for a local Human Rights organisation believed the ICC had cleared the UPDF.

82 ICG (2010), 24.

couple of years back in northern Uganda. They include rape, the abuse of civilians, and engagement in illicit activities like teak logging.[83] The army has so far been successful in keeping these matters internal by addressing this misconduct through court martials and disciplinary measures. According to Human Rights organisations interviewed on the ground, these measures tend to be intransparent though. In the past, those guilty of atrocities were often simply redeployed elsewhere and many cases of misconduct were not investigated in depth or even at all. The army has repeatedly stated, as quoted above, that it has its own accountability measures to make sure that misconduct and crimes committed by soldiers are investigated and prosecuted internally. An army official also claimed during an interview with the author that the ICC had not found sufficient evidence to link the UPDF to atrocities committed in northern Uganda. The fact that the ICC has not been prosecuting any government crimes can be expected to reinforce the perception both among the army[84] as well as in the population that the UPDF can keep up the current Modus Operandi without fear of repercussions from the ICC.

Conclusion

The case study of Uganda has shown how justice perceptions can have an influence on both national transitional justice concepts and international investigations. These perceptions include both perceptions of what kind of justice should be applied (retributive vs. restorative, cosmopolitan vs. traditional) as well as how justice is being applied (even-handedness, fairness). The impact of transitional justice is in particular influenced by perceptions in areas in which public opinion plays a role. This includes the educational functions of transitional justice, which are supposed to lead to more respect for the law and a strengthening of the rule of law as well as the reconciliation function of transitional justice. For the deterrence effects of international trials, the perception of justice also plays an important role. If a party does not believe it is being targeted by investigations, it will not be deterred from committing crimes. This also includes the isolation and marginalisation effects attributed in particular to international trials. These effects of transitional justice cannot be expected to take hold if people are not reached and convinced by the

83 Cakaj, L. (2011). The Lord's Resistance Army in the Central African Republic. *Conflict Prevention and Peace Forum.* Social Science Research Council. Institute for National Strategic Studies. Strategic Forum (National Defence University), online at: http://ndupress.ndu.edu/Portals/68/Documents/stratforum/SF-270.pdf (accessed June 2011).

84 People working in the Human Rights sector in Uganda have confirmed that the UPDF feels more or less immune against being held accountable for violations.

form of justice dispensed. Whose perceptions matter depends on which effect of transitional justice we are talking about. In terms of reconciliation, the victims and the war affected communities are those addressed by justice. For the education and isolation effects it is the entire nation or maybe even the international community.

The justice perceptions of the ICC and its international supporters are also shown to have an impact on national concepts of transitional justice. This effect is enforced by the complementarity regime under which the ICC operates. Complementarity means that the ICC can only investigate and prosecute a case if the same charges have not been or are not being prosecuted on the national level. The state in question must be shown to be unable or unwilling to prosecute the charges itself. As a result, states that have an interest in stopping ICC investigations within their jurisdiction will try to convince the court and its supporters that they are meeting international standards of criminal justice.[85] The ICC is thus a catalyst for international views of justice influencing transitional justice concepts in countries in which the ICC is active. As shown above, the ICC is in practice pushing countries towards more retributive models. This pressure comes to bear even in contexts in which the national predisposition tends more towards reconciliation, like in the case of Uganda. The results of that pressure are not necessarily positive. It led to the staging of sham trials, while the ICD prosecutions in Uganda raised issues of due process since the first defendant of the ICD remains in custody despite several court decisions to free him.

This case study has shown that perceptions of justice influence the impact of transitional justice. Yet these perceptions have only partly been internalized by quantitative surveys on transitional justice and trials in particular, namely in as far as they relate to variables already included in the models, like the power balance between victims and perpetrators. As such, the justice perceptions surrounding transitional justice are an important context variable that the research has so far not sufficiently taken into account. However, it is only one example for context variables that matter when trying to ascertain the impact and effectiveness of transitional justice models. Further qualitative research is necessary to identify and analyse these context variables. The results of this research will help to lay the foundations for future efforts to model transitional justice processes more accurately in order to inform the quantitative research needed to strengthen the empirical foundations of the field.

85 Uganda strived to do so by trying to strike an accountability compromise with the LRA that would be acceptable for the ICC. More recently, Kenya challenged the ICC's jurisdiction over crimes committed during post-election violence, referring in part to the principle of complementarity.

Allan Rutambo Ngari

Dealing with the Legacy of Mass Atrocities in the Great Lakes: Rwanda, Burundi, and the Democratic Republic of the Congo

The field of transitional justice has been subject of much speculation and debate. Some posit that it has its origins in law, and particularly international law and comity, where the concepts of human rights violations, accountability for these violations and democratic values find their home. Others assert that to confine the field of transitional justice to law is not only erroneous but a reductionist and simplistic view of a host of other disciplines and factors that are at the heart of transitional justice mechanisms.[1] To understand transitional justice therefore, one has to search further than the treatises and digests of a library or the discourse of academics and philosophers, relevant as these sources may be. Composed of a wide spectrum of issues ranging from retribution to restoration, one of the key goals of transitional justice is to promote peaceful co-existence, foster the rule of law, and establish democratic values in society.

Over the past five decades, all African states have been or are in some form of transition – from colonialism, apartheid or oppressive regimes to democracy and the respect for the rule of law. If the term transitional justice is taken to signify "the full range of processes and mechanisms associated with a society's attempts to come to terms with a legacy of large-scale past abuses, in order to ensure accountability, serve justice and achieve reconciliation"[2], then it is necessary to assess the

---

1 For the theoretical discussions of Transitional Justice see: Teitel. R. (2000); Elster, J. (2004), *Closing the Books. Transitional Justice in Historical Perspective*, Cambridge: Cambridge University Press. For a categorization of Transitional Justice mechanisms and retrospective justice see also: Pettai, E.-C., Pettai, V. (2015). *Transitional Justice and retrospective justice in the Baltic states. Cambride: Cambridge University Press (especially the first chapter); Buckley-Zistel, S., Beck, T. K., Braun, Ch., Mieth, F. (eds) (2014). Transitional Justice Theories. New York: Routledge. For the legal view on Transitional Justice: McAuliffe, P. (2010).* 'Transitional Justice and the Rule of Law: The Perfect Couple or Awkward Bedfellows?' Hague Journal on the Rule of Law 2, no. 2, pp 127–154; van der Merwe, H., Baxter, V., Chapman, A. R. (eds) (2009). *Assessing the impact of transitional justice*. Washington D.C.: United States Institute of Peace Press.

2 United Nations Rule of Law, *Transitional Justice,* online at: http://www.unrol.org/article.aspx?article_id=29.

context and progress achieved in the above-mentioned three countries in these terms and in the light of the idea that transitional justice has been a stated objective of those in power.

Applied specifically to Burundi, the Democratic Republic of Congo (DRC), and Rwanda, the term "transitional justice" might translate as the progression from a state of armed violence to one in which democratic institutions, values, and practices are the norm. With reference to contextual developments, which have occurred since the political transitions in each of these countries, advances in this domain have been slow, non-existent or only partial. All of these advances, or lack thereof, are underpinned by the political ideology prevalent at any given period in each of these countries. Some fifty years after attaining political independence from colonial rule, and an average of twelve years into transitions from conflict to relative peace (better expressed as "negative peace", retaining most of the factors which initially gave rise to conflict), these countries are beset with instability and the region remains volatile.

This chapter sets out to explore the effectiveness of efforts to institute transitional justice mechanisms in these three countries of the Great Lakes Region and to assess their achievements, successes, and remaining obstacles.

It addresses the transitional justice processes in the region and notes that in all respects, these processes, although providing a measure of dealing with past mass atrocities, have been negatively impacted by the political leadership. A cursory glance at the processes undertaken in these countries reveals that attempts to address the serious crimes perpetrated, divisions among citizens, and violations of the rule of law have not been consistent. A more nuanced study of transitional justice in the Great Lakes shows that constraints have been placed by each of the governments on transitional justice mechanisms. For instance, Du Toit comments: "Rwanda's post-genocide period has been characterized by a unique approach to transitional justice programmes of unprecedented scope and variety, allied to the lack of democratic reform and political power-sharing."[3] The International Crisis Group reports that following the 2010 communal, parliamentary and presidential elections in Burundi, "the new government has inherited serious governance problems – growing corruption, lack of an independent justice system, weak oversight institutions and a stalled transitional justice agenda."[4] Similarly, politics and transitional justice processes are not strange bedfellows in the DRC. The composition of

3 Du Toit, F. (2011). *Reconciliation and Transitional Justice: The case of Rwanda's Gacaca Courts*. Cape Town: Institute for Justice and Reconciliation, p. 4.

4 International Crisis Group (2011). 'Burundi: From Electoral Boycott to Political Impasse.' Brussels: ICG, p. 1.

the Truth and Reconciliation Bureau (2004–2006) mirrored that of the Transitional Government born of the Sun City Accords, with a One-plus-Four formula in which the five components (the Presidential Coalition, the RCD,[5] the Maji-Maji,[6] civil society, and the so-called "unarmed opposition") were equally represented. The Bureau therefore included individuals who bore responsibility for crimes committed in the course of successive wars in the Congo, which negatively impacted the Truth and Reconciliation Commission's (TRC) credibility and ability to function. Current efforts on the part of DRC civil society networks, lobbying for the establishment of accountability and truth mechanisms, risk failure if the State does not commit to the process.

This chapter argues that while political imperatives have forced changes of regime in the three countries now removed from a state of open warfare, the ideals enshrined in the notion of "transition" are not fully realized, resulting in a state of latent and unresolved tension. Based on the experiences of the three countries concerned, it is suggested that regimes currently in power have been unable to transcend the politics of the past, in spite of peace agreements and attempts to establish (Burundi/DRC), or make effective (Rwanda), transitional justice institutions.

The first part of this chapter examines challenges facing the three countries in the Great Lakes region. It then presents cross-cutting responses to these challenges from a transitional justice perspective, setting the stage for a more detailed exposition of the country-specific issues to be discussed in later chapters. The chapter concludes with an analysis of the tensions between law and politics in transitional justice initiatives in the Great Lakes.

Challenges facing the Great Lakes

Challenges of Ethnicity

Rwanda faced a dual challenge after the genocide pertaining to the socio-economic reconstruction of a devastated country and promoting reconciliation in a deeply divided society. Barely fifteen years have passed since the foundation of the National Unity and Reconciliation Commission (NURC), mandated with, as the name suggests, promoting national unity and reconciliation.[7] Healing and reconciliation

---

5 *Rassemblement Congolais pour la Democratie.*

6 Maji Maji is an armed rebel group that was based in the east of the DRC formed to defend their local territory against other armed groups.

7 The Commission's name may be misleading. The NURC bears the name of a truth commission in the sense of Priscilla Hayner's book: Hayner, P. (2010). *Unspeakable*

require several generations to accomplish. However, one might pause to reflect on the government's attempt to eradicate ethnic sentiment through outlawing the expression of a lived reality. Trenchantly stated: can an overarching ethos of "Rwandanness" emerge in a context of severely curtailed, and managed, political participation? The question takes on greater significance when considering the failure on the part of the regime to entertain accusations of the eradication of Hutu ordinary citizens during the 1994 Rwandan Patriotic Front's (RPF) onslaught, and the ensuing attacks on refugee camps in the DRC in the aftermath of the genocide.[8]

Thus, dual ethnic histories continue to prevail in Rwanda, unrelieved by a sense of common history and a people who appear to be in constant fear of unsettling the political status quo. Competing claims to victimhood during the 1994 genocide have added a layer of complexity to the rift between the ruling political elite and opposition groups. Undemocratic practices, including the detention of political opponents, journalists and activists, reinforced by contentious laws on "Genocide Ideology" and "Divisionism"[9] have alienated a growing number of Rwandans and given rise to a variety of opposition groups ranging from the "traditional" Hutu constituency, to some of the founding members of the RPF gathered under the banner of the Rwanda National Congress (RNC) who claim to advocate on behalf of all Rwandans for the establishment of a national dialogue on the country's future, and inclusion of the Hutu voice in the genocide narrative.[10]

---

truths. Transitional Justice and the Challenge of Truth Commissions. London, New York: Routledge.

8 On the issues of Rwanda's campaign against genocide ideology, governance and the critique of both by academics and Human Rights organizations see: *Waldorf, L. and Straus, S. (eds) (2011). Remaking Rwanda. State Building and Human Rights after Mass Violence. London, Madison: University of Wisconsin Press; Eltringham, N. (2004). Accounting for horror. Post-genocide debates in Rwanda. London: Pluto Press; Gahima, G. (2013). Transitional Justice in Rwanda. Accountability for Atrocity. New York: Routledge; Peskin, V. (2011). 'Victor's Justice Revisited. Rwandan Patriotic Front Crimes and The Prosecutorial Endgame at the ICTR.' In: Waldorf, L. and Straus, S. (eds) (2011): Remaking Rwanda. State Building and Human Rights after Mass Violence. London, Madison: University of Wisconsin Press, pp. 173–183; Reyntjens, F. (2013): Political Governance in Post-Genocide Rwanda, Cambridge: Cambridge University Press.*

9 The Rwandan Minister of Justice, Tharcisse Kagurama, has admitted to the vagueness of the laws following calls by Amnesty International to review the law on Genocide Ideology, online at: http://www.amnesty.name/en/library/asset/AFR47/002/2011/en/ef7cd1a3-d1db-46da-b569-818b7555b83b/afr470022011en.pdf.

10 'Kayumba Nyamwasa demande -t -il pardon?' *Jambo News*, online at: http://www.jambonews.net/actualites/20110616-kayumba-nyamwasa-demande-t-il-pardon/

Thus in spite of the implementation of powerful national institutions for reconciliation (NURC) and accountability (Gacaca justice), one observes a paradox in which Rwandans continue to lobby for a new democratic order.

In Burundi, there is a widening gap between the political elite and civil society activists, who have championed a transitional justice agenda for the country since the signing of the Arusha Peace Agreement in 2000. The promise of the 2005 democratic elections, characterized by a shift in political power to the Hutu ethnic majority, were quickly dashed as those in power reverted to political infighting. Transitional justice appears to be faltering on two counts: the misinterpretation of founding documents enshrining the transitional justice process to come, and the human factor, comprising jockeying for key political posts, corruption and non-democratic practices, including vote-rigging during the 2010 presidential and legislative elections which conferred a parliamentary majority to the government and left Burundi without an effective opposition.

Some progress, however, can be seen in Burundi. At the time of writing this chapter, Act No. 1/18 of May 15, 2014 established the creation, mandate, composition, organization, and function of the much-awaited Truth and Reconciliation Commission. This is the only mechanism that has been established as a state-initiative to deal with the past in Burundi. There have been concerns, however, that the ruling party *Conseil national pour la défense de la démocratie-Forces de défense de la démocratie* (CNDP-FDD) did not involve the opposition parties in the development of said law, while earlier comments from civil society on the draft law were not considered in the revision of the text. The process of establishing the Burundi TRC from the establishment of a Technical Committee to drafting the law was criticized as non-consultative and exclusionary of key stakeholders. Burundi has been under international pressure to oversee the establishment of a Truth and Reconciliation Commission and a Special Tribunal for Burundi that would deal with individual criminal responsibility of those suspected to have committed international crimes. In all these processes, the ruling party has marginalized civil society in contravention of one of the key clauses of the Arusha Agreement.

Challenges Relating to Governance

In the DRC, relations between the ruling party and the political opposition are at an all-time low. Indeed, constitutional amendments forced through parliament confer a direct advantage on the incumbent President.

> *The amendments scrap the second round of voting during presidential elections. The president will now be elected in a single vote, with a simple majority. A candidate can become*

president even if they only get a minority of the total votes cast during an election, with the other candidates splitting the rest of the votes.

Opposition parties have argued that eliminating the second round will diminish their chances of unseating incumbent President Joseph Kabila by making it harder for the opposition to unite behind one candidate during a single round[11].

With the consolidation of intelligence networks, brazen assassinations of Human Rights activists, and leaders of opposition parties either behind bars[12], in exile or lacking a clear political vision for the future of the DRC, there has been no break with past practices and it is clear that Mobutu has left a lasting imprint – from the development of a personality cult around a "Father-President" who deems himself irreplaceable, a trait which has been adopted by all successive Presidents. Indeed, it may be pertinent to say that this style of leadership permeates all levels of Congolese political culture, from the level of State President to that of Provincial Governor.

Challenges Related to the Demobilization and Reintegration of Armed Militias

At a regional level, numerous armed non-state actors operate within and across national borders of these three states. These insurgencies reinforce and feed each other, severely hampering the regulation of cross-frontier arms flows. Partly fuelled by undemocratic political processes in the respective countries, utilized by rival neighbouring states, and provided with a lifeline through their access to mineral resources, these insurgencies become self-perpetuating. Furthermore, they have been vectors of rapid social change including, amongst others, chronic humanitarian crises, social dislocation, war economies, aid-dependency and perpetuation of the child-soldier phenomenon in spite of international legal frameworks prohibiting the use and enslavement of child soldiers.

The presence of armed militias in the North and South Kivu provinces continues to pose a serious threat to instability in the DRC. Members of the Democratic Forces for the Liberation of Rwanda (FDLR) are well-entrenched in many areas. Their return to Rwanda is predicated upon a successful reintegration process, yet many allude to the failure of political dialogue in Rwanda and a manipulated justice process possibly compromising their safety, should they opt to return.

---

11 'Parliament Approves Constitutional Amendments', online at: http://congonewsagency.com/index.php/2011/01/16/parliament-approves-constitutional-amendments/.

12 Mouvement pour la Liberation du Congo (MLC) leader Jean-Pierre Bemba is currently standing trial at the International Criminal Court.

Meanwhile, the FDLR continue to be a threat to harmonious civilian living in the east of the DRC and its boarder areas with Rwanda.

Since the formal withdrawal of foreign military forces from the Kivus in 2003, three successive military operations have been launched to dislodge FDLR groups. The first, dubbed *Umoja Wetu (Our Unity)*, was launched in late February 2009 by a coalition of Rwandan and Congolese armed forces. Far from reaching its stated objective, it resulted in a further dispersal of FDLR groups throughout the two provinces, widely-reported instances of Human Rights abuse, and large-scale displacement of civilian populations in the vicinity of the operation.

The second, called *Kimya*[13] *1* and *Kimya 2*, received logistical support from the then UN Mission in the DRC, *la Mission des Nations Unies en République démocratique du Congo*

(MONUC). In the light of numerous abuses (sexual violence, pillaging) on the part of some units of the Congolese armed forces,[14] denounced by the group of UN experts in late 2009, the UN made a strategic but temporary withdrawal from all but logistical support of FARDC units.[15]

MONUC's operation *Amani Leo* (Peace Today), which targeted rebel forces in North and South Kivu, was officially launched in January 2010, but did not begin until late February: MONUC obtained this time to ensure that military operations are truly joint and that the army and its local leaders formally commit to protecting the people instead of attacking them. A Joint Monitoring Committee (FARDC, MONUC, and NGOs) was established for this purpose in March 2010, yet none of the commanders responsible for the violations of Human Rights have been prosecuted.

Successive operations have been launched by the *Mission de l'Organisation des Nations Unies de stabilisation en République démocratique du Congo* (MONUSCO),[16] including "*Amani Ya Kweli*" (Real Peace), and they are intended to deploy mobile operational bases and conduct patrols in the territories where

13 *Kimya* (kiSwahili) translates as 'silence' or 'fear'.

14 Les Forces Armées de la République Démocratique du Congo (FRRDC).

15 Letter dated December 10, 2008, from the Chairman of the Security Council Committee established pursuant to resolution 1533 (2004) concerning the Democratic Republic of the Congo addressed to the President of the Security Council, online at: http://daccess-dds-ny.un.org/doc/UNDOC/GEN/N08/618/77/PDF/N0861877.pdf?OpenElement.

16 MONUSCO was the successor of MONUC. In July 2010, the UNSC renamed MONUC by approving UNSC res. 1925.

Human Rights violations are known to be common; they also aim to fill the void resulting from restructuring problems within the FARDC.

The process of accelerated Army integration ("*brassage accéléré*") in North and South Kivu has had very limited success. Merging the forces of the *Conseil national pour la défense du peuple* (CNDP)[17] and the Maji-Maji with national Army units has had its own set of challenges, particularly given that these forces have opposed each other militarily and ideologically in the past. All indications are that CNDP forces are unwilling to be deployed outside the Kivu provinces and have to a large degree maintained their own command structures within the integrated units. This state of affairs has important implications for transitional justice in the DRC, and calls for an interrogation of that country's Amnesty Laws, which de facto confer impunity.

Cross-cutting all of the above are the opportunistic agendas and shifting alliances of convenience which characterize relationships between the numerous armed groups in the Kivu Provinces. Formerly providing support to the FARDC and Maji-Maji militias during the war against Rwandan occupation, some FDLR groups continue to collaborate with some Maji-Maji groups and elements of the national Army. Their hold on mineral-rich areas fuels their resistance to repatriation, while the fact that many have integrated local communities poses a conundrum: twenty years after the massive influx of Rwandan Hutus, including participants of the genocide, to Eastern DRC, the classification of children born to these groups on DRC territory poses an acute challenge.

Other parts of the DRC also experience the wrath of armed rebel groups: in *Province Orientale*, the persistence of the *Forces de résistance patriotique pour l'Ituri* (FRPI) and other groups speaks to a deep malaise within the national Army. In *Province Equateur*, thousands were displaced as a result of armed violence

17 The *Conseil national pour la défense du peuple* was established by former General of the Congolese army Laurent Nkundabatware (better known as Laurent Nkunda), a Tutsi whose declared agenda was to protect the minority rights of Congolese citizens of Tutsi ethnicity. Discredited by the commission of widespread Human Rights abuses by his forces, he was arrested in January 2009 by Rwandan forces and is currently under house arrest in Rwanda. Rwanda has not responded to the DRC's requests for his extradition to face trial for war crimes committed in the Congo. The CNDP was then led by Nkunda's former second-in-command, Bosco Ntaganda, who was wanted by the ICC on war crimes charges and surrendered to the US Embassy in spring 2013, from where he was transferred to the ICC. 'A surprising surrender.' *The Economist*, 13.3.2013, online at: http://www.economist.com/blogs/baobab/2013/03/bosco-ntaganda.

that broke out in 2009, and over 100,000 people continue to seek refuge in the neighbouring Republic of Congo.

For its part, the Congolese National Army is faced with the challenge of low morale, low levels of training and equipment, and unreliable salaries. In many instances, units are unpaid, particularly those geographically distant from the capital. Furthermore, it is composed of disparate groups, including some of the Maji-Maji and other armed militias operating in the Kivus. This is complicated by collaboration with FDLR units in many parts of the east, and the refusal of some former militia members to be integrated into the post-war DRC Army structures. Thus, the "army" of Congolese Tutsi General Laurent Nkunda, was under house arrest in Rwanda as early 2009, and was under the control of his rival, General Bosco Ntaganda, another Congolese Tutsi officer, currently in the custody of the ICC following a bizarre sequence of events where he found his way to the United States Embassy, and later transferred him to The Hague in compliance with the ICC's arrest warrant against Ntaganda for crimes against humanity committed in the Ituri District.[18]

Complex cross-border dynamics are also evident in those parts of South Kivu which are adjacent to Burundi: following the breakdown in communications between the Government of Burundi and the political opposition after the elections in 2010, alliances have been reignited between Burundi's FNL and Maji-Maji groups operating in the region of South Kivu, which now serves as a rear-base for the launching of FNL raids on Burundian territory.

Challenges Related to Reconciliation

The delicate balance between the poles of justice and reconciliation is of particular relevance in the Great Lakes countries and has generated much discussion and controversy. The inability to obtain consensus stems from the very nature of the conflicts and the means by which power was transferred from previous regimes to those now in power.

To a large extent, the peace processes, embarked upon with the manifest intent of bringing together all sides in the conflict(s), have laid the basis for these diverging positions: the Arusha Peace and Reconciliation Agreement for Burundi, signed

---

18 It is worth noting here that the US never ratified the Rome Statute and even inclined countries, which were beneficiaries of US military aid, to conclude bilateral agreements obliging those countries to transfer US citizens to the US, rather than the ICC, in case of ICC investigations against them. For the tumultuous relation between the US and the ICC, see: Scheffer, D. (2013). *All the Missing Souls: A Personal History of the War Crimes Tribunals.* Princeton: Princeton University Press.

in 2000 by all political parties and armed rebel movements with the exception of the Party for the Liberation of the Hutu People – Forces for National Liberation (PALIPEHUTU-FLN), came into existence before cease-fire negotiations had been terminated; PALIPEHUTU-FLN cadres continued their armed opposition to the transitional government, and to the post-transition CNDP-FDD.

Furthermore, subsequent legislation failed to reflect an important provision of the Agreement relating to immunity from prosecution. "In line with the provisions of Protocol II to the 2000 Arusha Peace and Reconciliation Agreement for Burundi providing for the interim period and transitional institutions, a Draft Law on Provisional Immunity for Political Leaders (2001) was discussed in Burundi, according to which members of political parties and movements signatory of the said agreement returning from exile shall be granted provisional immunity from penal prosecution for politically motivated offences committed during the period of 1 July 1962–28 August, 2000."[19] The Draft Law states: "This immunity does not concern crimes of genocide, crimes against humanity and war crimes".[20]However, the Draft Law was not adopted by Burundi's National Assembly. This state of affairs has jeopardized a common understanding of the transition in Burundi and been a bone of contention throughout Burundi's post-conflict history.

With reference to the DRC, the Lusaka Ceasefire Agreement of 1999[21] outlined the modalities for the withdrawal of foreign armed forces from the Congo, created ceasefire lines, and laid the groundwork for the Inter-Congolese dialogue. The Accords were signed jointly by representatives of the DRC Government, the RCD, the *Mouvement de libération congolais* (MLC), opposition parties (referred to as the unarmed opposition) and civil society. This followed negotiations, which took place under the auspices of the international community (in which South Africa played a leading role). It is of note that two principal armed groups were excluded from the agreement: the Maji-Maji and the FDLR; both entities continued fighting, exacting a heavy toll on civilian populations in the east of the country; the fact that they were officially referred to as "negative forces" did nothing to alter their hostility to the newly-established political order. While many of the Maji-Maji groups have adhered to the Army integration process, some groups remain on the periphery of the political process, while the remnants of the FDLR are subject to a complex set of circumstances, which have more to do with their nature as a foreign

---

19 International Committee of the Red Cross, Customary International Human Rights Law, online at: http://www.icrc.org/customary-ihl/eng/docs/v2_cou_bi_rule159.

20 *Draft law on Provisional Immunity for Political Leaders,* 2001, Articles 1–2.

21 Lusaka Ceasefire Agreement signed by the heads of states of Angola, DRC, Namibia, Rwanda, Uganda, Zambia, and Zimbabwe on July 10, 1999.

armed group, and the political dispensation in neighbouring Rwanda. Their political aim is not the integration into the structures of the DRC state apparatus, but to to return to Rwanda and regain power in Kigali. Their constituency is therefore not so much the public in DRC, but the public in the disperse Hutu exile community in other African and some non-African states and the Hutu in Rwanda.

The DRC's Truth and Reconciliation Commission (2004–2006) floundered on the rocks of its own internal contradictions, constituted as it was of all of the elements of the Lusaka Accords; the former armed rebel groups retained their control of territories held during the war and were not open to the principle of investigation of past crimes, or truth-seeking. These contradictions were carried over into the ill-fated Transitional Government, whose 1+4 composition made it inherently unstable.

Challenges Relating to International Criminal Justice

Prosecution of international crimes is one tool in a broad spectrum of transitional justice mechanisms available to a country in transition. What has emerged over the past two decades on the African continent is a preference, or sustained advocacy, for retributive models for dealing with gross violations of Human Rights and serious crimes of international concern. While such mechanisms have their rightful place in addressing the challenges faced by the countries in the Great Lakes in transition to democracy and the rule of law, it has been overstated by prosecutorial fundamentalists that transitional justice is solely retributive in nature. Of the three countries in the Great Lakes, only Rwanda has had to deal with the challenge of international criminal justice, which will be discussed in some detail below. Since the conclusion of the peace accords in Arusha for Burundi, the recommendation to establish a Special Tribunal for Burundi has not been acted upon for various reasons, including the lack of political will in Burundi to deal with its past in a retributive manner. The fears of the political class revolve around the implication of high-ranking political figures in the commission of serious crimes as indirect perpetrators or otherwise. On the other hand, the DRC has managed, although not ideally, to deal with serious crimes of international concern through its martial courts, whose jurisdiction has been extended to include these crimes. To a greater extent of success, the DRC has established revolving special courts (in the regions that have experienced greatest impact of the conflict) that focus on sexual and gender-based crimes. These courts have been successful in dealing with the menace of sexual and gender-based crimes committed by rebels and even military officers accused of committing these crimes.

What is clear at present is that Burundi and the DRC will have to deal with the consequences of a more proactive international community in the transition of these countries, which includes the effects of amnesty for perpetrators who are suspected of having committed acts that constitute one or more international crimes, namely war crimes, crimes against humanity or genocide. With the codification of the prohibition of amnesty for such crimes in the Rome Statute of the International Criminal Court (ICC), the complexities of balancing a truth-seeking mechanism, where perpetrators are granted some form of immunity for disclosing the truth, and a retributive mechanism, in which impunity for the commission of international crimes, are repressed. Somewhere in the middle of this complexity rest the rights of victims and affected communities of these crimes to see perpetrators punished, the victims' voices to be heard, and the crimes committed to be compensated – at least to some extent.

Retribution

Instituting criminal prosecutions for crimes committed during conflict are amongst the initiatives that are available within the spectrum of transitional justice mechanisms. The retributive theory of punishment in this context holds accountable perpetrators of gross violations of Human Rights as regulated by international Human Rights law and serious violations of the laws and customs of war regulated by international humanitarian law. During the conflicts in Rwanda, Burundi, and the DRC, millions of people were killed. In Rwanda, it is estimated that 937,000 people were killed in the hundred days of the 1994 genocide.[22] Over the period between July 1, 1962, when Burundi attained its independence from Belgium, to August 28, 2000, when the Arusha Peace Agreement was signed between the Government of Burundi and the many rebel forces in the country, hundreds of thousands of Burundians were killed.[23] In the DRC, the situation was similar: conservative figures estimate that millions were killed in the various conflicts between 1993 and 2002; indeed, the International Rescue Committee estimates up to 5.4 million excess deaths (deaths in

22 This is the number based on an official census of the Rwandan government, Hirondelle press release, April 5, 2004; See Van den Herik, L. J. (2005). *The Contribution of the Rwanda Tribunal to the Development of International Law.* Leiden: Martinus Nijhoff, p. 25.

23 See Boshoff H. (2010). 'Historical Overview.' In: Boshoff, H. Vrey, W. and Rautenbach, W. (eds.) (2010). *The Burundi Peace Process: from civil war to conditional peace*. Pretoria, South Africa: Institute for Security Studies, pp. 3–9.

excess of normal national mortality rates) since 1998, due to the direct and indirect consequences of war[24].

In all these conflicts in the Great Lakes, the sanctity of life and the respect for Human Rights have been abrogated. There can be no justification for such violations in war or in peace time. Owing to the total or partial judicial collapse caused by conflicts of such nature, each of these three countries is severely limited in effectively addressing the violations against its own citizens. In the Rwandan genocide, for example, judicial officers were specifically identified and many killed. The annihilation of custodians of the judicial system made it impossible for Rwanda to then address the violations on its own. Two years went by between the take-over of power by a transitional government dominated by the RPF in 1994 and the start of the first judicial actions against perpetrators of the genocide,, during which the basic infrastructure of the state had to be restored. But even then, Rwanda quickly reached the limits of its judicial capacity: after several huge waves of incarcerations, it quickly appeared that the country had no means to safeguard that prisoners were accused and could defend themselves. Those who were had to wait for years for their trials, incarcerated under conditions which made even their mere survival difficult.[25] Rwanda was pressured by international Human Rights groups, donor countries, and the UN to improve the fates of tens of thousands of prisoners, whose guilt could neither be proved or disproved (because of the lack of judges, prosecutors and sometimes even indictments and case files), but could also not be freed, because they constituted a potential security threat for the new government. Finally, in 2002, Rwanda embarked on a novel route to transitional justice, entrusting the Gacaca courts (lay courts for settling civil disputes) with criminal proceedings: Prisoners, who admitted their crimes in front of such a publicly deliberating lay court, could exchange their prison term for communal work – if their victims and the people from the respective community accepted their guilty plea. This quite unique scheme, which mixes retributive and restorative approaches, not only helped to empty the prisons again, but also relieved the state administration from the burden of guarding and feeding overcrowded detention facilities, thus contributing to the economic (and often even physical) reconstruction of the country.[26]

---

24 International Rescue Committee, IRC Congo Mortality Survey 2007, online at: http://www.rescue.org/resource-file/irc-congo-mortality-survey-2007.

25 *Gahima, G. (2013): Transitional Justice in Rwanda. Accountability for Atrocity. New York: Routledge, describes these dilemmas at length.*

26 The Gacaca courts and their impact on Rwandan society are subject to fierce disputes among scholars. For a rather positive account: *Clark, P. (2010). The Gacaca Courts, Post-Genocide Justice and Reconciliation in Rwanda. Justice without Lawyers. Cambridge,*

History is very clear on how violations of such a nature have been dealt with by the international community. The allied powers of the Second World War set up the International Military Tribunals of Nuremberg and Tokyo to deal with individuals accused of committing crimes. Seen as a form of victor's justice, these two tribunals received numerous criticisms, the major one being that these tribunals applied laws retrospectively. Nevertheless, a precedent was set with these two tribunals and almost half a century later, the international community under the auspices of the United Nations Security Council established the International Criminal Tribunal for Rwanda (ICTR). The ICTR was created "to promote national reconciliation and maintain peace in Rwanda by bringing to justice perpetrators of genocide and other serious violations of international humanitarian laws."[27] In his response to a question on the ICTR's biggest success, Karegyesa states that "…the greatest success of the ICTR has been deterrence of crimes and accountability."[28] The ICTR is the first court to try a genocide case since the Genocide Convention was adopted in 1948. Riddled with controversy and criticism ranging from the prosecution of only one party to the conflict in Rwanda, namely the Hutus, to the lack of effective cooperation with the Government of Rwanda, Karegyesa concedes that "…the jury is still out on whether the ICTR has contributed to peace and reconciliation in Rwanda."[29]

Protocol II on Democracy and Good Governance of the Arusha Peace and Reconciliation Agreement provides a procedure for the establishment of an international mechanism to respond to genocide, war crimes, and crimes against humanity that took place in Burundi as part of its transition.[30] An International Commission of Inquiry for Burundi (the Commission) had the mandate to investigate these

---

New York: Cambridge University Press. The sceptics are: Reyntjens, F. (2013). Political Governance in Post-Genocide Rwanda, Cambridge, New York: Cambridge University Press; Waldorf, L. and Straus, S. (eds) (2011): Remaking Rwanda. State Building and Human Rights after Mass Violence. London, Madison: University of Wisconsin Press.

27 UN SC Resolution 995/94; See Magnarell, P. J. (2000). *Justice in Africa: Rwanda's Genocide, its Courts, and the UN Criminal Tribunal.* Aldershot: Ashgate, pp. 59–70, 64.

28 Richard Karegyesa is the Chief of Prosecutions at the UNICTR; See: Bouwknegt, T. (2011). 'Prosecuting 'genocidaires' in Arusha.' *International Justice Tribune*, July 20, p. 4.

29 Bouwknegt (2011), 4.

30 Article 18 (1) on combating impunity during the transition, Protocol II on Democracy and Governance of the Arusha Peace and Reconciliation Agreement provides:
"In accordance with Protocol I to the Agreement, the transitional Government shall request the establishment of an International Judicial Commission of Inquiry which will investigate acts of genocide, war crimes and other crimes against humanity and report thereon to the Security Council of the United Nations."

serious crimes of international concern and report to the United Nations Security Council. The Final Report of the Commission emphasized that as a result of historic narratives in the country, Burundian criminal law and criminal procedure may not adequately respond to serious crimes committed in Burundi during the conflict.[31] The recommendations of the Commission noted in strong terms the "...overriding ethnic confrontations and total insecurity throughout the country."[32]

The Final Report of the Commission concludes that "...acts of genocide against the Tutsi minority were committed in Burundi in October 1993."[33] The extent of homicide in Burundi is however wider than the annihilation of one ethnic group. It is noteworthy that at the time of writing of the Final Report, it was well established that "...among the...adult population of Burundi, tens, if not hundreds, of thousands of individuals from both ethnic groups have at one time or another committed homicide."[34] Despite the need for a Special Tribunal for Burundi as provided in the Arusha Peace and Reconciliation Agreement, there has not been sufficient goodwill on the part of the government of Burundi to establish this Tribunal. The Tribunal, if it existed, would be poised to address serious crimes of an international concern that have been committed in Burundi. The Tribunal would have an international character in which an independent prosecutor and the possibility of international judges and other staff members would be contracted to avert political interference of the criminal trials.

The advent of the ICC in the DRC signifies the growing concern of the international community on the culture of impunity on the African continent. The DRC is a party to the Rome Statute that established the ICC and referred the situation in the country to the ICC Prosecutor in 2004.[35] There are dissenting opinions

---

31 The Final Report notes that "[n]o amount of reforms or resources can have any effect as long as every citizen faces the ever present and very real danger of death at the hands of members of either ethnic group, and as long as every citizen is convinced that his own ethnic group is under attack by people who have repeatedly shown that they do not hesitate to commit mass murder."

32 Final Report of the International Commission of Inquiry for Burundi (further: Final Report) (2004), para. 492 available from the United States Institute of Peace; online at http://www.usip.org/files/file/resources/collections/commissions/Burundi-Report.pdf.

33 Final Report (2004), para. 496.

34 Final Report (2004), para. 494.

35 ICC Press Release. 2004. 'Prosecutor receives referral of the situation in the Democratic Republic of Congo', online at http://www.icc-cpi.int/menus/icc/situations%20and%20cases/situations/situation%20icc%200104/press%20releases/prosecutor%20receives%20referral%20of%20the%20situation%20in%20the%20democratic%20republic%20o%20congo.

on the efficacy of the ICC to address impunity gaps in the DRC, however. For instance, it is widely believed that the few selected for investigation and prosecution represent a single divide in the political conflict between the parties that were involved in the conflict.

The report on serious violations of international humanitarian law in the DRC between 1993 and 2003, compiled by the UN High Commission on Human Rights, implicates a number of states and armed rebel groups operating in the region with the commission of war crimes and crimes against humanity. The report fell short of implicating other states such as Rwanda in being complicit in acts that verge on genocide. The report is a scathing indictment of the government of Rwanda, which gained legitimacy from the 1994 genocide against the Tutsi population. On its part, Rwanda has called the report "malicious, offensive and ridiculous".[36] The report notes that there is an international legal duty to prosecute persons suspected of committing serious crimes in the DRC and explores the option of a mixed judicial mechanism consisting of national and international members. The report also urges that the DRC judicial authorities should act to investigate and prosecute applying the principles of universal jurisdiction.

Truth-Seeking

Truth-seeking is widely considered a crucial component of transitional justice processes.

Hayner observes that "…the desire for truth…is powerful and seemingly almost universal, to judge from the wide range of context where these same demands have emerged."[37] The establishment of truth commissions is not novel to the Great Lakes. There have either been failed truth commissions, as in the case of the DRC, where the commission's work was severely impeded by the political affiliations of its commissioners, or there has not been sufficient political will to set up such a commission as in the case of Burundi. The Arusha Peace and Reconciliation Agreement for Burundi provides that "in accordance with Protocol I to the Agreement, a National Truth and Reconciliation Commission shall be established to investigate Human Rights abuses, promote reconciliation and deal with claims

36 Shyaka, A. (2008): 'Justice and Reconciliation in Post-Genocide Rwanda. Assessing the Impact of the International Criminal Tribunal for Rwanda.' *The Review of International Affaires*, LIX, no. 1130–1131, April/September 2008, pp. 15–25.

37 Hayner, P. B. (2011). *Unspeakable Truths: Transitional Justice and the Challenge of Truth Commissions*. New York: Routledge, p. 6.

arising out of past practices relating to the conflict in Burundi."[38] As mentioned above, the Burundi TRC has been established but has yet to commence operations at the time of writing.

Rwanda, on the other hand, has not had a formal truth commission in accordance with western standards. Waldorf however informs us that "…when the idea of incorporating the Gacaca into genocide trials was first discussed, local scholars proposed using the institution instead as a Rwandan version of a truth commission."[39]

Victims and Affected Communities

The victims' rights movement has begun taking a prominent position in discussions surrounding transitional justice, and rightly so. There is no doubt that in the Great Lakes region, there have been gross violations of Human Rights and serious violations of international law. the civilian population has borne the brunt of warring parties in the various conflicts in the region. Although the victims of these violations are most affected, their needs have often been relegated to the periphery in the discussions on transitional justice. Foremost in addressing the rights of victims is redress for the harm that they have suffered. When dealing with victims and the communities affected by international crimes, processes of reparations feature significantly. The subject of reparations has become increasingly important in national and international politics.[40] As Doak emphatically puts it, if we are serious about legitimizing transitional justice in the eyes of victims and communities, then we need to think more carefully about the emotional harms that victims suffer and the impact that such processes may carry.[41]

In addressing the rights of victims and affected communities of the various conflicts in the Great Lakes, it is therefore necessary to consult this group of people and assess what their particular needs are. Community dialogue on issues such as reparations plays a definitive role in reconciliation. By their inclusive nature, this form of consultation creates avenues for exposing the types of violations the

38 Article 18 (2), Protocol II, Arusha Peace Agreement.

39 Waldorf, L. (2006). 'Mass Justice for Mass Atrocity: Rethinking Local Justice as Transitional Justice.' *Temple Law Review*, 91, no. 1, pp. 1–88.

40 Rombouts H. (2004). *Victim Organisations and the Politics of Reparation: a case study on Rwanda*. Antwerp, Oxford: Intersentia, p. 1.

41 Doak, J. (2011). 'The Therapeutic Dimensions of Transitional Justice: Emotional repair and victim satisfaction in international trials and truth commissions.' *International Criminal Law Review*, 11, pp. 263–298.

civilian population has suffered and if managed well, makes perpetrators constructively engage with the victims towards healing wounds from the past. Within a national criminal justice system, victims of international crimes must participate in the activities that seek to determine the cases involving them. In addition, victims must be guaranteed reparation for the harm they have suffered.

Since the adoption of the Rome Statute of the ICC, the rights of victims of international crimes have been advanced. Not only do victims have the right to reparations, victims also have the right to participate in legal proceedings at the ICC. The ICC has also defined the concept of complementarity between the ICC and national criminal justice systems. In brief, the principle confirms that the primacy of jurisdiction for the investigation and prosecution of international crimes rests with national criminal justice systems. There is a move at present to extend the discussions and debate on complementarity to include the participation of victims in legal proceedings and their reparation in national criminal justice systems.

Traditional Justice

Traditional or community-based reconciliation and accountability mechanisms do not feature prominently within national and regional transitional justice and reconciliation frameworks – with the notable exception of Rwanda. This is in part due to the perception that such mechanisms, being regionally-specific or community-focused, could only have a limited impact and are not appropriate for dealing with wide-scale gross violations of Human Rights. Furthermore, within Human Rights circles these mechanisms are often critiqued on the grounds of their perceived retrograde or conservative nature, or on the grounds of inadequate gender and youth representation.

At the same time these mechanisms have important strengths, not least that they are able, through a tangible presence in communities across the continent, to reach where weak or over-committed national and international justice mechanisms fail – whether through a lack of capacity, credibility or cultural suitability. They are furthermore well suited to lend popular support and legitimacy to efforts to build the rule of law. They are also able to provide continuity and sustainability to reconciliation efforts that are too often associated with once-off national events as in the case of a truth commission or an international tribunal. Seen in this light, traditional justice mechanisms have the potential to enhance the range of options available for dealing with dilemmas faced during transitions.

Pending the establishment of national or international mechanisms for justice in the DRC, traditional community reconciliation mechanisms have come into play (notably in Ituri) and have been remarkably effective in rebuilding community ties across ethnic and military fault lines. Similar positive outcomes have been observed in the Ruzizi Plain of Eastern DRC, where trust-building initiatives between *Banyamulenge* (Congolese Tutsi) and other ethnic communities were strengthened through local solidarity structures.

The International Committee of the Red Cross (ICRC) claimed that by August 1996, Rwanda had about 80,000 Hutu crammed into prison facilities.[42] By then, the judicial capacity of the country to handle the increasing number of suspected *génocidaires* had all but crumbled. In reaction to these overwhelming facts, traditional justice mechanisms in Rwanda have played a significant role in responding to the atrocities and promoting a measure of reconciliation. Gacaca courts, which are traditional avenues for justice used by the Rwandan people, were creative ways to complement the formal justice systems. The Gacaca courts in Rwanda, however, went through a significant metamorphosis from the system used in times of old.

Magnarella notes that in Burundi, the judicial staff had been reduced to around twenty investigators and a few secretaries and law clerks.[43] To prosecute the tens of thousands of Burundians who committed acts of genocide and other serious crimes in the conflict in that country would be impossible for any judicial system, let alone Burundi's, which was on the brink of total collapse. While the Arusha Peace and Reconciliation Accord for Burundi (2000) stipulates the "establishment by the United Nations Security Council of an international criminal tribunal", it is debatable whether the political will exists to implement such a mechanism. With many of the members of Burundi's *Bashingantahe* traditional system having compromised themselves during the 20-year conflict, it is difficult to envisage its integration into transitional justice mechanisms at the present time.

It is acknowledged that women and children suffer most in armed conflicts. Femmes Africa Solidarité note that "although most Burundian women could not be said to have participated directly in the events that led to the present conflict, they have nonetheless been worst affected."[44] Mostly placed out of combat, women and children are used as porters and sex slaves. In some instances, women and children are incorporated into the ranks of rebel movements. In times of transition, the Disarmament, demobilization and reintegration process (DDR) must be sensitive to the reintegration of women and children into society. It is important to also bear in mind that sexual and gender-based violence is a weapon in conflicts,

42 Magnarell (2000), 71.

43 Magnarell, (2000), 72.

44 Femmes Africa Solidarité (2001). *Engendering the Peace Process in Burundi: Women's Best Practices in Africa.* Oxford: New Internationalist Publications Ltd., pp. 59–64, 59.

and that the shame and stigma that victims endured should be carefully managed, especially in instances where DDR is implemented.

In the DRC, armed groups raped men with objects in order to assert themselves in the communities and cause deep embarrassment and shame to the victims and the communities who were subjected to full viewing of these crimes. It is important that these victims are involved in the process of dealing with these crimes and that their plight, including medical concerns, are met with concerted efforts for redress. Men and boys are particularly vulnerable in the context of sexual and gender-based violence, since in most African countries, it is taboo to address such a topic. Equally concerning is that there is very little support for this category of victims from the established institutions such as hospitals and even civil society and humanitarian organizations.

Conclusion

While the gender courts in the east of the DRC have dispensed a form of justice to the victims of sexual and gender-based violence by making decisions on the guilt of military personnel responsible for these forms of violence, these courts are not civilian courts and do not deal with crimes beyond the military ranks. Efforts to establish a Special Chamber dealing with international crimes committed in the territory of the DRC and laws relating to the protection of victims and witnesses have not been successful. There is a general lack of political will to establish such bodies, and when the government initiates bills of law in the National Assembly, the process is not inclusive of other key stakeholders within the political and civil society domain to ensure that the laws are aimed at effectively and efficiently dealing with the past atrocities in the DRC. On its part, the ICC's interventions in the cases concerning Thomas Lubanga Dyilo, Germain Katanga, Ngudjolo Chui, Callixte Mbarushimana and now Bosco Ntaganda have dispensed a measure of justice in the east of the DRC where the worst crimes took place, but also have their limitations in addressing the justice concerns the very victims that the processes are aimed at.[45] While community-level initiatives initiated by civil society have assisted the affected communities of the conflict in commencing dialogue on avenues for reconciliation, these efforts are limited to achieving redress for victims and justice for the violations that the community have endured.

---

45 Ngari, A. (2014). 'Hope deferred: abrupt end to the Katanga case fails victims'. *ISS Today*, online at: http://www.issafrica.org/iss-today/hope-deferred-abrupt-end-to-the-katanga-case-fails-victims.

While Burundi has established a Truth and Reconciliation Commission, it remains to be seen whether the commission will establish narratives of the truth concerning the serious crimes and atrocities that the Burundian people have faced in the past. The failure to establish a Special Tribunal and laws relating to victims and witness protection continues to threaten the government efforts for establishing a truth-seeking mechanism. These mechanisms are aimed at complementing each other and ensuring that each mechanism functions at the optimum level of their mandates.

Rwanda remains the only country in the region and on the continent to have successfully used a purely localized mechanism to address the legacy of genocide in the country. The Gacaca system of justice in Rwanda has certainly been etched into history as a locally owned, developed and run process that effectively dealt with the mid- and lower-level perpetrators of the genocide in that country. As the country built its judicial and investigatory capacity over the years, it has been able to adjudicate matters related to the most responsible individuals who planned, organized and executed the genocide. There have been a number of legislative reforms, chief among them being the abolition of the death penalty in Rwanda that has allowed for the extradition of many Rwandans alleged to have been *genocidaires* and living in other countries. On its part, the ICTR has concluded its functioning but a number of fugitives remain at large.[46] The Mechanism for International Criminal Tribunals (MICT) does, however, have the mandate to try these individuals once they have been apprehended and surrendered to the MICT.

Overall, the selected transitional justice mechanisms in the region have failed to have a durable impact on the political, social and economic challenges which persist in each country. These efforts have unfortunately not addressed the deep-rooted issues underpinning successive cycles of conflict. The law-making processes in the Great Lakes have an inherent inclination to protect the regimes in power. With international community/law interference (justified or otherwise) in the sovereignty of each of the States in making their own laws, there is arguably a limited chance for local ownership of transitional justice programmes in the Great Lakes.

46 Nine fugitives remain at large. Of these, three have been earmarked for trial by the MICT: *Félicien* Kabuga, Protais Mpiranya and Augustine Bizimana. The remaining six, Fulgence Kayishema, Charles Sikubwabo, Ladislas Ntaganzwa, Aloys Ndimati, Ryandikayo and Phénéas Munyarugarama, will be referred to Rwanda following the ICTR Prosecutors recommendation.

Jan Hofmeyr

Restorative Justice in Post-Apartheid South Africa. The Truth and Reconciliation Commission and its Deferred Promise

The Promotion of the National Unity and Reconciliation Act 34 of 1995[1] paved the way for the creation of the South African Truth and Reconciliation Commission (TRC). The Commission was mandated to investigate gross Human Rights violations that were committed with a political motive between 1960 and 1994. Importantly, this mandate extended to both sides of the conflict, namely the apartheid state as well as the liberation movements in instances where it was implicated in such conduct.

With its ultimate objective of creating a new society, premised on national reconciliation as a product of justice, the Commission set out to unearth the truth relating to extreme Human Rights violations that occurred during this period by allowing victims to testify about their experiences. The TRC defined 'victims' as direct survivors or relatives or dependents of people who suffered gross Human Rights violations, which included torture, murder, severe ill treatment, abduction, aggravated assault, and detention that resulted from their political affiliations within the circumscribed period.[2] As such, victims were defined quite narrowly in terms of exposure to extreme Human Rights violations cases. Those that experienced other apartheid cruelties, such as forced removals, house arrest, prosecution for accessing so-called white amenities, and economic marginalisation on the basis of inferior education or job reservation, were therefore excluded from this understanding of the term 'victim'.

The provision of conditional amnesty to perpetrators became a much criticized and controversial component of the South African TRC. Some continue to regard its inclusion as an unnecessary compromise related to the country's negotiated transition, although many of the critics also concede that the destruction of evidence prior to the transition made the inclusion of this provision an undesirable,

1 Parliament of the Republic of South Africa (1995) Promotion of National Unity and Reconciliation Act, No. 34 of 1995; Shea, D. (2000). *The South African Truth and Reconciliation Commission.* Washington: USIP; Du Bois-Pedain, A. (2007). *Transitional Amnesty in South Africa.* Cambridge: Cambridge University Press.

2 Parliament of the Republic of South Africa (1995).

but necessary requirement to obtain truths that would otherwise not have been uncovered. For alleged perpetrators to qualify for amnesty, they were required to make a full disclosure of their activities; such activities had to be of a political nature; they had to be proportional; and they had to be executed on behalf of a known political organization. Those who complied were indemnified from any further prosecution.[3] While it is therefore true to say that the South African TRC process was essentially restorative by nature, it had the backing of a retributive threat to those who failed to comply with the provisions for amnesty. Nonetheless, this arrangement, which essentially made the alleged perpetrator answerable to the state and not the victim (amnesty did not require any restorative gesture from the perpetrator towards the victim), may have watered down the most potent restorative traits of this process.

Whether this has been a successful arrangement to get to the heart of the truth remains an open question. A large number of suspected perpetrators never applied in the knowledge that evidence was destroyed, while the failed prosecutions of the former Minister of Defence, Magnus Malan, and the head of the apartheid state's chemical warfare unit, Wouter Basson, for the same reasons, arguably compromised citizens' confidence in the justice system. Although there were some successful prosecutions, such as that of police Colonel Eugene de Kock, some observers felt that ultimately the foot soldiers bore the brunt for the instructions of their political principals. In early 2015, De Kock succeeded in obtaining parole after successive failed applications over several years.

Volumes have already been written about this primary criticism of the South African TRC: the contention that the process prioritized the rights of perpetrators above that of victims and that the aggressors, as a result, benefitted more than the Commission's intended beneficiaries.[4] There is substance to such critiques. Some maintain that only the tip of the iceberg has been uncovered as far as gross Human Rights abuses are concerned, let alone the types the types of abuse that were excluded or did not fall within the TRC's allocated timeframe. Yet, there is little doubt that the Commission lifted the veil on the brutal character of the apartheid regime. This, in turn, has had a profound impact on the post-apartheid narrative. No South African, including the beneficiaries who previously claimed

3 At the conclusion of the process, 7112 amnesty applications were received of which 849 were granted. See Du Bois Pedain (2007), 80–84.

4 Mamdani, M. (1998). *When Does Reconciliation Turn into a Denial of Justice?* Sam Nolutshungu Memorial Series: Human Sciences Research Council; Mamdani, M. (1996) 'Reconciliation Without Justice.' *Southern African Review of Books*, Nov/Dec, pp. 3–5.

that they were oblivious of the regime's cruelty, could henceforth say that they 'did not know.'

The Institute for Justice and Reconciliation's SA Reconciliation Barometer, an annual national public opinion survey which gauges the sentiments of South Africans towards reconciliation and nation-building, shows for example that in 2013, 77 per cent of South Africans agree that apartheid was a crime against humanity and 72 per cent said that it wrongly oppressed the majority of South Africans.[5] The corresponding figure for white South Africans regarding the two measurements was 53 per cent and 50 per cent.[6] These figures for the overall population are high, and while they may be lower for white South Africans, more than half of this group now also acknowledge that the nature of the system which they benefitted from has impeded on the lives of others.

The article now turns to the Commission's recommendations that relate to individual and long-term reparations, because they speak directly to the restorative nature of the process, but also to the ethos of the post-apartheid government. Moreover, as Hamber notes, reparations, together with the exchange of amnesty for the truth, and the space provided for victims to tell their stories, formed the core of what made the TRC.[7] The comments here regarding reparations will be limited to the question of monetary compensation. Unlike its capacity to make decisions on the extension of amnesty, the TRC's recommendations with regard to reparation remained just that: recommendations. It did not have any jurisdiction in the determination of the process and even less so in terms of the amounts awarded to victims. As such, the question of the extent and nature of these recommendations became an issue of political will. And how it unfolded can, arguably, also be regarded as a gauge of the more general approach that the post-apartheid state took to the restoration of those marginalized by the previous regime.

After the TRC

Given the pervasive nature of the apartheid system and the recognition by the TRC that its duration and mandate may have limited the number of apartheid

5 Wale, K. (2013). *2013 SA Reconciliation Barometer Survey Report: Confronting Exclusion – Time for Radical Reconciliation.* Cape Town: Institute for Justice and Reconciliation.

6 Wale (2013).

7 Hamber, B. & Kibble, S. (1999). 'From Truth to Transformation: The Truth and Reconciliation Commission in South Africa.' *Catholic Institute for International Relations Report*, online at: http://www.csvr.org.za/index.php/publications/1714-from-truth-to-transformation-the-truth-and-reconciliationcommission-in-south-africa.html.

victims that were able to testify before it, it did recommend symbolic reparations to facilitate the communal process of remembrance and community rehabilitation programmes aimed at promoting healing and recovery. The Commission also explicitly recommended individual payments to victims or their closest relatives. It provided for urgent, short-term, reparations with a monetary value of between R2,000 and R6,000, where immediate and critical needs existed, but it also proposed long-term payments of between R17,000 and R23,000 per annum over six years for individuals identified by the TRC.[8] In addition, the Commission recommended that the government broaden its scope for reparations to include victims of Human Rights abuse that fell within the mandate of the Promotion of National Unity and Reconciliation Act, but did not have the means to testify before the Commission. In terms of the former, 16,500 individuals received payments by 2002.

However, in response to the recommendation regarding long-term reparations, President Thabo Mbeki indicated in April 2003 that the government would only make a once-off payment of R30,000 to the designated persons. A President's Fund was created for this as well as for the payment of community reparations. Critics, among them the Institute for Justice and Reconciliation's (IJR) Fanie du Toit, were unanimous in their contention that the once-off payment was completely inadequate. Du Toit notes that when considering that many lost their ability to work and continued to live with their past trauma, "the R30000 was more an insult than a relief".[9] By the end of 2012, the government paid out this money to 16,397 of the 21,769 people that were identified by the TRC as victims.[10] Furthermore, no additional attempts were made to follow up on the TRC's recommendation to track down those victims who were not able to testify before the Commission. This has been the case, despite the relentless work of organized civil society organizations, such as the Khulumani Support Group, which continue to document and represent the interests of apartheid era victims.

---

8 Hamber, B. (1998). 'Repairing the Irreparable: Dealing with double-binds of making reparations for crimes of the past.' Paper presented at the African Studies Association of the UK Biennial Conference "Comparisons and Transitions" at SOAS, University of London, London, September 14–16, 1998, online at: http://www.csvr.org.za/docs/trc/repairingtheirreparable.pdf.

9 Du Toit, F. (2013). 'No closure to a hurtful past', *The Star Online,* online at: http://www.iol.co.za/the-star/no-closure-to-a-hurtful-past-1.1489995#.VF87tvmUdN1.

10 Department of Justice and Constitutional Development (2012) 'President's Fund Annual Report.' Online at: http://www.justice.gov.za/reportfiles/other/presfund-anr-2011-12.pdf.

Not only the sum of the reparations payments, but also the way in which the fund has been administrated (or not) in general since its inception provided important insights into the way in which the government has dealt with the recommendations of the TRC in the years following to its creation. The fact that it dragged its feet for almost eight years before it published regulations for community reparations for comment in 2010, following significant pressure from victims' lobbying groups, such as the Khulumani Support Group, the IJR, and the Centre for the Study of Violence and Reconciliation (CSVR), bears testimony to the degree of commitment that the government has shown towards the individual victims and communities deserving of reparations.

The proposed regulations for the disbursement of the funds, which at the time totalled R1 billion, involved very little consultation with victim's groups, and even less time to respond.

In a submission to the Department of Justice, which published the proposed regulations in the Government Gazette, the South African Coalition for Transitional Justice noted that the regulations seem to have shelved the idea of further individual reparations at the cost of communal reparations or community rehabilitation (terms that have been used interchangeably) in 18 communities.[11] The criteria for their selections are undefined, but the proposed services to be rendered, including the provision of proper schooling and health infrastructure as well as skills development support, seem to be responsibilities that the government would have to fulfil in marginalized communities across South Africa anyway. As such, one has the impression that the Fund is merely being used as another 'budget line' for government expenditure, rather than symbolic reparation to direct victims of apartheid era excesses. According the Coalition, the government's proposals only provided for a "small group of victims who made statements to the TRC rather than the thousands who legally qualify as victims of gross Human Rights violations", which is at variance with the TRC's caution against setting up a "privileged group of victims" after completing its operations. Some read more sinister motives into the belatedly published regulations. According to them, the fund allocations have little to do with victim interests and everything with government incompetence. Labelling them dubious, community activist Koketso Moeti suggests that instead of addressing the plight of apartheid era victims, the regulations will provide the scope for badly-run municipalities to be bailed out or to pay for infrastructure

11 South African Coalition for Transitional Justice (2010). 'Press Release: South African Coalition for Transitional Justice urges further efforts to engage victims of pardon applicants.' Online at: http://www.link2media.co.za/index.php?option=com_content&task=view&id=10048&Itemid=12.

funding backlogs at national and provincial government levels, thereby conflating development with apartheid era reparations.[12] If accurate, this approach is nothing short of cynical and communicates the lack of commitment for the institution and processes related to the Truth and Reconciliation Commission.

Behind it may lie a widely-held belief within the governing party that reparations to individuals do not make sense when the black majority, as a collective, has been disadvantaged by apartheid. This contention is not without merit. Even today, the average black household income is only 16 per cent of that for white households. Inequality, as expressed in terms of the Gini coefficient, is 0.70 and is largely still manifested in racial terms.[148] It is this difference between the rich and the poor that keeps citizens in present-day South Africa divided. In successive rounds of the SA Reconciliation Barometer, including the most recent survey, a majority of respondents has indicated that income inequality is the primary source of division between South Africans. 28 per cent indicated that this is the case, while 21 per cent flagged race, and a further 16 per cent attributed division to the polarising influence political parties have on people's perception of each other.[13] This does by no means imply that class has overtaken race as the defining hallmark of South African social relations, because the two still largely overlap. It does, nevertheless, suggest that income inequality has become the single most important determinant of such relations in the eyes of ordinary South Africans.

Economic justice, in other words the creation of a more inclusive and equitable economy, in which more South Africans have access to decent employment and the opportunity to shape their futures, should therefore be the principle priority of the South African state. This should, however, be addressed through appropriate macroeconomic and developmental policy, which must be clearly differentiated from restorative justice and the broader transitional justice project. Both are important and should complement each other, but are, nevertheless, distinct. Economic policy should address poverty and material inequality, that is to say economic injustice, like many other developing countries are doing around the world. This is not the function of reparations, like those proposed by the recently-released government regulations, or even the more far-reaching proposals of the TRC. The number of both the individuals and communities earmarked to benefit are restricted, even if one includes those that did not testify before the TRC. On

12 Moeti, K (2010). 'The Unfinished Business of the TRC'. *Thought Leader Blog*, online at: http://www.thoughtleader.co.za/koketsomoeti/2014/11/05/the-unfinished-business-of-the-trc/,[148] Statistics South Africa (2011). *Census 2011*. Online at: http://www.statssa.gov.za/publications/p03014/p030142011.pdf.

13 See Wale (2013).

the level of individual beneficiaries and communities, reparations should assist them to make up, at least in part, for the material losses that they have suffered as a result of apartheid Human Rights abuses. And even though money cannot return the life of a departed loved one, the monetary amount awarded should symbolically honour the sacrifice that has been made. But more broadly and probably most importantly, their symbolic significance should contribute to laying down a solid normative foundation for post-apartheid governance. It should symbolize a state that keeps its word, that cares, that respects human dignity, and that allows citizens to participate in shaping their own destiny. This creates predictability and trust in the political system and its leaders, even if citizens have to forfeit material security in the short to medium term as a result of macroeconomic constraints. However, although 54 per cent of respondents in the 2013 SA Reconciliation Barometer Survey felt that they could trust the country's leaders to do what is right, 63 per cent indicated that the country's leaders did not really care about people like them, and 54 per cent felt that there was no way to make disinterested leaders acknowledge their plight.[14] These findings suggest a perception of imposition rather than consultation – this same mentality was also a hallmark of the ethos of the apartheid state. Whether it is the massacre at the Marikana mine, where striking miners were killed en masse by police[15], or the publicly broadcasted murder of Andries Tatane[16], a community activist slain while protesting for better living conditions a year earlier, there is striking evidence for the state's lack of compassion.

Given the multiple criticisms that have been levelled at the absence of sufficient retributive measures to bring alleged apartheid criminals to book for their misdemeanours, the South African Truth and Reconciliation model had to redeem itself through its restorative ability. Yet it seems that the symbolic significance of this necessity has been lost on the present government. Also, having been criticized by the TRC for violent Human Rights abuses within ANC detention camps, it appears that the current government prefers to create its own narrative in which it is the author of the country's freedom and the values enshrined in its constitution. In this narrative, its leaders stood as giants at the forefront of the struggle and where the trials and tribulations of ordinary citizens were cast in the shadow of the party's presence. By taking away the individual's right to reparations and

14 See Wale (2013).

15 Tolsi, N. (2013). 'Marikana: One year after the massacre'. *Mail and Guardian Online*, online at: http://marikana.mg.co.za/.

16 City Press (2013). 'Andries Tatane killed again'. *City Press Online*, online at: http://www.citypress.co.za/citypress-says/andries-tatane-killed-again/.

replacing it with a vague model containing many responsibilities that are typically ascribed to a state otherwise as well, it has lost an important opportunity to change the trajectory of the country's politics.

This author concurs with Du Toit when he notes on the question of reparations that "[T]imeous and generous reparations would have been the right thing to do. It would have kept our promise to those who paid the highest price for our freedom. We have failed that test. Not only does this jeopardise the legacy of one of the world's most potent political achievements, but it leaves a gaping hole in our nation-building project".

Conclusion

When compared to other major political transitions of the twentieth century, South Africa's peaceful transformation to a democratic society has been described as a political miracle. One only needs to look to the north at the case of Rwanda, which in the same year witnessed one of the worst genocides of the century. But for the miracle to be consolidated, it needed to establish a new normative order that would replace the cycle of dispossession and violence that preceded it. The entrenched nature of the country's intergenerational trauma precluded simple solutions where the rule of law could from one day to the next be imposed to regulate the behaviour of citizens, who have been divided and in mostly antagonistic relationships with each other for centuries. And even if this had been possible, the destruction of evidence during the last days of apartheid would have made the retributive criminal prosecutions extremely difficult.

South Africa's approach was therefore a novel one; one that recognized its limitations and required trade-offs, such as the provision of conditional amnesty, which may not have been palatable for many judicial purists, but proved to be most practical in the circumstances at hand. During the period in which the Commission was in session, the uncompromising execution of its mandate did not win it many friends among the political stakeholders with a vested interest in its outcome. It was often the target of criticism by politicians, but also others who questioned the fairness of its procedures and functioning. There may be merit to some of these points of criticism, concerning, for example, the treatment of victims testifying before the commission. Yet, much of the blame that is today directed at the TRC, which it is being held responsible for the increasingly polarized nature of post-Mandela South Africa, is misdirected. Instead, more critical questions should be levelled at the commitment of the country's political elite to create an entrenched normative post-apartheid order which places human dignity at its centre. How committed was it to using its resources in order to send a clear symbolical message to those identified by the TRC – but also by South Africans more broadly – that it is a state that does not tolerate Human Rights abuse, and where it does occur, it will unequivocally choose the side of the victim?

Indeed, the country's achievements over the past 20 years have been significant, but the growing political fragmentation in its society obstructs solutions to deep-lying poverty, and the growing social inequality threatens these accomplishments. Far from being unified, the country often seems to be fighting itself, rather than the raft of developmental challenges it is facing. Bargaining, more often than not, has become a zero-sum game, in which parties battle to the bitter end to win at all costs.

The TRC was never meant to transform South African society, but rather to be a catalyst that would allow the state to change the quality and nature of relations between its citizens. It opened up the possibility for inclusive solutions. With all the shortcomings of an ambitious social experiment, the Commission has fulfilled its catalytic role during the transitional years. Halfway through the second decade of the new millennium, a deeply divided South Africa is in desperate need for a return to this ethos.

Anna Grzywacz

Transitional Justice in East Timor: Timorese Political Pragmatism and Its Effectiveness

The issue of transitional justice in East Timor has been widely described in the literature.[1] However, much of this literature focuses on the effectiveness of the solutions proposed by the UN, criticism of the organization or analysis of how this institution's solutions were questioned by society, and how the government of East Timor introduced its own solutions and standards to reconstruct the state and nation. In the theoretical discussion about transitional justice, several approaches clash with each other: the conviction about the existence of certain universal tools and mechanisms that can be applied to almost any transition is confronted with the frequent beliefs of local actors, according to whom every situation needs a unique approach in order to lead to positive results on the ground. This clash is reflected in the current debate about top-down judicial intervention by the International Criminal Court versus bottom-up initiatives; and it often overlaps with the cleavage between supporters of restorative versus retributive justice, as set out in the Patrick Wegner's chapter about Uganda in this book. There also is a lawyer-driven strand in transitional justice, which argues in favour of certain norms and values that should be universally applied and which is confronted by a more anthropological way of thinking (supported by many political scientists), which sees the purpose of transitional justice not in the necessity to strengthen universal norms and values, but in the sustainability of the post-transition situation.[2] In other words, the latter's focus is not so much on whether transitional

1 DeShaw Rae, J. (2009). *Peacebuilding and Transitional Justice in East Timor.* Boulder: Lynne Rienner Publishers; Ottendörfer, E. (2013). 'Contesting International Norms of Transitional Justice'. *International Journal of Peace and Violence,* 7, no.1, pp. 23–35; Harris Rimmer, S. (2010). *Gender and Transitional Justice: the Women of East Timor,* London, New York: Routledge; Kent, L. (2012). *The Dynamics of Transitional Justice. International Models and Local Realities in East Timor.* London, New York: Routledge; Drexler, E. (2009). 'Addressing the Legacies of Mass Violence and Genocide in East Timor and Indonesia'. In: Hinton, A., O'Neill, K. L. (2009) (eds). *Genocide: Truth, Memory and Representation.* Durham: Duke University Press, pp. 219–246.

2 Some authors argue that transitional justice should enhance and facilitate reconstruction and economic development, while others concentrate on the need to build a politically inclusive, stable and democratic society. For the first argument see: de Greiff, P.

justice is just, fair and lives up to certain universal standards, but whether it is efficient and leads to sustainable democratization and strengthens the rule of law.

A similar approach to transitional justice is political pragmatism, which results from concerns about the consequences and effects of prosecutions on the consolidation of peace, democracy[3] and development in the country. The purpose of this chapter is to analyse the situation in East Timor and to look at how the politics of pragmatism has been understood by the Timorese government. The chapter argues that East Timorese politicians favour restorative justice over retributive justice in the name of stability and reconstruction.

This chapter is divided into several parts. First, it describes the relation between restorative and retributive justice, which are often treated as contradictory or not related to each other. Then, after a historical outline of the conflict in East Timor, the transitional justice mechanisms used in this country are presented, together with their perception by both the government and Timorese public. The last part shows the social problems and tensions resulting from unresolved issues, which also shows in how far Timorese political pragmatism was effective.

Restorative and Retributive Justice as Complementary Elements of Justice

Restorative and retributive justice must not be seen as complementary. Their primary objective is to provide a notion of accountability, while respecting the rights of victims, including the search for truth about the past (truth-seeking).[4] Restorative justice programmes aim to address conflicts by involving the victim and the offender as well as judicial bodies, communities, and social networks[5]. "The core idea of restorative justice is that the people most affected by a problem decide

and Duthie, R. (2009) (eds.). *Transitional Justice and Development. Making Connections.* New York: Social Science Research Council. For the second: Lincoln, J. (2001). *Transitional Justice, Peace and Accountability: Outreach and the role of International Courts After Conflicts.* New York: Routledge and Bachmann, K. and Fatić, A. (2015). *The UN International Criminal Tribunals. Transition without Justice?* London, New York: Routledge.

3 Lincoln (2001), 24.

4 Cf. Garcia-Godos, J., Lekha Sriram, C. (2013). 'Introduction'. In: Lekha Sriram, C., Garcia-Godos, J., Herman, J., Martin-Ortega, O. (2013) (eds). *Transitional Justice and Peacebuilding on the Ground. Victims and Ex-combatants.* London, New York: Routledge, p. 2.

5 United Nations (2006). *Handbook on Restorative Justice Programmes.* (Criminal Justice Handbook Series). New York: UN, pp. 4–5.

among themselves how it should be dealt with."[6] Restorative justice programmes are more flexible than criminal justice processes, and victims can express their needs or expectations in a less formal way than they are allowed to do that during trials. By participating in such a process, both the victim and perpetrator can reconcile on terms adapted to the victim's needs. Retributive justice is defined as a criminal justice process, it "refers to the repair of justice through unilateral imposition of punishment, whereas restorative justice means the repair of justice through reaffirming a shared-values consensus in a bilateral process"[7]. For Roger Duthie, transitional justice promotes trust between individuals, groups and institutions in society. Prosecutions can generate trust between citizens and public institutions by restoring the rule of law. Institutional reforms, such as vetting procedures, can be seen as an effort to make public institutions effective and restore the trust in them. Moreover, justice and reconciliation initiatives can be used to help directly at the local level through the reintegration of former militaries, policemen, and secret service agents into society, thus enhancing trust in state institutions.[8] In such cases, it is difficult to separate the issue of transitional justice from the country's development in general, as some transitional justice measures can undermine, while others can bolster the rule of law, democracy, and economic development. As Jessica Lincoln argues, "the decision to uphold a norm of accountability should only be made if it is likely to be effective in achieving substantive ends; war crime trials are therefore not a goal in themselves but are to be pursued only if they assist in the attainment of pragmatic substantive goals (peace and justice)".[9]

Outline of the Conflict between Indonesia and East Timor

East Timor achieved its independence from Portugal in 1974. In 1975, Indonesia took advantage of the internal conflicts in East Timor which followed independence and annexed the country, occupying it with more than thirty-five thousand soldiers. Although the international community never recognized the annexation by Indonesia, on May 31, 1976 Indonesia appointed an interim government of

---

6 Johntone, G., Van Ness, D. W. (2007) (eds). *Handbook of Restorative Justice.* Portland: Willan Publishing, p. xxi.

7 Bukuluki, P. (2011). *Negotiating Retributive and Restorative Justice in Conflict Transformation Efforts*, Zürich, Berlin: Lit-Verlag p. 43.

8 Duthie, R. (2005). 'Transitional Justice and Social Reintegration.' Paper prepared for the Stockholm Initiative on Disarmament Demobilisation Reintegration (SIDDR), Working Group 3: Reintegration and Peace Building meeting, April 4–5, 2005, p. 3.

9 Lincoln (2001), 24.

East Timor, which decided to integrate with the Indonesian state.[10] East Timor became Indonesia's 27th province.

The independence movement – the Revolutionary Front for an Independent East Timor (Frente Revolucionária de Timor-Leste Independente, FRETILIN) – fought against the Indonesian forces. Estimates of the number of victims caused by the conflict (including those who starved to death) oscillate between tens of thousands and two hundred thousand.[11] Much of the low-level violence during the late 1970s and 1980s did not attract international attention but nevertheless destroyed the country. Massive Human Rights violations were committed by the Indonesian armed forces against the supporters of Timorese independence. The international community did not react until November 1991, when Indonesian security forces opened fire against a demonstration near the Santa Cruz cemetery in Dili, killing an estimated fifty to two hundred people.[12] The resistance leader José Alexandre "Xanana" Gusmão was captured and sentenced in 1993 to life imprisonment (the verdict was later amended to twenty years in prison). In 1996, two Timorese, Carlos Filipe Ximenes Belo, apostolic administrator of Dili, and José Ramos-Horta, a spokesman of the East Timorese resistance movement, received the Nobel Peace Prize for their efforts to restore justice and peace.[13] A growing number of non-governmental and parliamentary groups in Western countries began to exert pressure on their countries' governments, supporting East Timor independence.[14]

Indonesia had always objected to the direct inclusion of Timorese politicians in the conflict negotiations, arguing that East Timor had expressed its opinion in 1976 when the Timorese government decided to become a part of Indonesia. The actions that were taken, such as accession to the UN's annual All-Inclusive Intra-East Timorese Dialogue (AIETD), which began in 1995, were based on

---

10 The provisional government was in fact Indonesian and not Timorese.

11 McCloskey, S. (2000). 'Introduction: East Timor – From European to Third World Colonialism'. In: Hainsworth, P., McCloskey, S. (2000) (eds). *The East Timor Question. The Struggle for Independence from Indonesia.* New York: I. B. Taurus, pp. 3–4.

12 United Nations (2004). *The United Nations and East Timor: Self-Determination through popular consultation.* New York: United Nations Publications, p. 4.

13 Kingsbury, D. (2009). *East Timor. The Price of Liberty.* New York: Palgrave MacMillan, pp. 60–65.

14 Martin, Ian (2001). *Self-determination in East Timor. The United Nations, the Ballot, and International Intervention*. Boulder: Lynne Rienner Publishers, p. 19, online at: http://elibrary.kiu.ac.ug:8080/jspui/bitstream/1/140/1/Self-Determination%20in%20East%20Timor%20The%20United%20Nations,%20the%20Ballot,%20and%20International%20Intervention%20%28International%20Peace%20Academy%20Occasional%20Paper%20Series%29.pdf.

the assurance that dialogue would not question the current political status of East Timor. Over time, the independence movement became stronger, and in April 1998, the National Council of Timorese Resistance (NCTR) was founded under the leadership of Gusmão, who continued his political activity from prison. Under international pressure, the Indonesian government decided that Gusmão would be released. In August 1998 Indonesia accepted East Timor as an active part of the tripartite negotiation process, chaired by the UN Secretary-General.[15] Representatives of the UN AIETD organized a meeting with Timorese leaders in August of that year, with the aim of preparing negotiations over a mutual agreement.[16] Jakarta agreed to such a solution. The creation of the East Timorese Consultative Council, which was to have twenty-five members, ten from both sides and five appointed by the UN Secretary-General, was approved.[17] Their aim was to accompany and coordinate the transition process. Under UN auspices, a referendum was carried out in August 1999 and despite the pressure from the Indonesian government, most of East Timor's residents opted for independence. As a result, the Indonesian army destroyed around seventy per cent of the infrastructure and killed more than a thousand people. Indonesian forces were ordered to destroy as much as possible. Some of the messages left by these forces in the ruins of Dili declared "A free East Timor will eat stones" and "Slowly but surely, this place will fall apart".[18] Indonesian forces did not respect any Human Rights. The crimes committed were severe enough to incline some observers to label them genocide.[19] Under the impression of the atrocities, the Australian government lobbied the United States (US) government and the UN to obtain support for an Australian-led intervention force, the aim of which was to end violence. Under the double pressure of international isolation and economic decline, the Indonesian government agreed to withdraw its troops from East Timor, opening the way to an Australian-led UN force with a Security Council mandate.[20] In October of that year, the United Nations Transitional Administration in East Timor (UNTAET)

15 Martin (2001), 19.

16 Marker, J. (2003). *East Timor: A Memoir of the Negotiations for Independence.* Jefferson: McFarland, p. 175.

17 Martin (2001), 68.

18 Quotes are from Scott, C. (2001). 'East Timor: transition to statehood.' *Catholic Institute of International Relations (CIIR) Comment*, London, p. 4; Mydans, S. (1999). 'Refugees are joyful in a Dili of Ashes'. *New York Times*, September 21, 1999.

19 Nevins, J. (2005). *A Not-So-Distant Horror: Mass Violence in East Timor.* Ithaca, New York: Cornell University Press, pp. 217–218.

20 UNSC resolution 1264.

was established. It was mandated to reconstruct the country and over two years later, the Administration transferred its authority to East Timor, which became independent.[21]

The ravaged country was committed to finding a way to effectively deal with crimes and Human Rights violations committed in the past. East Timor has used many transitional justice measures, national and international ones, to achieve that ambitious goal.

Mechanisms of Retributive and Restorative Justice Implemented in East Timor

In October of 1999, at the request of the Commission on Human Rights, the UN Secretary-General appointed the International Commission of Inquiry on East Timor to prepare a report and evaluation of events. One month earlier, Indonesia had established the National Commission of Inquiry on Human Rights Violations in East Timor, which aimed to gather information on Human Rights violations committed during the years of Indonesian occupation. At the beginning of 2001, a report was published. It claimed the responsibility of the Indonesian armed forces for the crimes and demanded the establishment of a special court to prosecute perpetrators.[22] Abdurrahman Wahid, at the time president of Indonesia, in consultation with the Secretary-General of the United Nations, proposed the establishment of a local court. In August of 2001, the *Ad Hoc* Human Rights Court in Jakarta was established by a decree issued by the next Indonesian president Megawati[23].

Subsequent to reservations about the court's proceedings, the Special Panels for Serious Crimes in East Timor were established in 2000[24]. Their jurisdiction included acts of genocide, war crimes, crimes against humanity, murder, sexual offences and torture. This was the first case in which a local court wielded such broad jurisdiction. The jurisdiction of the panels over murders and sexual offences was limited to crimes committed between January 1 and October 25, 1999, which

21 Gunn, G. C. (2011). *Historical Dictionary of East Timor.* Plymouth: Scarecrow Press, pp. 20–21.

22 UN (2001). *Yearbook of the United Nations 2000.* Volume 54, New York, pp. 754–755.

23 Purdey, J. (2008). 'Legal Responses to violence in post-Soeharto Indonesia.' In: Lindsey, T. (2008) (ed.). *Indonesia. Law and Society.* Toronto, Singapore: Irwin Law (The Federation Press), pp. 521–523.

24 See: UNTAET, 'On the Establishment of Panels with Exclusive Jurisdiction Over Serious Criminal Offences'. UN Doc. UNTAET/Reg/2000/15, June 6, 2000, online at: http://www.un.org/en/peacekeeping/missions/past/etimor/untaetR/Reg0015E.pdf.

was the period of the most severe violence in East Timor, which was stopped by the creation of the UNTAET.[25] The panels completed their activities after the publication of the last judgment in April of 2005. Eighty-four defendants were convicted, but the panels failed to judge high-ranking perpetrators, who most likely will never be brought to justice. Most of them now live in Indonesia and are sheltered by the lack of an extradition agreement between the two countries.[26]

East Timor is an example of a country where truth commissions operated at the same time as a criminal tribunal. The Committee on Reception, Truth and Reconciliation in East Timor (Comissão de Acolhimento, Verdade e Reconciliação, CAVR) was established by the UNTAET regulation in July 2001[27]. It was created to complement the activities of the Special Panels. It had a broad right to issue subpoenas and to pose the requirement of testifying under oath, the right to seek and receive information, both at home and abroad. The committee had the right to request a search warrant in order to obtain evidence. The UNTAET decree created a procedure called the Community Reconciliation Process, which allowed offenders of minor crimes to be granted immunity and helped them to return to society in exchange for a voluntary confession, testimony and comprehensive social work or public apology.[28] The perpetrators of the most serious crimes were deprived of this possibility and their cases were transferred to the Office of the General Prosecutor with a request to initiate criminal proceedings. The commission had to cooperate with the Attorney General, and, if necessary, give the attorney access to the collected information[29].

CAVR's main aim was to establish the truth about the violence and Human Rights abuses, including the context, causes and reasons which led to the violence,

---

25 Bassiouni, M. C. (2011). *Crimes Against Humanity. Historical Evolution and Contemporary Application.* New York: Cambridge University Press, pp. 247–253.

26 Schlicher, M. (2005). 'East Timor Faces up to its Past. The work of the Commission for Reception, Truth and Reconciliation'. Aachen: Missio 2005, pp. 13–16, online at: http://www.missio-hilft.de/media/thema/menschenrechte/studie/25-osttimor-en.pdf.

27 See: Comissão de Acolhimento, Verdade e Reconciliação, online at: http://www.cavr-timorleste.org/en/cavr.htm.

28 McAuliffe, P. (2008). 'East Timor's Community Reconciliation Process as a Model for Legal Pluralism in Criminal Justice'. *Law, Social Justice and Global Development Journal*, 12, issue 2, pp. 1–21; online at: http://www2.warwick.ac.uk/fac/soc/law/elj/lgd/2008_2/mcauliffe/mcauliffe.pdf.

29 See Kent, L. (2004). 'Unfulfilled Expectations: Community Views on CAVR's Community Reconciliation Process.' Judicial System Monitoring Programme, Dili, online at: http://www.cavr-timorleste.org/otherFiles/Lia%20Kent_Report.pdf.

but also to identify all of the conflict parties involved in these abuses.[30] All these findings were included in the report entitled *Chega!* (in Portugese: no more, stop, enough[31]) issued by CAVR in 2006.[32] The report is organized thematically to provide all information about the violence committed in East Timor. The most important part of the report is section 7, which presents a catalogue of all of the Human Rights violations. The report was prepared with the involvement and help of Timorese victims and, although it is not legally binding, it is regarded as an important part of the healing process.

Chega! was perceived as an impressive effort to construct a dialogue, mainly based on the memoirs of the Timorese people. Its authors did therefore not regard it as an authoritative account, but claimed to give voice to the victims and to include their perspective in the process of creating an inclusive understanding of Timorese history and nation building.[33]

The report also contained recommendations. It urged the governments to set up a reparations programs, to erect memorials for the victims and to launch forensic inquiries into mass graves and investigations about the whereabouts of disappeared persons. The international community was asked to distribute and promote the report as widely as possible, to support governmental reparations, the truth-telling process and the return of Timorese cultural goods, which had been robbed during the violence. Special attention was paid to the responsibilities of countries "who gave military backing to the Indonesian Government between 1974 and 1999 and who are duty bound to uphold the highest principles of world order and peace and to protect the weak and vulnerable", namely the US, Great Britain and France.[34] The report also requested to prosecute perpetrators of the violence prior to 1999 and if necessary, to create an international tribunal for East Timor.[35] The report also included some far-reaching and far-fetched appeals

---

30 Commission for Reception, Truth and Reconciliation (CAVR) (2005). *Chega! Final Report of the Commission for Reception, Truth and Reconciliation*. Dili: Commission for Reception, Truth and Reconciliation, p. 7, online at: http://www.cavr-timorleste.org/chegaFiles/1162273558-Chega!-Report-Executive-Summary.pdf.

31 Online at: http://www.cavr-timorleste.org/en/chegaReport.htm.

32 The commission held eight national hearings, conducted 1,048 research interviews, and received 7,760 victim statements.

33 Webster, D. (2007/2008). 'History, Nation and Narrative in East Timor's Truth Commission Report.' *Pacific Affairs* 2007/2008, 80, no. 4, Special Forum: East Timor's Truth Commission, p. 582.

34 Part 11 of *Ghega!* Report, p. 4. online at: http://www.cavr-timorleste.org/chegaFiles/finalReportEng/11-Recommendations.pdf.

35 CAVR: Chega! (2005), 12.

to both governments and the population, for example to promote and protect Human Rights, support the proliferation of a universal Human Rights culture, strengthen civil society, parliamentarianism, the judiciary, and religious associations, to remove violence from political life, and to consider a follow-up to CAVR.[36] Most of the recommendation were never implemented.

CAVR was not assessed very well by the victims. Their criticism focused primarily on the limited mandate, the institutional deficits, the low degree of social participation, which was due to the lack of awareness about CAVR.[37] Some victims complained about too low verdicts for the perpetrators or the lack hereof due to the legal shelter some perpetrators had found in Indonesia. Both of these aspects are the basis of the negative evaluation of the commission by some authors.[38]

But the CAVR report was also rejected by Indonesia in January 2006. The Indonesian government did not agree with the report's negative assessment of Indonesian politics. In Indonesia, the report was also received negatively because of the document's retrospective of the events following the referendum in 1999, which were to be addressed by a joint Commission of Truth and Friendship (CTF). Some Indonesian politicians spoke very critically about the report, including the president's spokesman Dino Patti Djalal, who condemned the report for being distorted and making unfair accusations.[39] Foreign Ministry spokesman Yuri Thamrin rejected the recommendations as unrealistic and impractical.[40] President Gusmão also criticized parts of the report. He admitted that the lack of prosecution may be an obstacle in building a democratic and stable state, but also found too much idealism in the report.[41] With regard to the appeal to investigate and prosecute more crimes committed after 1975, he argued that this could destabilize the country.[42] He also refuted the request for the establishment of an international tribunal, because "it will be meaningless if we have all the perpetrators in jail, but the people continue to face high infant mortality, endemic and

36 CAVR: Chega! (2005), 13.
37 Kent (2004), passim.
38 Hamutuk, L. (2003). 'Reviewing the East Timor Commission for Reception, Truth and Reconciliation (CAVR)'. *La'u Hamutuk Bulletin,* 4, no. 5.
39 *The Jakarta Post,* January 20, 2006, online at: East Timor and Indonesian Action Network: http://www.etan.org/et2006/january/14/20ri.htm.
40 'RI Dismisses Report on Timor Atrocities during Occupation'. *The Jakarta Post,* January 20, 2006.
41 Kent, L. (2012). *The Dynamics of Transitional Justice. International Models and Local Realities in East Timor.* Abington, New York: Routledge, p. 133.
42 Kent (2012), 133.

epidemic diseases, without decent housing, without clean water and food."[43] In other words – he gave priority to reconstruction needs over the need for justice. He was not alone. Taking into account the need to maintain good relations with Indonesia, Timorese political leaders have focused primarily on economic development, social justice and building democratic structures, creating an atmosphere of forgiveness as the best way to stabilize the country.[44] They were also forced to embark on that path by the lack of international support for possible alternatives. In 2004, president Gusmão stated: "I say don't force East Timor to punish. Have an international tribunal. The international community should deal with punishment of crimes, not East Timor."[45] These words should not be read as an attempt to transfer responsibility, but rather as a statement on the fact that a small and weak emerging state lacks the conditions to tackle the judicial challenges of a transition from a violent past to a more peaceful present, especially if hampered by and dependent on a more powerful neighbour.[46]

The Social Consequences of Forgiving and Forgetting

When it became independent, East Timor was almost a failed and destroyed state. The first years of rebuilding the political, social and institutional fundaments can retrospectively be regarded as a success.[47]

The Government of East Timor adopted a national development plan, the implementation of which was to ensure the consolidation of peace in the country. The document entitled "Goodbye Conflict, Welcome Development" showed that the transition focused more on long-term development objectives and strategies than on overcoming the past.[48] The development plans included a number

---

43 Castel, H. (2013). 'Maximizing Transitional Justice Opportunities: the Case for East Timor's CAVR'. In: Mayersen, D.; Pohlman, A. (2013) (eds). *Genocide and Mass Atrocities in Asia. Legacies and Prevention.* London, New York: Routledge, p. 76.

44 Pigou, P. (2003). *Crying Without Tears: In Pursuit of Justice and Reconciliation in Timor-Leste: Community Perspectives and Expectations.* New York: International Centre for Transitional Justice, online at: www.ictj.org/downloads/Crying_Without_Tears_designed.pdf.

45 Rimmer (2010), 58.

46 Braithwaite, J., Charlesworth, H., Soares, A. (2012). *Networked Governance of Freedom and Tyranny: Peace in Timor-Leste.* Canberra, p. 204. Stanley, E. (2009). *Torture, Truth and Justice. The case of Timor-Leste.* London, New York: Routledge, p. 110.

47 See Government of East Timor (2013): *Goodbye Conflict, Welcome Development, AMP Government Snapshot (2007–2012).* IV Constitutional Government, Dili.

48 Government of East Timor (2013).

of priorities. Among those, "safety and security" scored much higher than "access to justice", according to an retrospective assessment.[49] Since independence, parliamentary elections have been held twice (2001, 2007), as have presidential elections (2002 and 2007), all of which took place in a relatively peaceful way with a high voter turnout (over eighty per cent). In 2010, the first local elections were carried out.[50]

However, East Timor's post-transitional focus on reconstruction and development also came with a price tag. Reconstruction and developing the judiciary and its independence and autonomy were no priority, and transitional justice, with its components of prosecuting the perpetrators, was postponed and sidelined in the name of the country's stability and nation building. One might argue that such a course of events was hardly able to establish the principles of accountability, judicial independence and the separation of powers in Timorese society, which may be the reason why the judiciary is so often criticized by the public.[51] In the transition process, short-term security imperatives were favoured by the government over the long-term and more costly processes to ensure the independence of judicial institutions within which peace was being built.

---

49 Timor-Leste Ministry of Finance (2010). *Development Partners Meeting, Background Paper*, pp. 10–11, online at: http://timor-leste.gov.tl/wp-content/uploads/2010/04/2010-TLDPM-Background-Document_-04.04.10_EN1.pdf.

50 Timor-Leste Ministry of Finance (2010), 9.

51 Graydon, C. (2005). 'Local Justice Systems in Timor-Leste: Washed up, or Watch this Space?' *Development Bulletin*, no. 68, pp. 66–70; also Grenfell, L. (2009). 'Promoting the Rule of Law in Timor-Leste.' *Conflict, Security & Development*, 9, no. 2, pp. 213–238; Grenfell, L. (2006). 'Legal Pluralism and the Rule of Law in Timor-Leste'. *Leiden Journal of International Law*, no. 19, pp. 305–337.

Gjylbehare Bella Murati

A Surrogate State's[1] Approach to Transitional Justice - The Kosovo experience

Since June 1999, the territory of Kosovo has been under the interim administration of the United Nations Mission in Kosovo (UNMIK), which engaged in the complex task of post-conflict peace-building.[2] Established pursuant to Security Council Resolution 1244, UNMIK was empowered to temporarily exercise complete sovereignty over the territory of Kosovo, including performing basic civilian administrative functions; overseeing the development of provisional institutions for democratic and autonomous self-government (pending a political settlement); and protecting and promoting Human Rights. Until 2005, its structure comprised four pillars, each assigned to different tasks[3]: Pillar I was in charge of Police and Justice and Pillar II of Civil Administration, both under the direct leadership of the Special Representative of the UN Secretary-General (SRSG), who represents the United Nations in Kosovo; Pillar III was responsible for Democratization and Institution Building and led by the Organization for Security and Cooperation in Europe (OSCE); Pillar IV, led by the European Union (EU), was in charge

1 The term "surrogate state" comes from the Kosovo Ombudsperson. See, Special Report No. 1. *On the accountability with international standards of UNMIK Nr; 2000/47 On the Status, Privileges and Immunities of KFOR, UNMIK and Their Personnel in Kosovo*, issued on August 18, 2000, para. 23.

2 There is political disagreement over the name of the territory. Albanians refer to the territory as Kosova while Serbia as Kosovo or Kosovo and Metohija. The latter term dates to the abrogation of Kosovo autonomy in March 1989. In order not to take a political stand, the appellation Kosovo will be used throughout this work.

3 The major tasks of UNMIK included: 'Performing basic civilian administrative functions where and as long as required; Organizing and overseeing the development of provisional institutions for democratic and autonomous self-government pending a political settlement, including the holding of elections; Transferring, as these institutions are established, its administrative responsibilities while overseeing and supporting the consolidation of Kosovo provisional institutions and other peace-building activities; Supporting the reconstruction of key infrastructure and other economic reconstruction; Maintaining civil law order, including establishing local police forces and meanwhile through the deployment of international police personnel to serve in Kosovo; Protecting and promoting Human Rights.'

of Reconstruction and Economic Development.[4] The SRSG was entrusted with absolute power to exercise the legislative, executive, and judicial power over the administering entity, and as such enjoyed the maximum civilian executive powers envisaged by UNSC Resolution 1244.

Soon after the proclamation of independence,[5] the UNMIK was expected to fully cede power to the EU, but legal grounds for a structured transition have been lacking. The lack of unanimity within the United Nations Security Council to endorse the new resolution, which would establish the legal grounds for deploying a new EU mission in Kosovo, has brought new sets of problems to the functioning of the newly created state. However, until a temporary solution is found, the UN Secretary-General has made a decision on the basis of UN Security Resolution 1244 to reconfigure the United Nations presence in Kosovo and as such enable the deployment of a new EU mission.[6]

In light of the above, the European Union's Rule of Law mission in Kosovo (EULEX) has been deployed and formally operates under the authority of a

---

4 Pursuant to UNMIK Regulation 2001/9 on the Constitutional Framework for Provisional Self-Government in Kosovo, May 15, 2001, a number of competencies were transferred to local government institutions. However, the SRSG had continued to exercise powers and responsibilities in the legal field, over law enforcement institutions, and the correctional service to conclude agreements with states and international organizations in all matters within the scope of UNSCR 1244 (1999).

5 In 2005, the UN Secretary-General appointed the former Finnish President, Mr. Marti Athisaari Special Envoy for the Kosovo status process, which was to determine the future political status of the UN administered territory. On March 15, 2006, Mr. Athisaari announced a settlement proposal which involved the internationally supervised independence of the country. Almost a year later on February 17, 2007, the Kosovo Parliament declared independence. The proposed settlement places Kosovo under EU supervision comprising an International Civilian mission (ICO) responsible for implementing the above mentioned plan, and the EULEX law and order mission responsible for administering and developing the rule of law in the country.

6 The very process of reconfiguration of UNMIK lacks transparency and clarity. On August 18, 2008, an agreement was signed between UNMIK and EULEX on the transfer of certain parts of UN mission property to EULEX. It related to the transfer or sale of certain assets, vehicles, and facilities which were used by UNMIK. Due to the lack of transparency, there is still insufficient clarity about the content of this agreement in the public. Most people have understood it as a document which stipulates the details of the reconfiguration process; however, it has been stressed by the UNMIK spokesperson that this is a purely technical agreement and that the signing of the Memorandum of Understanding between UNMIK and EULEX on the transfer of competences is a separate issue, which has still not been scheduled.

reconfigured UNMIK, at the same time retaining a neutral stance towards the status of Kosovo.[7] Pursuant to its mandate, it provides technical assistance and support to the Kosovan authorities in the rule of law, in particular in judicial, police and customs matters. Though it is considered to be a technical mission, it retains a number of limited executive powers.[8]

Acting as a surrogate state UNMIK was empowered to exercise all legislative and executive authority and to take responsibility for the administration of justice.[9] In this regard it took the responsibility of establishing a justice system scheme in order to ensure the prosecution of all those responsible for the atrocities committed in the past, with the sole aim of bringing justice to the victims-survivors that would enable them to embark on a so-called recovery journey. In doing so, it engaged itself in both retributive and restorative justice.

This chapter looks into the specificities of the transitional justice system of a country placed under an international territorial administration. In this context, it aims to explore the flaws of UNMIK's transitional justice tools by highlighting the link between its mandate and its undertakings. It sheds light on the shortcomings surrounding the formalized justice institutions used by the international actors for recovering society from past abuses.

Taking into consideration the above, it argues that transitional justice should not be seen in the frame of criminal trials only, but rather as a complex enterprise consisting of different elements, which together make post-conflict recovery successful.

The Instruments of Transitional Justice

The transitional justice landscape includes a range of different mechanisms and models that have been developed throughout history, whose aim was to confront legacies of gross Human Rights violations.[10] Recently, a new trend emerged in

---

7 UN Security Council Resolution 1244, which created UNMIK, is therefore still in force and it remains to be seen what tools will be used to enforce the resolution's legal requirements. The new EU mission has widely been rejected by the Serb minority, which suddenly showed a willingness to accept UNMIK's authority.

8 Additional information regarding EULEX's mandate in Kosovo, see www.eulex.eu.org.

9 See UNMIK, Regulation No. 1999/1 on the authority of the Interim Administration in Kosovo (July 25, 1999), para. 1.1: "all legislative and executive authority with respect to Kosovo is vested in UNMIK and is exercised by the Special Representative of the Secretary-General." All UNMIK Regulations can be found online at: www.unmikonline.org.

10 Crossley-Frolick, K. A. (2011). 'Transitional Justice and Security Sector Reform: The Role of the EU and Other Multilateral Institutions in Building Kosovo's Police Force',

response to the wave of democratization of the societies caused by different political changes, namely the fall of communism, the end of the bipolar balance of power as well as a number of internal and international conflicts.[11] In view of the above, several mechanisms emerged reflecting different political and philosophical dimensions of transitional justice.

Retributive justice, which entails the restoration of justice by means of prosecuting those responsible for gross Human Rights violations, retains a vital role in the field of transitional justice.[12] Retributive justice is characterized by two types of formalized judicial institutions, namely international tribunals and internationalized courts, better known as hybrid courts, although it also can be met out by national courts and even through administrative means, such as, for example, vetting, screening and in the form of re-education and symbolic exclusion.[13]

International and internationalized tribunals both deal with a criminal prosecution as an imposition of punishment on perpetrators, aiming to establish a culture of accountability, and in so doing end a culture of impunity. They claim to shed light on intense Human Rights abuses and help society establish peace, justice, and reconciliation. They are both associated with Western, liberal democracy, although their measures, methods and procedures are also applied in national jurisdictions of states with different roots and traditions.[14]

Yet despite such similarities, internationalized/hybrid courts have received little attention in international justice literature. Most of the literature is focused on the justice provided by international tribunals or international criminal courts. The following section provides an overview of the internationalized court's practice in Kosovo.

---

paper prepared for delivery at the 2011 European Union Studies Association Biennial Meeting, March 3–5, 2011, Boston, MA, USA. Online at: http://www.euce.org/eusa/2011/papers/12i_dursun-ozkanca.pdf.

11 Teitel, R. (2003). 'Transitional Justice in a New Era'. In: *Fordham International Law Journal*, 26, p. 894.

12 After the Second World War retributive justice was seen as a universal value of primary importance: Teitel, R. (2003). 'Transitional Justice Genealogy'. *Harvard Human Rights Journal*, no. 16, pp. 69–94.

13 Stan, L. (2008). *Transitional Justice in Eastern Europe and the former Soviet Union: Reckoning with the communist past.* London, New York: Routledge; Mayer-Rieckh, A. and de Greiff, P. (2007). *Justice as Prevention: Vetting Public Employees in Transitional Societies.* New York: The Social Science Research Council.

14 Hybrid tribunals were created on behalf of and in cooperation with Cambodia and Sierra Leone, too.

Assessing UNMIK's Approach to Transitional Justice

Retributive Measures

Each post-conflict situation is different and complex. But in many post-conflict situations, the state is controlled by an elite, in which the former military plays an important role. The post-conflict situation is characterized by political instability and the lack of sufficient security measures on the ground, which hampers economic recovery, in particular foreign investment. The judiciary, the state administration, and the police are usually weak.[15]

Therefore, such a situation requires an immediate reaction, e.g., the establishment of security on the ground, disarmament of combatants, and restoration of the rule of law including the establishment of a proper criminal justice mechanism for dealing with perpetrators of war crimes and other Human Rights abuses. In many cases, the scheme in question implies the establishment of adequate institutions and fair procedures with a proper approach to the crimes that various atrocities constitute. It encompasses various dimensions of justice, both judicial and non-judicial aspects that deal with legacies of the violent conflict.[16]

However, this is a difficult task, as very often it is not easy to obtain the truth about crimes committed during an armed conflict, not because of a lack of evidence, but because of the unwillingness of the responsible party to seek such evidence and release the necessary information. It is usually followed by a degree of ignorance and often bolstered by nationalistic beliefs and mythology. As a result, the lack of interest of the responsible party to deal with the past in a proper manner has an enormous effect on attempts to heal the wounds of the past.

Kosovo has faced large-scale atrocities that occurred during the 1998–1999 war committed by both paramilitary and military forces of the Federal Republic of Yugoslavia (FRY), amounting to war crimes, crimes against humanity, and genocide. After the arrival of the North Atlantic Treaty Organization (NATO)

---

15 Mesa Peinado, M. (2007). 'The Role of NGOs and society in Peace and Reconciliation Processes'. Centro de Invesigacion Para la Paz, online at: http://www.ceipaz.org/base_datos.php?item=313&buscador=%25&autorSearch=Peinado

16 Anderlini, N., Pampelconway, C. and Kays, L. (2004). *Transitional Justice and reconciliation, Inclusive security, Sustainable Peace: A toolkit for Advocacy and Action, Justice Governance and Civil Society.* London: Women Waging pace, International Alert, p. 8, online at: https://www.ndi.org/files/Toolkit%20for%20Advocacy%20and%20Action%20IIS.pdf.

forces, the FRY machinery had to withdraw, and with it those who were the most responsible for gross Human Rights violations during the war.[17]

On the other side, many individuals belonging to Serbian and Roma minorities experienced severe violence in the aftermath of the withdrawal of the FRY forces, including murders, abductions, mass arson and destruction of property based on the assumption they had been allied with the former Serbian machinery in the violence against the Albanian population.[18]

Following its establishment, UNMIK was confronted with a much broader challenge: overcoming the legacy of gross and systematic violations of Human Rights committed by the Milošević regime and building a society based on the rule of law. Among the first steps undertaken were the disarmament, demobilization and reintegration of ex-combatants, and the resettlement and reintegration of refugees and internally displaced persons.

In addition, it particularly focused on re-establishing the judiciary and building a new police force. Within such a framework, the so-called internationalized/hybrid court system was established and empowered to deal with the abuses committed during the war.[19] It comprises both national and international components.[20]

---

17 The Kosovar past consists of many layers which involve oppressions, inter-ethnic clashes and wars. Suffering resulting from this past has never been acknowledged properly either by the parties involved in those conflicts, nor by the international community. Consequently, it caused revulsion, intolerance and a deep division between the Albanian and Serbian population. However, the 1998–1999 armed conflict brought new waves of violence and deepened the rift between Albanians and Serbs. Thousands of people were killed, more than 4,000 disappeared and over 2,000 were detained.

18 For more details see the report published by Amnesty International, *Prisoners in our own homes, Amnesty International's concerns for Human Rights of minorities in Kosovo/Kosova.* April 30, 2003. See also, O'Neil, W. (2002). *Kosovo An Unfinished Peace.* Boulder: Lynne Reinner Publisher, p. 75. O'Neil served as a Human Rights adviser to the SRSG. He argues that in order to avoid such a situation UNMIK should have declared martial law, "with carefully circumscribed limitations on certain Human Rights as permitted under international law".

19 Besides exercising legislative and executive authority, the UN Security Council empowered UNMIK with the responsibility for the administration of justice. See UNMIK, Regulation No. 1999/1, note 3, para. 1.1: "All legislative and executive authority with respect to Kosovo is vested in UNMIK and is exercised by the Special Representative of the Secretary-General."

20 The domestic trials in post-conflict societies often lack legitimacy because of their judicial systems which are perceived not to be independent and impartial, and as such are unable to prosecute cases of complex and organized crimes. On the other hand, the international *ad hoc* tribunals have been criticized for only building international

The initial intention of the international community was to establish the Kosovo War and Ethnic Crimes Court (KWECC), an internationally-led, *ad hoc* tribunal, but this was abandoned following several rounds of negotiations between the international community and Kosovan representatives. The idea had been to establish the KWECC, which was to have concurrent, primary jurisdiction over serious violations of international humanitarian law, including war crimes, genocide, crimes against humanity and other serious crimes committed on political, ethnic or religious grounds during the armed conflict in Kosovo, starting from January 1, 1998.[21] However, the whole idea was received with much skepticism by both the domestic and international communities. While the domestic community mainly feared the potential complications of having an additional judicial layer between the domestic system and the International Criminal Tribunal for the Former Yugoslavia, which allegedly would be more likely to initiate criminal investigations against Albanians who had participated in armed conflict, the international community was mainly concerned about the security of court personnel and the costs of the court.[22]

On May 27, 2000, a hybrid court system option was chosen and thereafter systematically introduced,[23] enabling the appointment of international judges

---

case law but not vital domestic capacity, as their positive effects do not reach the affected society. Consequently, hybrid courts have been presented as the appropriate fora to judge perpetrators offering legitimacy by providing ownership without affecting independence and impartiality, prosecuting more perpetrators in less time and at lower costs while also building domestic capacity. In this regard, such models have been introduced outside Kosovo in East Timor in the Crimes panels of the District Court of Dili and in Sierra Leone in the Court for Sierra Leone. For more about the hybrid court model, see Nouwen, S. (2006). 'Hybrid Courts, The hybrid category of a new type of international crimes court'. *Utrecht Law Review*, 2, no. 2. See also *Rule of Law tools for post-conflict states, Maximising the Legacy of Hybrid Courts.* Office of High Commissioner for Human Rights, Report 2008, online at: http://www.ohchr.org/Documents/Publications/HybridCourts.pdf (further: OHCHR 2008).

21 Petriello, L. T. and Wierda, M. (2006). *Lessons from the Deployment of International Judges and Prosecutors in Kosovo.* New York: The International Centre for Transitional Justice, p. 11. See also Marshall, D. and Inglis, S. H. (2003). 'The Disempowerment of Human Rights-Based Justice in the United Nations Missions in Kosovo'. *Harvard Human Rights Journal,* 16, p. 95.

22 Petriello, Wierda (2003), p. 12.

23 In accordance with UNMIK Regulation 2000/6 on the Appointment and Removal from the Office of International Judges and International Prosecutors, promulgated on February 15, 2000; Amending UNMIK Regulation 2000/6 on the Appointment and Removal from the Office of International Judges and International Prosecutors, promulgated on

and prosecutors to serve in domestic courts.[24] They formed part of the domestic judiciary and as such were grafted onto the domestic judicial system, applying a compound of international and national substantial and procedural law.[25] The involvement of the international judges came as a result of a continuing failure by local judges to conduct fair trials, in particular in serious cases involving victims belonging to minorities.[26]

In this regard, the international judges mainly served to deal with war crimes as well as cases involving ethnic crimes. However, very often they were engaged in matters characterized as politically motivated cases. It was left to their sole discretion to select and take responsibility for new and pending cases within the jurisdiction of the court to which they had been appointed.[27] At the same time,

---

May 27, 2000; and UNMIK Regulation 2000/64 on Assignment of International Judges/ Prosecutors and /or Change of Venue, promulgated on December 15, 2000.

24 The hybrid court system became a common practice in post-war societies. For instance, it was also introduced in East Timor (the Serious Crimes Unit and Special Panels for Serious Crimes pursuant to Regulation No. 2000/15) and Bosnia and Hercegovina (the Special War Crimes Chamber established pursuant to an agreement concluded between the Office of the High Representative of the International Tribunal for the Former Yugoslavia and the national authorities). See OHCHR 2008, 3. Furthermore, there are some cases where the United Nations were invited by a specific country to establish a hybrid tribunal within their judicial system. This was the case for the Special Court for Sierra Leone (based on an agreement between the United Nations and the Government of Sierra Leone concluded in 2002) and the creation of the Extraordinary Chambers in Cambodia to try the main leaders of the Khmer Rouge (under an agreement concluded in 2003 by the United Nations and the Government of Cambodia to create Extraordinary Chambers in the courts of Cambodia). For more on hybrid courts, see Romano, C. P. R., Nollkaemper, A. and Kleffner, J. K. (2004). *Internationalized Criminal Courts. Sierra Leone, East Timor, Kosovo, and Cambodia.* Oxford: Oxford University Press.

25 After the establishment of the new International Presence in Kosovo in 2008 (the European Union Rule of Law Mission in Kosovo, EULEX), UNMIK judges and prosecutors were replaced by EULEX judges acting under the umbrella of the Assembly of EULEX judges, the self-governing body established pursuant to Art. 4 of the Law on Jurisdiction, 2003/03 L 53.

26 O'Neil (2002), 88.

27 Section 1.2 of UNMIK Regulation 2000/64. The selection of the cases was performed in cooperation with the Head of the Judicial Department.

a strict case-monitoring practice[28] was instituted which enabled international prosecutors to resurrect cases abandoned by their Kosovan counterparts.[29]

After the establishment of a new International Presence in Kosovo in 2008 in the form of EULEX, UNMIK Judges/Prosecutors were replaced by EULEX judges acting under the umbrella of the Assembly of EULEX judges.[30]

As everything else, transitional justice in Kosovo was placed under the control of the international community. Due to the nature of conflict, it was clear from the very beginning that such an endeavour would require the intervention of a third party, seeing as the domestic actors were unable and unwilling to give an adequate response to the atrocities committed on their behalf.[31] Subsequently, UNMIK took the responsibility of putting an end to impunity, restoring respect for the rule of law and to a certain extent becoming a cornerstone of sustainable peace and democratic transition.[32]

In this regard the hybrid court system was seen as the only possible judicial mechanism which could address the needs of both those directly affected by the crimes, namely the victims and their families, and those who had committed the crimes or allowed them to happen.

Although such a model was seen as guarantor of best practices for prosecuting past atrocities, its effective contribution to this goal remains controversial. The challenges confronting this court are threefold. The method of selecting judges and guaranteeing their security of tenure are of particular importance for the independence of the court system. At the beginning of the mission, local judges were appointed for terms of six months. Later it was, however, decided to extend their terms to the end of the UN mission.[33] Despite the extension of the local judges' terms of office, its actual duration still remained uncertain since nobody knew how long the UN Administration would be in place. Such practices were incompatible

---

28 UNMIK Regulation 2001/2, amending UNMIK Regulation 2000/6, *on the Appointment and Removal of International Judges and Prosecutors,* January 12, 2001.

29 Hartmann, M. (2003). 'International judges and Prosecutors in Kosovo'. Special Report 112, United States Institute of Peace, p. 2.

30 The self-governing body established pursuant to Article 4 of the Law on Jurisdiction, 2003/03 L 53.

31 See, e.g., the legal basis for the establishment of the International Criminal Court (ICC). The complementary principle enshrined in the Rome Statute obliges a State Party to prosecute persons accused of war crimes. However, if a State is unable or unwilling to fulfil this duty, the ICC will assume jurisdiction (art.17910 (a)).

32 United Nations (2008). *Rule of law tools, for post-conflict states, Maximizing the Legacy of Hybrid Courts.* Geneva: United Nations Publication, p. 4.

33 Hartmann (2003), 8.

with international standards, which demand a fixed tenure until a mandatory retirement age or the expiry a term of office.[34]

Yet the appointment of the international judges required a different method than the appointment of domestic judges. They were selected through a selection procedure specific to UNMIK and appointed by the SRSG for six-month renewable terms, which was the standard term for all mission personnel working with the UN Department of Peacekeeping Operations. However, the selection procedure lacked transparence since it was completely concealed from the outside world. The short terms of office constituted a serious threat to judicial independence and to the quality of the administration of justice.[35]

Due to the lack of security of tenure, both the international and local judges became vulnerable to the influence of those who might affect their employment prospects.[36] Since the re-appointment of both national and international judges fell under the sole discretion of the SRSG, one could easily get the impression that such re-appointments might have depended on the performance assessments of the SRSG's offices. Judges whose judicial career is not secure are more likely to be vulnerable to external influences, which may seriously influence the adjudication process. As stated by Sir Gerard Brennan, Chief Justice of Australia, "judicial independence is at risk when future appointment or security of tenure is within the gift of the Executive".[37] It implies that judicial appointments by the executive can assure judicial independence only if security of tenure is guaranteed, if not permanently, then at least for a reasonable period of time.[38] Thus short-term judicial appointments threaten the independent functioning of a hybrid court. Where an executive has the authority to appoint and remove judges and prosecutors, the judiciary is consequently relegated to an inferior position. As such, a judge may render decisions not in accordance with the law, but in order to not antagonize UN

34 Points 11 and 12 of the UN Basic Principle on the Independence of the Judiciary.

35 "This is a serious matter of concern", said Marek Antoni Nowicki, Ombudsperson in Kosovo, who further stressed that "the short term appointments may affect their ability to act impartially". Interview with Marek Antoni Nowicki, conducted on October 3, 2004 in Prishtina.

36 Security of tenure involves a long-term appointment; it guarantees that a judge can be removed from his/her position only with good cause or a breach of ethical rules. For a detailed explanation, see: Shetreet, S. and Deschenes, J. (1985) (eds.). *Judicial Independence, The Contemporary Debate.* Dordrecht: Martinus Nijhoff Publishers, p. 19.

37 Brennan, F. G. (1998). 'The State of the Judicature'. *Australian Law Journal 72,* pp. 34–35.

38 See Meron, T. (2005). 'Judicial Independence and Impartiality in International Criminal Tribunals'. *The American Journal of International Law*, 99, p. 361.

member states and his own state in particular. In this context, the job uncertainty may oblige judges to be driven by their careers and not by judicial conscience or a reading of the law.[39]

This has led to recognition that the legal cordon ensuring the independence of an international judge is rather fragile. The very essence of such a reality enhances the probability of opting for 'self-preservation' instead of observing standards of justice. Further challenges the hybrid court in Kosovo faces are the lack of jurisdiction over perpetrators residing in the northern part of Kosovo and Serbia proper as well as the difficulty to obtain evidence regarding alleged crimes committed by former Kosovo Liberation Army members. These have mitigated the success of the courts in bringing to trial suspected perpetrators.[40] As a result, more than thirty trials concerning war crimes have been conducted before internationalized courts in Kosovo.[41] To date, courts have been unable to secure the presence of the

---

39 Meron (2005), 360.

40 The northern part of Kosovo is mainly inhabited by the Serbian community, which is concentrated in four municipalities: Leposavić, Zubin Potok, *Zvečan* and the Mitrovica part of the town in the north. The population of this area has been opposing the installment of UNMIK administration since the beginning.

41 E.g., in 2000, the District Court in Mitrovica sentenced Nenad Pavićević, accused of having committed war crimes, to 20 years' imprisonment in absentia. The District Court in Prizren sentenced Artan Hasani to 15 years' imprisonment for the murder of a Serbian woman called Stana Srdić. In 2000, Dragan Jovanović, Srdjan Aleksić, Vlastimir Aleksić, Branislav Popović and Tomislav *Vučković*, all accused of having committed acts of genocide, escaped from the Detention Centre in Mitrovica. As of today, the responsible Serbian authorities have not taken any steps to extradite them to the UNMIK authorities. The international trial chamber of the District Court in Mitrovica sentenced Miroslav *Vučković* to 12 years' imprisonment for war crimes against civilians. In 2001, the District Court in Prizren sentenced two persons called Jovanović and Kolašinac to 20 and five years' imprisonment, respectively, for committing war crimes against civilians. In 2003, before the international panel of the District Court of Prishtina/Priština, a trial was conducted against the "Llapi group". This group included former KLA Commander of the "Llapi zone", Rustem Mustafa, who was sentenced to 17 years' imprisonment. The former Commander of the KLA military police, Nazif Mehmeti, was sentenced to 13 years, Latif Gashi, who was in charge of KLA intelligence, was sentenced to 10 years and Nami Kadriu, a former military policeman, was sentenced to 5 years' imprisonment. In 2002, an international panel of the District Court in Peja/Peć presided over a trial conducted against the "Dukagjini group" consisting of former KLA soldiers. Idriz Balaj was sentenced to 13 years' imprisonment, Daut Haradinaj to 5 years, Bekim Zekaj to 3 years, and Ahmet Elshani and Ramush Ahmeti to 3 years' imprisonment. On May 12, 2005, the District Court of Prishtina/Priština sentenced

alleged perpetrators. Many of them have simply returned to their normal lives and professions in Serbia.

In addition, the lack of restrictive rules that prevent others from interfering in judicial conduct convey the fragility of the judicial system in resisting to external pressure. For instance, some former judges reported cases involving political interference, which they experienced during their stay in Kosovo. For the most part, of the interference was intended to halt an investigation or influence a desired judicial outcome of in cases involving the prosecution of "certain persons", mainly those involved in war crimes or corruption.[42] In addition, some UNMIK officials admitted the existence of outside pressure, which according to them coerced judges into giving in to these demands.[43] Yet while cases involving crimes conducted by the members of Serbian forces did not make it to trial, several trials have been carried out by UNMIK and EULEX judges involving former Kosovo Liberation Army (KLA) members.[44] However, many cases are stalled due to a continuous interference in the judicial process, the collective refusal to acknowledge any wrongdoings on the part of the former KLA forces, the incapability of prosecutions to secure sufficient evidence as well to ensure the physical security of witnesses, etc.[45] Subsequently, the war crimes trials have become the subject of

three out of five men belonging to "Kaqaniku group", former KLA soldiers to 20 years' imprisonment.

42 A Swedish judge, C. Karphammar, who used to work as a judge and as a prosecutor in Kosovo, stated that he "directly knows of several cases in which UN and KFOR senior officials opposed or blocked prosecution of former Kosovo Liberation Army members, including some now in KPC (TMK)… The investigations were stopped at a high level", and for the entire time he worked in Kosovo, "the judiciary was not allowed to work independently" Quoted in O'Neil (2002), 91.

43 It refers to the case of Zoran Stanković a former Serb policeman, who was accused of taking part in the Račak massacre in January 1999. O'Neill (2002), 91.

44 "Prosecutors and investigators of EULEX are currently investigating a total of 76 war crime cases. Out of them, 51 are in the phase of the preliminary investigations and 25 are officially under investigation", Krasniqi, B. a spokesperson for the EULEX mission in Kosovo, in Kosovo struggle to prosecute war crimes 20.03.2012, online at: http://www.setimes.com/cocoon/setimes/xhtml/en_GB/features/setimes/features/2012/03/20/feature-03.

45 A former UNMIK official says that in some cases judges were exposed to external pressure and consequently had to give up prosecutions. He refers to the case of Zoran Stanković, a former Serb policeman who was accused of taking part in the Račak massacre in January 1999. Moreover, some former international judges have reported cases involving the political interference they experienced during their stay in Kosovo, reflecting the intention of halting an investigation involving the prosecution of "certain

political negotiations between local and international political actors, which indicates that many alleged crimes may remain unresolved and untried.[46] In August 2015, a new law was passed allowing the establishment of the Special Tribunal with the jurisdiction to prosecute war crimes allegedly committed by former KLA members.[47] The Tribunal will have a seat in Kosovo, but proceedings will take place in a special chamber in The Hague. The separate judicial chambers will hold files and sensitive records and it will be exclusively run by international staff. The authority to appoint judges and prosecutors to this tribunal has been given

---

persons". O'Neill (2002), 91. Moreover, though Kosovo has enacted a witness protection law (enacted in 2012) it still lacks its proper implementation. According to the Interior Ministry spokesman the law will be put into effect in 2013. "The full implementation of the law will begin after the Unit for Witness Protection is established and the law is completed with other legal acts", statement can be found online at: http://www.setimes.com/cocoon/setimes/xhtml/en_GB/features/setimes/features/2012/03/27/feature-03 Consequently, due to the lack of adequate protection measures, many witnesses testifying in war crime procedures are continuously exposed to various forms of threat. Meanwhile, EULEX, the Rule of Law mission has developed its own Witness Protection Unit operating both inside and outside the country. The suspicious death of the key witness Agim Zogaj (who was found hanged in the park, in Germany, where he was placed) in the trial process involving a former KLA commander had raised many suspicions about the functioning of the unit as a whole, in particular its ability to offer adequate protection to witnesses. Agim Zogaj had allegedly committed suicide as a consequence of the continuous threats exercised upon him after his initial testimony given in the above mentioned case.

46 On the other hand, several high-ranking Serbian officials have been tried before the International Criminal Tribunal for the Former Yugoslavia (ICTY), which has supremacy over domestic courts. However, similarly to hybrid courts, the effectiveness of international criminal prosecutions lacked support from the state government, which reluctantly refused to support the prosecution of their benefactors and warlords. Unfortunately, all successive Serbian governments have shown an ambiguous attitude when it comes to fully cooperating with the ICTY and for this reason has been reported several times to the Security Council for non-compliance. It has been proven that international criminal justice is the product of political compromise and as such is not immune from political interests. Moreover, its legal framework does not provide a sufficient guarantee that it fulfills the task of justice, since there are no specific legal sanctions, aside from reporting non-compliance to the United Nations Security Council, which may pressure the non-compliant state into fulfilling its obligations arising from an order or verdict rendered by an international tribunal.

47 Bilefsky, D. (2015). 'Kosovo Parliament votes to allow war crimes court.' *New York Times,* August 4, 2015, online at: http://www.nytimes.com/2015/08/05/world/europe/kosovo-parliament-votes-to-allow-war-crimes-court.html?ref=world&_r=0.

to EULEX. The Special Court is not yet operational. It remains to be seen how effectively and fairly it will dispense justice.

Having an international character, the hybrid courts operate in a normative framework and understanding of internationally designed justice and have consequently proven to not be collectively understood and shared by the communities affected by the armed conflict. For example, similarly to its government, the majority of the Serbian population continues to hold negative attitudes towards international judiciary. Historical circumstances, especially the adverse effects of the NATO intervention in 1999, have created an atmosphere of doubt, distrust, and disrespect towards international institutions.[48] On the other hand, the trust in the internationalized judiciary is gradually decreasing among the Albanian population as well, in particular after the extradition of former KLA officers the the ICTY.[49] Large parts of the Albanian population believe that the internationalized judiciary is trying to establish a sort of political balance between Belgrade and Prishtina in order to improve its reputation among the Serbian population. The impression is created that by prosecuting former KLA soldiers, the international community is trying to criminalize the liberation war in Kosovo by lumping together liberators and oppressors.[50]

Restorative Justice Measures

Given the complexity of the process, most crimes committed during a war go unpunished.[51] This raises the question whether prosecutions are the best method of redressing past abuses in the context of transitional justice. Is there any other option that would complement the prosecution? It is in this context that so-called

---

48 See the survey conducted by International IDEA, *South East Europe Public Agenda Survey* in 2002, available at www.idea.int/press/pr200220404.htm. Compare also with the chapter by Klaus Bachmann in this book.

49 Bachmann, K. and Fatić, A. (2015). *The UN International Criminal Tribunals. Transition without Justice?* New York, London: Routledge, pp. 93, 103; according to the authors, positive attitudes toward the ICTY in Kosovo (by Kosovo Albanians) decreased from 83.8 per cent in 2002 to 67.04 per cent in 2011.

50 Such opinions have been expressed during demonstrations organized by war veterans since 2004 regarding the arrest of KLA solders.

51 As already stressed by the Secretary-General, "In the end, in post-conflict countries, the vast majority of perpetrators will never be tried, whether internationally or domestically". See, UN Security Council (2004). *The Rule of Law and Transitional Justice in Conflict and Post-conflict Societies.* Report of the Secretary-General, United Nations Document S/2004/616, August 2004, para. 46.

restorative justice has emerged. It deeply differs from retributive justice as it mainly focuses on repairing the harm caused by a crime,[52] and is characterized by dialogue and negotiations among the parties.[53] This process includes entire communities, offenders, victims and survivors. It is frequently carried out by truth commissions whose primary goal is "to demonstrate or underscore a break with a past record of Human Rights abuses, to promote national reconciliation, and/or obtain or sustain political legitimacy."[54] Restorative justice particularly focuses on acknowledgement, reparation and compensation for atrocities, aiming to restore relations both between victims and perpetrators, and within the broader community to which they belong. It includes a range of actions, such as collecting documentations of past abuses, conducting research and advocating accountability, providing legal assistance to victims and creating a new, inclusive narrative, whose aim is to delegitimize the atrocities of the past, to foster common understanding of this past and to bolster the unity of the community, which undergoes transition. At present, the above mentioned methods serve as bridges which link the past of deeply divided nations characterized by conflict, suffering and injustice to a future based on a proper response to violations, the restoration of honour and dignity to victims, and the assurance of a recognition of Human Rights and the possibility of coexistence. Together, they all help build a path that leads to reconciliation. Taking into consideration its mandate, it is widely believed that besides prosecution, UNMIK authorities should have been equally engaged in restorative justice, in particular with regard to the need of clarifying the fates of missing persons, dealing with sexual violence cases and material reparation in order to help prosecutions as well as criminal justice trials complete their tasks.

But the demand of civil society for the enactment of a law on missing persons which would address the overarching problem of missing person's issues was simply ignored by the relevant UNMIK authorities. Only in 2011 did the Kosovan authorities promulgate the Law on Missing Persons.[55] However, the law failed to

---

52 Daly, K. (2000). *Restorative justice in Diverse and Unequal Societies,* Flinders University Symposium on Criminal Justice in Diverse Societies, Adelaide, *Law in Context* 17(1): pp. 167–90.

53 Daly (2000), 167–190.

54 Hayner, P. (1994) defines truth commissions as "bodies set up to investigate a past history of violations of Human Rights in a particular country". Hayner P. (1994). 'Fifteen Truth Commissions (1974–1994), A Comparative Study', *Human Rights Quarterly* 16, pp. 597–655; Hayner, P. (2010). *Unspeakable truths. Transitional Justice and the Challenge of Truth Commissions.* London, New York: Routledge.

55 Law no 04:L-023 enacted on August 31, 2011.

impose upon all competent organs in Kosovo the obligation to provide assistance and available information to family members searching for their missing relatives "under threat of sanctions". The main competency has been vested in the hands of a governmental unit composed of various governmental agencies.[56] Moreover, the law fails to empower victims to demand compensation for the harm suffered.

Overall, this law may give some hope to the relatives of the individuals that went missing as a consequence of crimes committed by members of the Kosovo Liberation Army, but regrettably not to the relatives of the Albanian victims. At the moment, they are left in the dark as to the whereabouts and condition of their relatives, as this information remains in the hands of the Serbian government.[57] Taking into consideration the political constraints between Kosovo and the Serbian government, it is doubtful whether this issue can be advanced without external political pressure.[58] Meanwhile, criminal proceedings will be exposed to lengthy proceedings pending the identification and exhumation of dead bodies as the main evidence to prove the culpability of perpetrators for the disappearances and the murders committed during the war.

In terms of material reparation, it is important to highlight that while some symbolic attempts have been made to address specific harms, little has been done with regard to material reparations such as financial compensation and restitution. The international governing structures did not feel responsible for setting up a reparation programme. Given the current state of relations between Serbia and Kosovo, it is unlikely that compensation will be paid by the Serb government to Kosovo victims in the near future.

The issue of sexual violence has been treated in a similar manner. Unfortunately, sexual violence and its effects continue to be an underestimated part of the war legacy. Sexual violence was widespread during the armed conflict. Apart from data collection conducted by various non-governmental organizations, no adequate surveys have been carried out by the successive authorities. The victim-survivors

---

56 Article 9 para. 1 of the Law on Missing Persons.

57 Regional governments never showed any serious commitment to the issue of missing persons and the field operations suffered from a lack of information and support. For more information, see Amnesty International (2009). *Burying the past, 10 years of impunity for enforced disappearances and abductions in Kosovo.* Amnesty International Report, online at: http://reliefweb.int/report/serbia/burying-past-10-years-impunity-enforced-disappearances-and-abductions-kosovo

58 Unfortunately, hopes are placed on the international community, whose political pressure may oblige Serbian authorities to release information presently within its possession with respect to the missing persons' fates and whereabouts.

have been left without protection and continue to be exposed to suffering due to the stigma attached to rape.[59] The engagement in such matters falls into the hands of powerless segments of society, namely women rights network.[60] For a long time, the victims of rape have been denied the status and rights given to other civilian victims such as invalids and veterans. In 2011, a law on the Status of Victims of War was promulgated, but it completely disregarded the approximately twenty thousand women estimated to have been victims of rape, leaving their basic needs undefined and their basic Human Rights unprotected.[61] In April 2014, the law was amended, and accordingly those who suffered sexual violence during the war have been categorized as victims of war, and are as such entitled to medical and financial assistance. It remains to be seen how the responsible authorities will implement this law in practice.

Although it made an enormous contribution to the establishment and development of democratic institutions and strengthened the civil sector, UNMIK's involvement in transitional justice exhibits serious flaws. Despite its willingness to comply with the normative needs arising from international law, the situation on the ground shows that very often, international norms have become part of

---

59 Kvinaa til Kvinaa Foundation (2012). *Hope of redress for survivors of rape during the war in Kosovo,* March 8, 2012, online at: http://www.equalpowerlastingpeace.org/2012/03/08/hope-of-redress-for-survivors-of-rape-during-the-war-in-kosovo/

60 Many of them refused to talk about their past out of fear of being marginalized. They were under constant pressure and many of them have been abandoned by their family and their husbands. Most of the victims have therefore chosen silence as the only way to survive. "The 22-year-old woman, married four months ago, said she was taken from this small southern village by Serbian forces, held for a day in the local police station, beaten, then threatened with death. But she was not, she said, raped, I am 100 per cent certain that they raped her," said Thaqi, 34, a farmer imprisoned by the Serbs for supplying weapons to the Kosovo Liberation Army, the Albanian guerrillas who fought Serbian forces. "I know that when women get in their hands, there is no chance to escape." Thaqi says his wife denies the rape because "she doesn't dare tell that kind of story." If she admitted it to him, he said, "I would ask for a divorce – even if I had 20 children." As his wife listened, silent and shamefaced, in a corner of their empty home, looted of all furniture and possessions by the Serbs, Thaqi added: "I don't hate her, but the story is before my eyes. I feel very cold toward her." Kissing her, he said, "is like kissing a dead body." See Bumiller, E. (1999). 'Kosovo victims must choose to deny rape or be hated'. *New York Times*, June 22, 1999.

61 In 2011, a law on the status and rights of martyrs, invalids, veterans, members of the Kosovo Liberation Army, civilian victims of war and their families, was promulgated. Essentially, it is meant to provide assistance to the victims of war. Law, 2011/04-L 054, promulgated on December 28, 2011.

a political game played by both international and local actors. Sadly, this has diminished the capacity of the internationalized court to disseminate rule of law values in society.

The failure of the international administration in Kosovo to adequately promote retributive justice and to apply restorative justice has seriously jeopardized the prospects for sustainable peace. However, despite its complexity, multiple shortcomings and weaknesses, the international community should continue to support the transitional justice process in the coming years and decades.

Part II: International Criminal Tribunals and the Prosecution of Mass Atrocities

Klaus Bachmann

The Loathed Tribunal: Public Opinion in Serbia toward the International Criminal Tribunal for the former Yugoslavia (ICTY)[1]

In the vast literature about Transitional Justice and International Criminal Law, international criminal tribunals occupy a special place, especially in the context of the "fight against impunity" that sees retributive justice as the main measure for addressing past atrocities and Human Rights abuses. International criminal tribunals *ad hoc* in particular are almost sheer retributive mechanisms – their focus on victims is subordinated to the objective of establishing guilt; they concentrate on the perpetrators, who are to be isolated from society, punished, and delegitimized for their past conduct. In contrast to the International Criminal Court (ICC), *ad hoc* tribunals were neither empowered to deal with victims' compensation nor were they given the task of establishing a record or narrative about the past (although some actors at International Criminal Tribunals (ICTs) intended to do this). The UN *ad hoc* tribunals were meant to be instruments for the prosecution of perpetrators[2] and nothing more, but nevertheless, their activities were accompanied by far-reaching hopes and expectations. They were tasked with "contributing to stability and peace"[3] and even to "reconciliation."[4] Both the International Criminal Tribunal for the former Yugoslavia (ICTY) and the International Criminal Tribunal for Rwanda (ICTR) also developed a number of additional objectives they wanted to achieve. By establishing outreach mechanisms,

---

1 The author would like to express his gratitude to the Polish National Center for Research (Narodowe Centrum Nauki) for facilitating the research on which this chapter is based by awarding him with research grant no. 2011/01/B/HS3/00801 (International Criminal Tribunals in a Comparative Perspective). This allowed him to travel to Belgrade, Sarajevo and Croatia, to collect the source data of the opinion surveys, and to talk to colleagues about them. The author would like to thank Zoran Pavlović, Irena Ristić, Aleksandar Fatić, Slobodan *Zečević* in Belgrade and Jan Muś in Poland, as well as Timothy Waters in Indiana and numerous staff members of the ICTY, including prosecutors and judges who were willing to discuss the issue with him.

2 See UNSC Resolution 827, which stipulates explicitly that the ICTY was established "for the sole purpose of prosecuting."

3 UNSC res. 808.

4 UNSC res. 955 (establishing the ICTR).

they intended to promote International Criminal Law, Human Rights and to fight denial.[5] To some extent, they became instruments of political transition, especially after the implementation of their completion strategy, which made the transfer of cases back to the local judiciary conditional upon the fulfilment of legal and institutional reform. This 'policy of completion' led to different outcomes in the countries under their jurisdiction ranging from shirking and measures aiming to circumvent the tribunal policy, to compliance.[6]

From a theoretical point of view, it could also be argued – and it often was – that ICTs even by only prosecuting and punishing perpetrators contributed to general deterrence and the delegitimization of the old political order (before transition), sublated vengeance, and helped transitional societies to draw a line between a bad past and a better future and to distinguish between positive attitudes and negative attitudes towards the past. Thus, ICTs were also seen as instruments of 'dealing with the past' and agents of social and moral change.

With the benefit of hindsight, one might doubt whether these respectable goals were realistic and could ever have been achieved. Public opinion polls conducted in the former Yugoslavia and Rwanda reveal high scores of rejection and criticism of the ICTY and the ICTR; reactions of the public to the most prominent verdicts were predominantly negative. Throughout the former Yugoslavia, the dominating pattern of dealing with the past remained untouched by the ICTY's judgments and decisions. According to this pattern, perpetrators from one community were heroes whereas perpetrators from an enemy community are seen as evildoers. Even more than twenty years after the outbreak of hostilities, this pattern is only questioned by small minorities in the communities which formed

5 Author's interviews with former ICTY outreach officer Refik *Hodžić* (now at the International Centre for Transitional Justice in New York) and ICTR outreach officer Innocent Kamenzi in Kigali, Rwanda, and with former ICTY and ICTR president Gabrielle Kirk McDonald, under whose presidency the ICTY outreach program was initiated (all interviews conducted in 2012). According to these interviews, the ICTY outreach program was first and foremost an attempt to deal with denial in the Prijedor region, where prisoner camps had been located and where the local population was in outright denial about the fact that any crimes or atrocities had taken place, despite the ICTY's guilty verdicts against the local camp commanders and staff members.

6 More on that issue can be found in Subotić, J. (2009). *Hijacked Justice. Dealing with the Past in the Balkans*. Ithaca, London: Cornell University Press, and Bachmann, K., Sparrow-Botero, T. and Lambertz, P. (2014). *When Justice meets Politics. Independence and Autonomy of Ad Hoc International Tribunals*. Frankfurt/M.: Peter Lang Int., as well as in Bachmann, K., Fatić, A. (2015): *The UN International Criminal Tribunals. Transition without Justice?* New York, London: Routledge.

conflict parties during the violent breakdown of Yugoslavia during the 1990s. In Rwanda, most citizens deny that the ICTR may have had any notable impact on transitional justice and reconciliation, because ICTR trials took place outside the country and in the shadow of mass prosecutions by the Rwandan judiciary, which started in 1996 and the Gacaca courts, which were created in 2002. In Yugoslavia, national prosecutions of war crimes started late and slowly and were often concentrated on suspects from outside the community whose judiciary had investigated crimes. Serb prosecutors investigated and prosecuted suspects from Croatia and Kosovo, Kosovo prosecutors indicted Serb suspects and the Croat judiciary was busy investigating Serb crimes rather than atrocities committed by Croatian units.[7] As Klarin has shown, the post-Yugoslav discourse on war crimes was one about heroes rather than victims, and the trials in The Hague were regarded as mechanisms by which a biased prosecution tried to harrass national heroes. The victims' perspective, so dominant in the international Human Rights discourse, among Human Rights NGOs and the wider public, was neglected even when victims of one's own community testified as witnesses.[8] The divergence between Western liberal-democratic, pro-ICL[9] and Human Rights-inspired values and the more materialist[10], in-group affirmative values of post-war societies, which were more attached to the collectivist notion of sovereignty than to individualist concepts of Human Rights, explains part of the failure of ICTs to achieve their own objectives and to fulfill the high hopes of their supporters. It was this divergence that is responsible for the unavoidable part of the ICTs' failure. Procedural shortcomings, unbalanced policies, and incoherent jurisprudence form the other part

---

7 About the domestic trials against war criminals in the former Yugoslavia, see: Subotić (2009), 57–62, 101–108, 140–146.

8 Klarin, M. (2009). 'The Impact of the ICTY Trials on Public Opinion in the Former Yugoslavia', *Journal of International Criminal Justice* 7 / 1, pp. 89–96. Probably the most controversial case was the sentencing of 143 Kosovo Albanian defendants on terrorism charges by a Serb court on the basis of some kind of collective guilt of crimes committed against Serb victims. The presiding judge admitted the lack of evidence concerning individual guilt but stated instead that "for the essence of a terrorism conviction, this is not necessary." Gordy, E. (2013). *Guilt, Responsibility, and Denial The Past at Stake in Post-Milošević Serbia. Philadelphia: University of Pennsylvania Press,* pp. 52–53.

9 The term Pro-ICL is defined as an attitude favouring international criminal justice and Human Rights over national justice and sovereignty.

10 Materialist values describe values (according to Ronald Inglehart's postmaterialism theory) whose aim is to facilitate survival as opposed to postmaterialist ones, which facilitate the improvement of the quality of life. See: World Value Survey: *www.worldvaluessurvey.org*.

of the equation that is often highlighted by the legal literature about the *ad hoc* tribunals.[11] This chapter will deal will a very specific link that rendered the ICTY's record so ambiguous. It tries to elucidate the local reactions to ICTY decisions and the perception of the population in one specific country crucial for the ICTY's possible failure or success: Serbia. The overarching question this chapters seeks to answer is: Why were Serb attitudes towards the ICTY so negative and at the same time so stable? Can this be explained – as some authors have tried to – by invoking Serb ethnocentrism[12], and a lack of trust in any kind of justice or is the Serb rejection of the ICTY rooted in a rejection of international justice (as opposed to national or local justice)? Alternately, could it best be explained by geopolitical orientations inclining Serbs to see the ICTY as a hostile mechanism whose main aim is not to do justice, but to subjugate Serbia to the rule of foreign powers?

Serbs and the ICTY

The negative attitude of the overwhelming majority of citizens in the Republic of Serbia towards the ICTY is well known. Opinion polls carried out on behalf of the OECD, but also polls conducted by academic institutions show almost complete distrust of the ICTY. Only in Republika Srpska is the rejection of the ICTY's proceedings and outcomes more severe than in Serbia or the State Union of Serbia and Montenegro. In a 2002 poll, carried out by the International Institute for Democracy and Electoral Assistance (IDEA) and the Organization for Security and Cooperation in Europe (OSCE), more than half of the respondents in the Federation of Bosnia-Hercegovina expressed trust in the ICTY, in Kosovo (which at that point was still a part of Serbia-Montenegro), this indicator was even 83.8 per cent, whereas trust was low in Croatia and Montenegro but lowest in Serbia and Republika Srpska.

---

11 Gordy (2013), 59–65.

12 The ethnocentrism claim often comes in disguise when authors reproach "the Serbs" not to confront their own past or to downplay past atrocities in order to keep an untainted image of their nation. See: Hoare, M. A. (2010). 'Bosnia-Hercegovina and International Justice: Past Failures and Future Solutions.' *East European Politics and Societies* 24, pp. 191–206.

Table 1: Trust in the ICTY across the countries under its jurisdiction 2002 (%)[13]

	Federation of Bosnia-Herzegovina	Croatia	Kosovo	Montenegro	Serbia	Republika Srpska
Trust in the ICTY	50,5	20,5	83,8	24,1	7,6	3,6

This variance across countries and entities of the former Yugoslavia[14] has been explained in different ways. Some authors argue that this is due to strong negationist tendencies among Serbs, who refuse to acknowledge the burden of history that – according to these authors – makes them the main collective culprit of the crimes perpetrated during the violent conflicts in the former Yugoslavia.[15] Others point to the slow pace of ICTY proceedings, its long trials and obscure decisions, or then explain Serb rejection by arguing that the ICTY had been imposed on Serbia (and other successor states) by 'the West', usually understood as the EU, NATO and, to a lesser extent, the United Nations.[16] In the following chapter, some

13 In this study, the following surveys were used: Institute of Social Sciences, Belgrade (ISS): JJM 133–1998, JMS 134–1999 S, JMS 137–2000 S, JMS 154–2000 S, Serbian Public Opinion October 2003, Yugoslav Public Opinion 2002, Yugoslav Public Opinion 2004, (can also be retrieved from www.gesis.org); Belgrade Center for Human Rights and Organization for Security and Cooperation in Europe, IPSOS – Strategic Marketing: Serbia 2009: Public Perception in Serbia of the ICTY and the national courts dealing with war crimes (only power point presentation was available), Stavovi gradjana prema MKS i sudjenjima za ratne *zločine – Hrvatska (only result summary was available), IDEA and OSCE Poll 2002 (only interactive data base was available, no source data file), Strategies of symbolic nation-bulding in West Balkan states 2011, source data available online at: http://www.hf.uio.no/ilos/english/research/projects/nation-w-balkan/ Throughout this chapter, the same labels and abbreviations of the ISS polls (JMS, JMM etc) are used, as are contained in the source files and in the Gesis Data Archive for the Social Sciences, where some of them were uploaded and are now available: www.gesis.org.*

14 The notion of entity is intended to describe a part of the former Yugoslavia that – in terms of its media system, population and administrative structure is distinct from other parts, but does not constitute a full-fledged country, diplomatically recognized by the international community (for example Republika Srpska in Bosnia-Herzegovina and Kosovo before its declaration of independence).

15 Hazan, P. (2004). *Justice in a Time of War. The True Story Behind the International Criminal Tribunal for the Former Yugoslavia.* Texas and Paris: Texas A&M University Press, p. 178.

16 Laughland, J. (2007). *Travesty. The Trial of Slobodan Milošević and the Corruption of International Justice.* London, Ann Arbor: Pluto Press.

of these allegations will be transformed into testable hypotheses that can then be checked against the survey data using the source data (as far as it was made available) for cross table analysis.

The most striking feature of all polls that were being analysed in the framework of this chapter, is the fact that none of the traditional predictors of political attitudes seem to play a role in determining respondents' opinions about the ICTY. There is not much variance in respondents' attitudes toward the ICTY, no matter whether they are rich or poor, residents of towns or villages, well or hardly educated. Gender does not matter, neither does age. What really does matter is ethnicity, or, as it was often labelled in the questionnaires, nationality. If one wants to predict a respondent's attitude towards the ICTY, one has to look at the nationality a respondent indicated in the poll: if he is a Serb, he will most likely have a negative attitude, if he is a Montenegrin, he will not trust it, if he is an Albanian or Bosniak, he will usually have more respect than Serb or Montenegrin respondents for the "Hague Tribunal". Looking at respondents' gender, education or social status does not make it much easier to predict their opinion about the ICTY. The same is true for the specifically Serbian issue of whether Slobodan Milošević should be transferred to the ICTY. The issue was most controversial after Milošević had lost the elections against Voijslav Kostunica in the autumn of 2000 and was forced to step down and acknowledge his defeat. In that situation, Serb public opinion was confronted with the same dilemma as other transitional societies: should the head of the *ancien régime* be prosecuted at home, amnestied, sent to an international court and prosecuted there?[17] The polls dealing with this issue cannot not be unambiguously interpreted in favour or against the ICTY,

---

17 An additional factor when deciding to submit a former ruler to a domestic court rather than an international one is usually the expected consequences for the interpretation of the recent past: If Milošević – or any other ruler who was forced to step down – was judged by a domestic court, he would have been accused of corruption and crimes committed in Serbia, rather than of international crimes (genocide, crimes against humanity, war crimes), although they were already part of the Yugoslav Penal Code since 1951. If judged by an international court, a former ruler risks an indictment including international crimes (international tribunals usually don't have jurisdiction over corruption issues), but important stakeholders, parties, and groups of interest also risk that such a tribunal elucidates crimes from the past for which guilt often cannot only be attributed to the ruler and his entourage alone. Judging a former ruler for corruption before a domestic court lowers the risk of a backlash to public opinion at home and enables a country to avoid 'dealing with the past' of people and groups other than the former ruler and his entourage. For the Yugoslav Penal Code and its provisions about international crimes, see: Donnelly, R. C. 'The New Yugoslav Penal

because the questions asked measure attitudes towards the ICTY as well as attitudes toward Milošević and his rule. This is illustrated by the following table:

Table 2: Attitudes towards Milošević and towards delivery to the ICTY (%) (Serbia 1999)

Milošević's delivery	Strong approval of his achievements	Somewhat approve his achievements	Somewhat disapprove his achievements	Strongly dissapprove his achievements	total
approve	0,5	0.6	3,5	42	46,5
disapprove	9,1	18,8	14,4	11,2	53,5
total	9,6	19,4	17,8	53,2	100

It is unsurprising that people who endorsed Milošević's political achievements were less likely to support his extradition. Almost none of them were in favour of his transfer. But also among those who disapproved of his politics (altogether 71.1 per cent), roughly a quarter opposed surrendering him to The Hague. This does not mean that those respondents were against punishing Milošević. Polls show quite a lot of support for prosecuting and judging Milošević at home, by the Yugoslav judiciary (despite the low trust respondents expressed in the Yugoslav or Serb judiciary, as we will see later). What is important here is the fact that quite a few of Milošević's opponents were against prosecuting him in The Hague. One has to take into account that attitudes toward Milošević must have been affected by general attitudes toward the Yugoslav past ('Yugo-nostalgia' versus 'modernization' for example), and – as we know from many surveys in Central European countries – such attitudes strongly vary across age groups and according to education, with younger and well-educated people in favour of modernization and older and less educated cohorts in favour of traditional values.

The other potential factor that could have affected respondents' attitudes toward Milošević's transfer was the issue of NATO air strikes in 1999. Violent clashes between the Kosovo Liberation Army on one side and the Serb police and later also the Yugoslav Army on the other side had triggered diplomatic interventions by the international community and the deployment of the so-called Kosovo Verification Mission.[18] In January 1999, the Mission discovered traces of a massacre in the village of Račak, allegedly committed by Yugoslav forces against the civilian

Code 1952'. *Yale Law School Legal Scholarship Repository*, online at: *digitalcommons.law.yale.edu/cgi/viewcontent.cgi?article=5749.*

18 The Kosovo Verification Mission was organized and carried out by the Organization for Security and Cooperation in Europe and included military and civilian observers.

population.[19] The events in Račak outraged public opinion outside Yugoslavia and many Western governments, and led to the Rambouillet negotiations, which failed. In order to coerce Yugoslavia (that is Serbia and Montenegro), NATO started a bombing campaign against Yugoslav military and civilian targets that inclined the Yugoslav leadership under Milošević to withdraw all Yugoslav and Serb armed forces from Kosovo and to agree to the deployment of a UN-led intervention force in Kosovo (called Kosovo Force, KFOR).[20]

One might assume that even for Milošević's opponents NATO's bombing campaign was an outrageous attack on the entire population and therefore "universally rejected."[21] But there is some evidence which suggests that such statements may at least not cover the whole picture of Yugoslav attitudes towards NATO bombing. As the following table demonstrates, public opinion in Serbia was far from being united against the airstrikes. Relatively more respondents blamed Milošević's and the then Yugoslav government for the conflict than the US president and NATO. To some extent, even some of Milošević's supporters must have regarded him at least partially guilty for the conflict with NATO. This does not openly contradict the claim about universal rejection of the airstrikes, but it shows how divided the population was about who was to blame for it.[22]

Table 3: Attitudes towards Milošević and NATO airstrikes[23]

Responsibility for conflict Serbia - NATO	**Attitudes (as percentage of those respondents who expressed an opinion)**[24]
Milošević and the ruling coalition	31,55
Clinton and NATO	27,74
both	35
neither	1,07
Don't know	4,64

19 As it later appeared (among others during *the prosecutor v. Milošević* and *the prosecutor v. Djordjević*), at least some of the casualties had been members of the Kosovo Liberation Army. See: Bachmann, K. (2011). 'When the court refuses to write history.' *Review of International Affairs.* vol. 62 (1143), pp. 5–33.

20 Daalder, I. H. And O'Hanlon, M. E. (2000). *Winning Ugly. NATO's War to Save Kosovo.* Washington D.C.: Brookings Institutions Press, pp. 137–182.

21 Gordy (2013), 21.

22 Some of the polls quoted by Gordy (2013), 22–25, indicate that at a later stage, in 2001, more respondents blamed the US for the bombing than the Milošević government.

23 Institute of Social Sciences, Belgrade: Yugoslav Opinion Poll (Serbia and Montenegro, including Kosovo) poll label JMS 134–1999 S.

24 Cases in which respondents refused to answer were excluded.

Whereas the first polls concerning Serb attitudes toward the ICTY are most likely tainted by interfering opinions about NATO bombing and attitudes toward Milošević as a politician, they already show a strong – though not dominant – tendency to hold Milošević accountable. But their preference was about judging him at home, rather than by the ICTY. In a poll from June 1998 – long before Milošević stepped down and was arrested – almost 20 per cent of respondents were in favor of fulfilling "all requirements of the international community" with respect to war crimes suspects' extraditions, whereas a much smaller number wanted to reject such requirements. The overwhelming majority of respondents wanted the Yugoslav authorities to make their own investigations (more than 30 per cent) and the Yugoslav judicial system to prosecute war criminals (almost 27 per cent).[25] A poll in February 2000 delivered almost the same values, only the percentage of those willing to fulfil all requirements of the international community had fallen to 14 per cent and the number of those preferring national prosecutions had slightly increased.[26]

Institutional Trust

Serb citizens' preference to judge war criminals at home rather than to deliver them to The Hague can be explained by two opposite factors linked to institutional trust. Serbs might have rejected the ICTY, because they saw it as an instrument of justice and generally mistrusted any judiciary, including their own. The second hypothesis goes in the opposite direction: Serbs may have rejected the ICTY because they trusted their own judiciary more than the international court. This hypothesis is often confirmed in cases where nationals of one country reject an ICT jurisdiction because they regard it as less reliable or as imposed from the outside and have more confidence in their own judges and prosecutors. The relatively high percentage of respondents who were critical toward Milošević but did not want him surrendered to The Hague is an indication of the possible validity of this hypothesis in the Serb case.

The Yugoslav survey of 1998 contained several questions about institutional trust. Pollsters asked respondents to rate their level of trust in several institutions (among others the federal government, the army, the police, and the judiciary) on a five item Likert scale.[27] By juxtaposing the distribution of answers to

25 Slightly more than ten per cent chose "don't know". JJM 133 from June 1998.

26 JMS 137, February 2000, with the same of "don't know" as in JJM 133.

27 A Likert scale is a symmetrical scale, with the neutral element in the middle and extreme positions at the lowest and highest positions, from which respondents can

both questions (the one about extradition of war criminals and the one about institutional trust), one can create values for Cramer's V, which measures the strength of association between both variables.[28] Roughly speaking, in our case Cramer V reveals that confidence in the Yugoslav judicial system is hardly related to respondents' attitudes toward extradition (Cramer V is at only .08 for that association). There is a slightly stronger link between attitudes to extradition and attitudes toward the federal government (V = .18) and trust in the Serb government (V = .17) and only a weak association between attitudes toward extradition to the ICTY and attitudes toward the police (V = .12). This is hardly surprising, since most respondents, asked about the institution they trusted most, either gave evasive answers or indicated "none". In this ranking, the army enjoyed the highest trust score with 24.31 per cent of all indications, whereas the judicial system obtained a depressing 1.82 per cent. For sure, Serbs did not regard their own judiciary as a good alternative to the ICTY: they distrusted their courts even more than the ICTY. When the trust questions were repeated in November 2000, the result was more or less the same. The highest V value appeared when relating attitudes toward extradition to attitudes to nongovernmental organizations (V = .24). The latter may be seen as an indication that respondents who express confidence in NGOs are more inclined to support extradition to the ICTY than those who mistrust NGOs.

The Serb survey of 2003 enables a comparison of the issue of trust in Serb institutions directly with trust in the ICTY. At that point, the ICTY was introduced into the surveys on the same basis as Serb institutions and other international institutions like the UN, NATO, the EU and the OSCE. By then, Cramer's V for trust in the judiciary had risen to .19, but still remained much lower than the strength of other associations. For instance, trust in the government and the president of Serbia was now linked to trust in the ICTY by a Cramer's V score of more than .30 and in the case of the police led to a V-value of .18.

---

choose the answer which suits them. Usually it has 5 items ranging from strong approval for a statement to strong disapproval. It is named after psychologist Rensis Likert.

28 Cramer's V is constructed as a measurement for the relation between two nominal variables. For the purpose of this chapter, Likert scales are treated as nominal, although one might argue that they also fulfill the requirements of an ordinal scale. Cramer's V can osciallate between 0 (no association between the variables) and 1 (perfect association). Values below .20 are usually treated as weak. See: Kühnel, S. M. and Krebs, D. (2010). *Statistik für Sozialwissenschaften.* Reinbeck bei Hamburg: Rowohlt, p. 356.

This altogether substantiates the rejection of the hypotheses linking Serb rejection of the ICTY to high confidence in their own judicial system. It is more likely that Serb objections against the ICTY were motivated by a lack of confidence in the judiciary in general – no matter whether international or local. It is also possible that mistrust in the ICTY and the refusal to extradite suspects to The Hague had nothing to do with attitudes towards justice and the judicial system, but was rooted in completely different attitudes. One of the possible causes was often emphasized by opponents and critics of the ICTY, who claimed that the tribunal was "biased" and "an instrument of a new world order" whose aim it was to subjugate Serbia.[29]

Geopolitical Orientations

Taking such views as points of departure, one can hypothesize associations between trust in the ICTY (or, respectively, support for extradition to the ICTY) and a pro-Western geopolitical orientation, which can be measured by questions about trust in NATO or the EU or as support for closer cooperation between Serbia and and these organizations or even support for a NATO or EU membership of Serbia. The 1998 poll (conducted in Serbia and Montenegro) contained a question about the need to "reintegrate Yugoslavia into the World and Europe" which was associated with support for the delivery of war crimes suspects to the ICTY on the level of Cramer's $V = .14$, hence not too strongly. However, in this poll, which did not directly ask about trust in NATO and EU, support for compliance with the ICTY seemed to be slightly connected to some specific value orientations, such as democracy and Human Rights (Cramer's $V = .16$). The link with responses to another question asking about the importance of restoring Serb pride and dignity, revealed an even stronger (but negative) association of $V = -.25$. When pollsters asked whether Serbia should rely more on the West, this relation became even stronger: now Cramer's V increased to .39, demonstrating a relatively strong link between pro-Western attitudes and support for cooperation with the ICTY.

In the first Serb poll of 2000, the question about the delivery of war crimes suspects to The Hague can be juxtaposed with a polarizing question that inclined respondents to decide either for integration with Russia and Belarus or the EU. The responses confirmed the relatively strong link between geopolitics and the attitude toward the ICTY: supporters of a pro-Western orientation were more

29 Laughland (2007), 7–32.

inclined to support extradition than those who wanted Serbia to come closer to the alliance between Russia and Belarus.

Additionally, it should be mentioned that 92.3 per cent of those who wanted to fulfil "all requirements of the international community" also supported EU integration, and 25.9 per cent of all those who supported EU membership were in favour of extradition. Only nine per cent of them opposed extradition and regarded the suspects as patriots. Most supporters of EU membership either avoided giving a clear answer or chose one of the more moderate options and wanted suspects to be delivered after domestic investigations or to be judged at home. Questions about confidence in NATO, EU and the UN in the same survey further confirmed the impression that the attitude toward the ICTY was to a large extent dependent on respondents' geopolitical opinions. For confidence in NATO, Cramer's V was at .24, for confidence in the UN it was even higher (V = .30), but the EU delivered the highest V-score of .34. Contrary to some Western European and Serb intellectuals (and later Milošević's defenders) who accused the ICTY of being an instrument of NATO victor's justice, Serb respondents seemed to associate the ICTY more strongly with the EU than with NATO – despite the fact that EU conditionality did not yet play a role.[30]

In the third poll carried out in Serbia in 2000, the same question about compliance with the international community's requirements was asked, but at that time, additional questions about trust were introduced, which facilitated the analysis of respondents' attitudes. Once again, a strong link between geopolitics and attitudes toward the ICTY resurfaced and was much stronger than the correlations between attitudes toward the ICTY and institutional trust. The latter had scored between V = .08 and .21.

30 About EU conditionality and the ICTY see: Börzel, T. and Risse, T. (2000). 'When Europe Hits Home: Europeanization and Domestic Change.' *European Integration Online Papers* 4, no. 15; Howell K. (2004). 'Developing Conceptualisations of Europeanization: Synthesising Methodological Approaches.' *Queen's Paper on Europeanization*, no. 3; Bachmann, K. and Fatić, A. (2015). *The UN International Criminal Tribunals. Transition without Justice?* London, New York: Routledge, pp. 157–190.

Table 4: Associations between attitudes toward extradition to the ICTY and geopolitical orientations in 2000

	Cramer's V
Trust in the UN	.24
Trust in the OSCE	.26
Trust in the EU	.24
Trust in NATO	.20
Should Yugoslavia aspire to admittance to EU	.33
Should Yugoslavia aspire to NATO membership	.43

The 2004 poll, conducted by the Institute of Social Sciences in Belgrade, which used five item Likert scales for the measurement of trust in international organizations and in the ICTY, confirmed these findings concerning the link between geopolitical orientations and attitudes toward international criminal justice.

The poll also contained a question that helps to explain the motivation of respondents linking negative attitudes toward the ICTY with anti-Western opinions: they regarded cooperation with the ICTY as a duty that had been imposed on the country against its will. Those who regarded cooperation as imposed mistrusted the ICTY, and those who saw it as voluntary tended to have a higher confidence in the Hague Tribunal than their opponents. Both sides could present good arguments: when signing and ratifying the Dayton agreements, all sides had also accepted the jurisdiction of the ICTY over their territory and had to endorse the obligation to surrender accused persons and to hand over evidence against them. However, critics of the tribunal often emphasized that the ICTY had been created by the UN Security Council in contravention of its powers and contrary to the UN Charter which only allowed the Council to create institutions designed to assist the Council in his tasks. Doing justice was no task conferred on the UNSC by the Charter and many Serbian critics used to argue that the ICTY should have instead been founded by the UN General Assembly.[31] These arguments were less important for the general public in Serbia than the pressure the US and the EU frequently exerted upon subsequent Serb governments. In 2000, the US had withheld financial aid for the new Serb government until Milošević was sent to The Hague; in the following years, the EU time and again urged Serbia to comply

31 See Gordy (2013), 59–65; and, for the legal arguments, Schabas, W. A. (2006). *The UN International Criminal Tribunals. The Former Jugoslavia, Rwanda and Sierra Leone.* Cambridge, New York, Melbourne, Madrid, Cape Town, Singapore, São Paulo, Delhi, Dubai, Tokyo: Cambridge University Press, pp. 48–53.

with ICTY demands before agreeing to trade liberalization, progress in the EU association process, and later in EU membership talks. This proved to a large extent successful, but the success for the ICTY came with a price tag – the tribunal became embroiled in power politics and diplomatic games and lost legitimacy in the eyes of Serbia's citizens.

Serb Public Opinion and the ICTY's Performance

The start of the new millennium was a watershed for the ICTY for several reasons. Firstly, after years of struggle with reluctant EU and NATO states and non-cooperative governments in the former Yugoslavia, the ICTY prosecutors managed to get hold of several high-ranking suspects, among them former head of state Slobodan Milošević. Secondly, with the Milošević trial public awareness rose – not only in international media, but also in Serbia. The Milošević trial was now not only being broadcast by the ICTY's satellite program (which was difficult to receive), but also by Radio and TV B92 – and the media in Serbia started to send their own correspondents to The Hague in order to cover the "trial of the century" (as it was often labelled) live and *in extenso*. A poll carried out by ISS in December 2002 revealed that the majority of respondents declared following the Milošević trial on television on a daily basis or at least regularly. Until then, the most senior suspect in the ICTY's docket had been Biljana Plavšić, the former president of Republika Srpska, who had concluded a plea agreement with the prosecution and thus reduced her own trial to a sentencing hearing which lasted only a few days. She pleaded guilty to crimes against humanity after the prosecution had dropped a genocide charge against her, causing outrage among victims' organizations in Bosnia. When the Milošević trial started, Serbian respondents already had a clear opinion about the ICTY record, formed on the basis of their general orientations about geopolitics and justice and the ICTY's performance, whose trials had concentrated on low ranking perpetrators from Bosnia, mostly Bosnian Croat and Bosnian Serb camp commanders and camp staff, who had abused and killed their prisoners.[32]

32 For the influence of those first trials on Serb public opinion and the perceived bias of the ICTY against Bosnian Croats and Serbs, see Bachmann, Fatić (2015).

Table 5: ICTY's bias as perceived by Serb respondents in December 2002

Statement put to respondents[33]	**Very convincing**	**Somewhat convincing**	**A little convincing**	**Not at all convincing**	**Doesn't know, refused to answer**	
Crimes committed by Albanians, Croatians and Bosnians are not prosecuted as vigorously as allegations against Serbs	65,58	14,73	5,81	4,65	9,22	100%
The prosecution in The Hague is amateurish and incompetent, so real justice cannot be achieved	35,5	22,4	12,09	18,99	11,01	100%
The Tribunal in The Hague represents the best legal standards the international community can organize, so justice will be done in a way which is fair for everyone	10	11,86	17,29	40	20,54	100%

33 Each question was preceded by an explanation of the following content: "Now I am going to read you some statements about the trial against Slobodan Milošević before the International War Crimes Tribunal in The Hague. For each statement, please tell me whether you consider it very convincing, somewhat convincing, a little convincing or a not at all convincing state."

As we can see here, the distribution of opinions about the ICTY more or less corresponded to the ICTY's performance: it had indicted more Serb Bosnians and Bosnian Croats than members of any other group, and so far no single Kosovo Albanian had been sentenced (or even completed his trial) by the ICTY.[34] Back in 2002, this disproportion was even more evident than today (by the end of 2015), when 63.7 per cent of all suspects who were convicted by the ICTY, are Serbs (either from Bosnia or Serbia proper), 21.25 per cent of all sentenced are Croats (almost all from Bosnia), but only 7.5 per cent of all convicted come from the Federation of Bosnia-Hercegovina and a mere 2.5 per cent from the KLA.

Ethnocentrism

The last factor whose salience is often evoked in the debate about Serb refusal to cooperate with the ICTY is ethnocentrism. According to this view, Serbs reject the ICTY because they refuse to 'deal with their past', to accept their share (whatever that is) of the crimes committed during the conflict and regard those who were transferred to the Hague Tribunal as heroes rather than as war criminals or suspects. A poll carried out in 2011 in all Yugoslav successor republics facilitates a comparison of different attitudes. It shows that the tendency in Serbia to regard (suspected) war criminals as heroes is still strong but completely overshadowed by Kosovo Albanians' inclination to regard their suspects as war heroes.

---

34 The first judgment against a Kosovo Albanian was issued in 2005 in the case of *the prosecutor v. Limaj et al.* and ended with one sentence and two acquittals.

Table 6: Attitudes towards the ICTY, own war criminals, national pride and European Integration 2011[35]

Measurement	**Serbia (in percentages)**[36]
Attitude toward the ICTY	–48.28 (negative attitude) +23.86 (positive attitude) **–24.42 (net approval/rejection)**
Criminals are our heroes	+46.87 (positive attitude) –21.23 (negative attitude) **+25.64 (net approval/rejection)**

35 The data for the following table were derived from the source data of the project "Strategies of Symbolic Nation-Building in West Balkan States", whose opinion polls were carried out in the second half of 2011. Details can be found online at: http://www.hf.uio.no/ilos/english/research/projects/nation-w-balkan/. In order to test the hypothesis, linking attitudes toward the ICTY to ethnocentrism, we used the question "Are you proud to be a citizen of Serbia/Croatia/Kosovo/Montenegro" (the question was not asked in the Bosnia and Herzegovina poll). Below, we indicate the positive and negative answers and the difference between both. "+" indicates the number of positive answers, "–" the negative ones. Both together usually do not amount to 100 per cent, because of evasive answers, refusals to answer and the method of the poll, which also offered respondents the possibility to answer "yes and no", which strongly inflated the amount of evasive attitudes. In order to test the hypothesis, which links attitudes toward the ICTY to the geopolitical orientation, we used the question "Do you think that European Integration is a good or bad thing for Serbia /Croatia, Montenegro/Bosnia and Herzegovina?" In order to test the hypothesis linking attitudes toward the ICTY to externalization of guilt or solidarity with perpetrators, we used the question "Our officials and soldiers indicted / sentenced by the ICTY or domestic courts are heroes, not criminals." As a measurement for respondents' attitudes toward the ICTY, we used the question "Cooperation with the ICTY is negative for Serbian/Montenegrin/Kosovo/Croatian national interests". In Bosnia and Herzegovina, this question was asked in a slightly different way: "Cooperation with ICTY is negative for Bosnia-Herzegovina." Respondents were then asked to agree or disagree. Where respondents were asked according to a Likert scale, positive and negative answers were pooled together. In Bosnia-Herzegovina, the poll was carried out in the whole country, but the question about ethnicity ("What is your ethnicity?") could be used to disentangle the different ethnicities, whose attitudes strongly differ. It must be kept in mind that results for different ethnicities do not necessarily correspond with results for the different entities, because the results for ethnicities also may include respondents who do not live in the entity in which their ethnicity is in the majority (for example Bosniaks living in Republika Srpska or Serbs living in the Federation of Bosnia-Herzegovina).

36 Evasive answers were neglected, therefore percentages do not add up to a hundred per cent.

Measurement	Serbia (in percentages)
Pride	+91.1 (positive attitude) -7.78 (negative attitude) **+83.32 (net approval/rejection)**
European Integration is a good thing	+40 (positive attitude) -32.19 (negative attitude) **+7.81 (net approval/rejection)**

According to the poll, a relative majority of Serbs was in favour of EU integration, and their overwhelming majority was proud to be Serb. A relative majority saw Serb ICTY suspects as heroes and almost half of those who expressed an opinion on the matter rejected the ICTY. A closer look at the poll statistics for other countries and entities reveals, though, that neither pride nor identification with the alleged heroes explain a negative stance toward the ICTY. In Kosovo, just as many respondents as in Serbia were proud to be Kosovo Albanians and even more regarded KLA suspects as heroes rather than perpetrators, but nevertheless supported the ICTY. Pride was high across all communities and so was the inclination to see own suspects as heroes (except for Montenegro, whose respondents were more critical toward their own community). Geopolitical orientations explain the Serb attitude toward the ICTY much better than pride, ethnocentrism or identification with the accused.

Table 7: Strength of association between attitudes towards the ICTY and ethnocentrism and geopolitical orientation in 2011 (as Cramer's V, outliers are highlighted by italics)

Cramer's V for attitude toward ICTY and...	Serbia	Croatia	Montenegro	Kosovo	Bosnia and Herzegovina (whole)
...attitude toward own war crimes suspects	*.52*	*.50*	.45	.15	.27
...pride of being a citizens of one's country	.15	.16	.17	.18	–
...attitude toward European Integration	*.35*	.18	.21	.14	*.36*

The table shows that positive attitudes toward own war crimes suspects makes it quite likely for a respondent to reject the ICTY, except for Kosovo, from which where few suspects were extradited or surrendered to the ICTY (and relatively few of them were later sentenced). Attitudes toward European integration are strongly associated with attitudes toward the ICTY in Serbia and Bosnia and Herzegovina, but not in the other countries and entities. For Serbia, which is the main focus of this chapter, the table demonstrates that – contrary to conventional wisdom – geopolitical attitudes explain Serb attitudes toward the ICTY much better than ethnocentrism. In other words, in Serbia (just as in the other parts of the former Yugoslavia) almost everyone is proud to be a member of his community, but this does not yet allow any interference, whether he also rejects or approves of the ICTY. If we know whether he or she is in favour of European integration or regards the ICTY as an instrument of "the West" for the subjugation of Serbia, than we can also quite safely predict whether the respondent will be for or against cooperation with the ICTY or express trust in the "Hague Tribunal."

One of the surveys covering all of the former Yugoslavia also deals with the issue of whether the ICTY's central message was endorsed (and if yes, how) by its audience in the different Yugoslav successor republics. This message is the claim, included in the trial judgment of *the prosecutor v. Krstic*, that in 1994, after the fall of the Srebrenica enclave, a genocide occurred, orchestrated by the amy of the Bosnian Serbs. The narrative about the Srebrenica genocide has become deeply embedded in the society and the public sphere of the Federation of Bosnia-Herzegovina, but also in the international community. Annual commemorations take place in Srebrenica, and Western media usually dedicate reports to the events of 1995 in July every year. In Serbia, the issue has been controversially discussed in the public sphere and in 2010 the Parliament of Serbia with a majority of one vote[37] issued a special resolution on Srebrenica, in which it condemned the events as crimes. The question of whether these crimes should be labelled as genocide or otherwise has become a litmus test in Serbian politics for patriotism and the attitude towards Serbia's past. The resolution refrained from calling Srebrenica a genocide.[38] In the Federation of Bosnia-Herzegovina, it is popular, especially in nationalist circles, to claim that all Serb crimes committed in Bosnia constituted genocide.[39]

37 See B92, online at: http://www.b92.net/eng/news/politics.php?yyyy=2010&mm=03&dd=31&nav_id=66160 (accessed March 31, 2010).

38 The text consists of one sentence: "The parliament of Serbia strongly condemns the crime committed against the Bosnian Muslim population of Srebrenica in July 1995, as determined by the International Court of Justice ruling." See: BalkanInsight March 31, 2010. http://www.balkaninsight.com/en/article/serbia-adopts-resolution-condemning-srebrenica-massacre.

39 See, for example: *Džunuzović, A. (2009). Lanet Olsun - Zločin nad Bošnjacima istočne Bosn. Sarajevo: Mladi Muslimani.*

But how was the ICTY message about the genocide in Srebrenica in July 1994 dealt with by Serbs? In no other case concerning the former Yugoslavia did the ICTY issue a similar verdict and instead convicted perpetrators for crimes against humanity and / or war crimes.[40] In the framework of the 2011 poll this question was also included in the questionnaire and put to respondents in – among others – Bosnia and Serbia. Here is the result:

Table 8: Genocide denial in Bosnia and Serbia in 2011 (as percentage of all respondents of an ethnicity)

Respondents	Agree with the genocide claim[41]	Reject the genocide claim	Percentage of evasive answers[42]
Bosniaks in Bosnia and Herzegovina	95	1,8	3,2
Croats in Bosnia and Herzegovina	76,8	3,4	19,8
Serbs in Bosnia and Herzegovina	13,8	57,6	29,2
Serbs in Serbia	25,51	33,4	41,09

The central message of the ICTY about Srebrenica is thus mostly accepted by those whose ethnic community is not negatively affected by it – by Bosnian Croats and of course by Bosniaks, whose collective identity is to a large extent based on victimhood. The target communities of the genocide verdict, the Serbs in Bosnia and Serbia, have hardly endorsed this message. It is strongly contested and rejected by Bosnian Serbs, where the percentage of genocide-deniers is much higher than in Serbia proper.

In sum, we can conclude that the ICTY's rejection by Serbs is first and foremost caused by geopolitical considerations, mistrust towards justice in general and

40 The so-called 98*bis* decision of the trial chamber in *the prosecutor v. Milošević* also contains the claim, that crimes in other municipalities in Bosnia can be regarded as forming part of a genocide. However, a 98*bis* decision is no judgment, it merely says (if it is positive for the prosecution) that the prosecution produced enough evidence for continuing the trial and that the defence has a case to answer. See: Meierhenrich, J. (2014). 'Beyond the Theater of International Justice: The Rule 98*bis* Decision in *Milošević*.' In: Waters, T. (2014) (ed). *The Milošević Trial. An Autopsy.* Oxford, New York: Oxford University Press, pp. 316–326.

41 The categories from the poll "agree" and "strongly agree" are aggregated as positive answers, the same was done with the categories of "disagree and strongly disagree."

42 Evasive answers were inflated because they also were given the possibility to answer "agree and disagree" and could refuse answers or claim not to know. All these answers are pooled together here as "evasive answers".

identification with the suspects, but not so much by ethnocentrism. Ethnocentrism, which is strong across the whole of former Yugoslavia, does not explain why Serbs reject the ICTY. This is best explained by geopolitical orientations – people who are in favour of EU and NATO membership tend to support extraditions to the ICTY more than those who are against a pro-Western foreign policy. Those who reject the ICTY do so because they regard it as biased against Serbia and as an instrument of the EU (rather than NATO or the UN) used in order to force Serbia into compliance with Western interests. Those who support the ICTY usually do so because they see it as a price to pay for EU integration.

Ana Ljubojević

The Vukovar and Ovčara Trials and Their Influence on Popular Narratives About the War in Croatia and Serbia

Recent history in Serbia and Croatia is more about each nationality's collective memory rather than common factual history. Mutually exclusive 'truths' about war and the committed atrocities quickly developed and were used by political elites and mass media for the creation of new national narratives that fragmented post-war societies. Other historical records were created by the International Criminal Tribunal for the former Yugoslavia (ICTY) and domestic courts prosecuting war crimes.[1]

This chapter analyses the impact of transitional justice mechanisms on the historical narratives and the creation of collective memory about the war. Taking Brooks and Gewritz's methodological approach, law is analysed here not as set of rules and policies, but as a source of "stories, explanations, performances, linguistic exchanges – as narratives and rhetoric."[2] Furthermore, law is given a dimension of "cultural discourse through which social narratives are structured and suppressed." Thus, attention is given more to the actual facts than legal rules of the procedure, and to the way language is used as much as to the idea expressed. While shaping reality through language, law uses distinctive linguistic methods, forms, and expressions and requires strategies of interpretation. During a trial, the predominant historical narrative of the audience may be constantly questioned and challenged so that 'reality' is always divided into various versions of truth. The popularity of such a narrative-based approach to law can be understood as a

---

1 The Yugoslav Penal Code, which was in force when most of the crimes were committed, included international crimes (genocide, crimes against humanities and war crimes). But due to the reluctance of the Republic of Serbia's Office of the War Crimes Prosecutor to indict high-ranking suspects, most cases tried in Serbia actually dealt with war crimes suspects. For an overview over the current state of affairs, see the latter's website: http://www.tuzilastvorz.org.rs/html_trz/predmeti_eng.htm.

2 Brooks, P. & Gewritz, P. (1998). *Law's stories: Narrative and Rhetoric in the Law.* Yale University Press, p. 1.

"loss of faith in the idea of objective truth and the widespread embrace of ideas about the social construction of reality."[3]

There is an important difference in the construction of historical narratives in the trials held before the ICTY and trials on the local level. While the ICTY indicted only high-ranking officials from military and political elites, domestic courts dealt with direct perpetrators. This research shows that the differences in legal proceedings and legal notions used in court have an impact on the way past events are framed by prosecutors and judges. It also shows that both – the way the law is implemented and the narratives are shaped in court – have an influence on how collective responsibility is conceived by the wider public.

The influence of transitional justice mechanisms on local societies can be measured through their impact on historical narratives triggered by war crime trials. The purpose of international criminal tribunals is not the creation of historical records, at least not in the first place, but often historical facts are used as background information in order to place a specific crime into a larger context. Several authors have analysed the way in which prosecutors, judges, and trial chambers deal with expert witnesses, amici curiae, the input from historians and political scientists and other specialists who appear in court either in order to bolster the prosecution or the defence arguments or who are called by the chamber in order to provide guidance for the judges.[4] They found that prosecutors and judges are often prone to writing history themselves, either in extensive indictments and judgments or when making speeches at the beginning or end of a trial. As Wilson demonstrates, they often invoke positivist notions of historiography that are widely contested by contemporary historians and attempt to create authoritative accounts of the past (and of the crimes which they adjudicate).[5]

In Serbia and Croatia, the instrument of transitional justice has been the prosecution of war crimes. The rationale behind this choice was to bolster transition to a stable democracy and to strengthen the rule of law.

Scholars like Peskin, Subotić, Akhavan, Orentlicher and others dealt with the impact that the international criminal tribunals had on the post-Yugoslav region

---

3 Brooks, P. & Gewritz, P. (1998), 12.

4 Wilson, R. (2005). 'Judging History: The Historical Record of the International Criminal Tribunal for the Former Yugoslavia.' *Human Rights Quarterly* 27, 3, pp. 908–942; Wilson, R. A. (2011). *Writing History in International Criminal Trials*. Cambridge University Press; Bachmann, K. and Fatić, A. (2015). *The UN International Criminal Tribunals. Transition without Justice?* New York, London: Routledge, pp. 232–240.

5 Wilson (2011), 1–23.

and its transition towards democracy.[6] Bearing in mind results of previous research, we conducted an analysis between the legal reasoning of the ICTY and Belgrade Special Court for War Crimes in order to establish differences in explaining the alleged causes of the war crimes and historical narratives proposed on those two levels. We also analyse whether such international and domestic historical narratives contributed to the specific framing of the cited institutions in the public sphere. Our main interest is to analyse the nature of framed historical narratives. In order to answer these questions, our research deals with the case study of two trials held for crimes perpetrated at Ovčara farm near Vukovar: one before the ICTY called "Vukovar hospital" or "Vukovar three", and one before Belgrade's Special Court for War Crimes named "Ovčara" trial.

Both Serbia and Croatia encountered serious problems in enabling fair trials for war crimes before domestic courts. Low domestic demand for normative change and a high degree of politicization of the judiciary have been a major problem from the beginning. For example, the Serb public largely refused to believe the Serbs had committed war crimes, and they blamed other nations and ethnic groups for starting the war. Political elites, the church, intellectuals, and the military, who had participated in the war either fighting in the field, giving orders or supporting the war effort symbolically, stayed in power after the transition and actively blocked transitional justice projects because of their own responsibility in creating, spreading and imposing war propaganda. Croatia institutionalized its official historical narrative about the Homeland War when in 2000 the Croatian Parliament approved the "Declaration on the Homeland War" as "just and legitimate defense" in order to "defend its internationally recognized borders against Greater Serbia's aggression."[7]

---

6 Peskin, V. (2008). *International Justice in Rwanda and the Balkans. Virtual Trials and the Struggle for State Cooperation*. Cambridge, New York, Melbourne, Madrid, Cape Town, Singapore, São Paulo, Delhi: Cambridge University Press; Subotić, J. (2009). *Hijacked Justice. Dealing with the Past in the Balkans*. Ithaca, London: Cornell University Press; Akhavan, P. (2009). 'Are International Criminal Tribunals a Disincentive to Peace?: Reconciling Judicial Romanticism with Political Realism.' *Human Rights Quarterly*, 31, pp. 624–654; Orentlicher, D. (2008). *Shrinking the Space for Denial: The Impact of the ICTY in Serbia*. New York: Open Society Justice Initiative, online at: https://www.opensocietyfoundations.org/reports/shrinking-space-denial-impact-icty-serbia.

7 Milekić, S. (2015). 'Croatian Law Should Penalise Attacks on War, Judge Says.' *Balkan Investigative Network*, March 20, 2015, online at: http://www.balkaninsight.com/en/article/croatian-judge-advocates-legal-definition-of-1990s-war; Batt, J., Obradovic-Wochnik, H. (2009) (eds). 'War crimes, conditionality and EU integration in the Western Balkans.' *Chaillot Paper* 116, p. 22, online at: http://www.iss.europa.eu/uploads/media/cp116.pdf.

In Serbia, the establishment of the War Crimes Chambers in 2003 was seen as an element strengthening the government, mostly because the public attitude towards the ICTY was extremely negative and the preferred strategy was the one of transferring trials back home. In Croatia, transfers of trials from the ICTY to Croatia under the ICTY's completion strategy were considered a political victory of sorts, because it reconfirmed transition to be successful and demonstrated the ability of the judiciary to deal with such cases and soothed public perceptions about the ICTY's alleged anti-Croatian bias. When the ICTY transfers a case to the local courts, the War Crimes Prosecutor in Serbia or Croatia adapts the indictment and adjusts it to the domestic legal system, endorsing the evidence gathered at the ICTY. This does not mean that the process is smooth and uncontroversial. In the "Ovčara" trial, the judgment in the first instance was overruled by the Serbian Supreme Court and in the "Lora" case in Croatia, none of the indictees were found guilty by the Split district court. Moreover, trials were organized almost uniquely against direct perpetrators, leaving so-called "impunity gap" between high-ranking officials brought before the international tribunal and the lowest-rankeding alleged criminals.

The Ovčara trial

On December 4, 2003, the War Crimes Council of the Belgrade District Court[8] issued its first indictment against eight alleged perpetrators of war crimes committed at a farm building in Ovčara, close to Vukovar, Croatia. Based on documentation handed over to the Serbian Authorities by the ICTY, the indictment accused members of the Territorial Defence of Vukovar (TO Vukovar) and the paramilitary formation "Leva Supoderica" of crimes committed against more than 200 prisoners of war, who had been transported from the Vukovar hospital to the Yugoslav Army barracks and then handed over to units of the Territorial Defence, who had beaten, tortured, shot, and buried them close to an old farm building.

Almost in parallel to the Serbian trial, three high-ranking officers of the former Yugoslav People's Army (YPA) were tried for the same events at the ICTY in The Hague. The indictment issued by the ICTY prosecution against Mrkšić, Radic and Šljivančanin[9] describes events dating from the beginning of the siege of Vukovar in late August 1991, the fall of the city to Serb forces, the forced removal of about

8 After the judicial reform, the Belgrade District Court became the High Court, therefore we will use hereafter its commonly used name: Special Court for War Crimes.

9 The initial indictment was confirmed on November 7, 1995, and later amended to include Slavko Dokmanović, mayor of wartime Vukovar. Following the death of the

400 non-Serbs from the Vukovar hospital, and the killing of at least 264 Croats and other non-Serbs.

In the third consolidated amended indictment against the "Vukovar three", the accused were held responsible for violations of the laws or customs of war as well as for crimes against humanity. YPA generals were accused of participation in a so-called Joint Criminal Enterprise (JCE), the alleged aim of which was the persecution of "Croats and other non-Serbs present at Vukovar hospital after the fall of the city, through the commission of murder, torture, cruel treatment, extermination and inhumane acts." The international tribunal's indictment also differed with respect to the nature of crimes and with regard to the criminal procedure used in order to prove those crimes. Namely, the "Vukovar three" were accused of crimes against humanity and violations of the laws or customs of war according to the Statute of the ICTY; therefore victims were presumed to be also civilians and not only prisoners of war. Thus, they were described as Croats or other non-Serbs. This ethnic dimension was not present in the indictment of the Ovčara trial held before the Belgrade Special Court for war crimes, where the victims were described as "prisoners of war."[10]

In addition, the ICTY indictment underlines that "each member of the Joint Criminal Enterprise worked in concert with each other and with other members of the JCE and acted either directly or through their subordinates, which included members of the YPA, the Territorial Defence of the co-called "Serbian Autonomous District/Srpska autonomna oblast/ Slavonia, Baranja and Western Srem" ("SAO SBWS"), TO of the Republic of Serbia, and volunteer and paramilitary units including those organized by Vojislav Seselj, all acting under the command of the YPA."[11] The choice to name paramilitary units "Serbian forces" bolstered the impression of an ethnicized background to the events in Vukovar. Although the Serbian indictment also mentions the YPA, claiming that "members of the Vukovar Territorial Defence (TO) and the volunteer unit 'Leva Supoderica'" were components of the then YPA, no army officer has ever been indicted for the Ovčara case before the Belgrade Court.

Moreover, the "Vukovar three" were charged on the basis of individual criminal responsibility and superior criminal responsibility, whereas the Serbian indictment dealt only with direct executioners. The detainees were transferred to Ovčara from YPA barracks, but the indictment issued by the War Crimes Prosecutor

---

fourth indictee, the indictment was changed three more times and was finalized on November 15, 2004.

10 Ovčara indictment at the Belgrade Special Court for War Crimes.

11 *The prosecutor v. Mrkšić et al.* ("Vukovar Hospital"), ICTY 95-13/1.

in Belgrade did not include any of the events before the arrival on the Ovčara farm and accordingly did not tackle the issue of their responsibility for various army officers that allegedly agreed to surrender the prisoners to the TO and the paramilitaries. Consequently, such a selective indictment cleared *a priori* any involvement in the crime of state institutions such as the army or the military police. However, both the indictment and the judgment saw the Vukovar TO and the paramilitary unit "Leva Supoderica" as components of the then YPA. The Serbian indictment described the Ovčara massacre as a separate episode of the war that was later on portrayed in the public sphere as an incident committed by paramilitary groups and local territorial defence units, thus relieving the state and the YPA of any blame for it.

The punishment that can be meted out for the offences described in the Serbian indictment is regulated by Article 144 of the Criminal Code of the Socialist Federal Republic of Yugoslavia (SFRY). Hence the rule of *tempus regit actum*, i.e. that the law that was in force at the time a criminal act was committed could be applied to the perpetrator of the criminal act. Yet when trying war crimes committed during the conflicts in the former Yugoslavia, as a general rule, the Serbian courts applied the 1993 FRY Criminal Code as the law more favourable to the accused. In Article 144 (war crime against prisoners of war) of the SFRY Criminal Code, the maximum punishment was the death penalty, whereas in the FRY Criminal Code the maximum punishment was twenty years of imprisonment.

The first instance judgment of the Ovčara trial in Serbia was rendered on December 12, 2005, but was reversed by the Serbian Supreme Court a year later and the case was put back on trial due to procedural mistakes. A new first-instance judgment was rendered by the District Court's War Crimes Chamber on March 12, 2009. On September 14, 2010, the Appellate Court in Belgrade confirmed the first instance judgment. Despite the appeals decision about retrial, the Ovčara case revealed the ideological core of the narratives about the events in Vukovar that had been popularized in the public arena. The indictment did not include YPA commanders, but the court was satisfied that the army "deliberately left prisoners to the members of the TO and the paramilitary." The Special Court for War Crimes' sentence established that the regular army of YPA did not take part in the crime at Ovčara and that its members did not know that colonel Mrkšić had decided to surrender prisoners of war to the TO. Members of the TO were convicted, but the YPA's responsibility vanished and Serbia as a state continued to evade a broader public debate about its responsibility in the war.

On the other hand, the case held before the ICTY brought charges for crimes against humanity, which requires the prosecutor to prove the perpetrators' knowledge of a widespread or systematic attack against the civilian population. The context is very important for assessing whether a crime was committed as part of such an attack or was unrelated to it. For example, when it was committed for purely personal reasons and without knowledge of what was going on around it. There is some controversy in the legal literature about the question of whether crimes against humanity require state action to be regarded as such, or whether non-state actors can also commit such crimes. Nevertheless, in the context of the war in Yugoslavia – and specifically Vukovar and Ovčara – it was quite obvious, that crimes against humanity, even if conducted by paramilitaries, were linked to state action anyway.

The trial of the "Vukovar three" before the ICTY commenced on October 11, 2005. Almost two years later, on September 27, 2007, the Trial Chamber rendered its judgment, convicting Mrkšić to 20 years of imprisonment, Šljivančanin to five years and acquitting Radic. Moreover, the Chamber, pursuant to Article 7(1) – individual criminal responsibility – found Mrkšić and Šljivančanin guilty on counts related to violations of the laws or customs of war, whereas they were found not guilty of crimes against humanity. Finally, their participation in a JCE was not proven beyond reasonable doubt and thus rejected. The Appeals Chamber judgment, rendered on May 5, 2009, confirmed the sentence for Mrkšić, but imposed a new sentence of 17 years' imprisonment for Šljivančanin. Šljivančanin, however filed an application for review of the appeal judgment and on December 8, 2010, the Appeals Chambers accepted new evidence and dropped the charges against Šljivančanin pertaining to murder as a crime against humanity. He was nevertheless sentenced to 10 years' imprisonment and granted early release in July 2011.[12]

On December 12, 2005, Serbia's Special Court for War Crimes rendered its judgment in the Ovčara case, sentencing eight persons to 20 years imprisonment (maximum penalty), three to 15, one to 12, one to nine and one to five years. Two were released due to a lack of evidence. As shown before, the ICTY indictment contained more severe crimes than the Special Court's indictment, but The Hague tribunal sentenced two indictees to much milder punishments compared to Special Courts' ones, and even released one of the accused. Nevertheless, despite the fact that no command responsibility was proven, nor perpetration of crimes against humanity or JCE, the frame used to describe the ICTY in the media was still anti-Serb or anti-Croat. Nevertheless, the Belgrade trial changed something: "We will not talk about the causes of war, this should be left to the course of history,"

12 ICTY-95-13-1-R1, Appeals Chamber Review Judgment of December 8, 2010, concerning Šljivančanin, onlinen at: http://www.icty.org/x/cases/mrksic/acjug/en/101208_review_judgement.pdf.

underlined judge Krstajić at the end of trial in Belgrade, "what is indisputable is the fact that crimes happened at Ovčara." For a long time, the official version of what had happened in Vukovar had been "liberation," then became "the Vukovar conflict" or the "Vukovar operation," and finally was labelled "the fall of the city." Even though the indictment for Ovčara was really narrow, some background information regarding the role of the army and the Yugoslav state were indisputably proven. One of the defendants made this clear in his statement in court. Predrag Dragović said: "I feel sorry for the victims and for the Serbian history."

Conclusion

The problem of judicial responsibility is tackled on two levels: international and domestic. The events in and around Vukovar were – at more or less the same time – dealt with by the ICTY and a domestic court for war crimes in Serbia. In The Hague, high ranking suspects were accused, whereas in Belgrade, the direct executors were charged. In contrast to the ICTY, the War Crimes Chamber in Belgrade could not prosecute crimes that were not included in the legislation at the time of the commission of the crimes. On the domestic level, the prosecution had no incentive to examine the context of the crime, as these are mostly relevant to cases of crimes against humanity and indictments including JCE or command responsibility. Instead, the Belgrade trial concentrated on each single crime. In those circumstances, the truth-telling capacity of the domestic war crimes trials is extremely limited.

Ostojić argues that it is "the pacification of the domestic political scene and the strengthening of democratic institutions that gradually improved prospects for establishing accountability."[13] This research supports the hypothesis that post-conflict societies accept the consequences of past atrocities but still do not take full responsibility for the crimes committed. Instead, twenty years of instrumental denial and subsequently little or no interest in dealing with the past 'cleared' the terrain for more objective and fair trials. In addition, historical knowledge and continuity with the past is broken in an attempt to create a new political community, cleared of past wrongdoings.

In Serbia, war crime trials persists to be a minor topic in the public sphere. There is a great deal of silencing and auto-censure about the nature of the war itself that balances between "possible responsibility for war" and "responsibility of the other party" and therefore trials are described mostly in a very technical,

---

13 Ostojić, M. (2011). *Between Justice and Stability. The Politics of War Crimes Prosecutions in Post-Milošević Serbia*. London: Ashgate.

seemingly objective manner. On the other hand, Croatian identity is strongly connected to the Homeland War and crimes are understood mostly as legitimate defence. Scholars like Peskin and Subotić explain the hesitant response to transitional justice mechanisms by pointing to the role of internal political struggle between nationalist and liberal political elites.[14] This chapter argues that instead of triggering truth-seeking and truth-telling processes that would lead to reconciliation, the focus on war crimes has multiplied the mutually exclusive historical narratives that are increasingly shaping collective identities. Politics of interpretative denial do not deny the raw facts; rather, "they are given a different meaning from what seems apparent to others."[15]

---

14 Peskin (2008), 61–91 and Subotić (2009), passim.

15 Cohen, S. (2001). *The Elementary Forms of Denial. States of Denial Knowing about Atrocities and Suffering*, Maiden: Blackwell Publishers.

Allan Rutambo Ngari

Foreign Judicial Intervention and the Media – The Case of the ICC and Kenya

While Kenya had experienced violence during previous election periods, the violence then had been sporadic and taken place mainly prior to the election date. The 2007 elections were markedly different. They were marred by violence shortly after the announcement of the presidential election results by the now defunct Elections Commission of Kenya. The violence that broke out in various parts of the country left over 1,300 people dead and over 600,000 internally displaced.

Under the chairmanship of H. E. Kofi Annan of the Panel of Eminent African Personalities, representatives of the two political parties, the Party of National Unity ("PNU") and the Orange Democratic Movement ("ODM"), their leaders (the two Principals) signed the National Accord and Reconciliation Act 2008 that paved the way for a Grand Coalition Government ("GCG") headed by the two Principals, Mr. Mwai Kibaki and Mr. Raila Odinga as the President and Prime Minister of the Republic of Kenya, respectively.

The Kenya National Dialogue and Reconciliation ("KNDR") initiative that was established by the two Principals agreed on a reform agenda that included undertaking constitutional, legal, and institutional reform and addressing accountability and impunity. Three commissions were initially established: (i) the Commission of Inquiry into Post Election Violence ("CIPEV"); (ii) the Truth, Justice and Reconciliation Commission (TJRC); and (iii) the Independent Interim Elections Commission. CIPEV, which was established in May 2008 under The Commissions of Inquiry Act, Cap 102 of the Laws of Kenya, is the most relevant of the three Commissions to consider in this chapter as it was mandated to "investigate the facts surrounding circumstances related to acts of violence that followed the 2007 Presidential Elections" and thereafter make recommendations within three months of its formation.[1] After receiving a 30-day extension[2] of its mandate, CIPEV delivered a report in October 2008 containing recommendations for *inter alia* the establishment of a Special Tribunal for Kenya that met international standards to try persons accused of committing crimes related to the post-election violence in

1 CIPEV created under the Commissions of Inquiry Act, Cap 102 Laws of Kenya on May 22, 2008, by Kenya Gazette Notice No. 4473 and 4474 of May 23, 2008.

2 Extension of Time Kenya Gazette Notice No. 8661 of September 11, 2008.

Kenya.[3] Failing to abide by the recommendations of CIPEV, the two Principals committed to referring the situation to the ICC in terms of Article 13 (a) of the Rome Statute.[4] Kenya signed the Rome Statute on August 11, 1999, and deposited its instrument of ratification on March 15, 2005.[5] As Kenya is a State Party to the Rome Statute, the ICC has jurisdiction over war crimes, crimes against humanity and genocide committed in the territory of Kenya after the entry into force of the Rome Statute in Kenya.[6]

In an historic decision the Pre-Trial Chamber of March 31, 2010 granted authorization to investigate a situation.[7] But it was the announcement of the identity of the six individuals in the Kenya I and Kenya II cases made on December 15, 2010 that had an impact on the social and political landscape in Kenya.[8] As will be discussed

below, an erroneous narrative that certain political and ethnic groups within the country were targeted for the political expediency of others began to emerge.

Another turning point in the ICC intervention in Kenya is the decisions of Pre-Trial Chamber II of January 23, 2012 confirming the criminal charges against six prominent Kenyans for their alleged roles in the planning and/or execution of the

---

3 Report of the Commission of Inquiry into the Post-Election Violence in Kenya, Government of Kenya Printers, October 2008, pp. 453–476.

4 Chapter 5, paragraph 5 of the CIPEV Report reads:"If either an agreement for the establishment of the Special Tribunal is not signed, or the Statute for the Special Tribunal fails to be enacted, or the Special Tribunal fails to commence functioning as contemplated above, or having commenced operating its purposes are subverted, a list containing names of and relevant information on those suspected to bear the greatest responsibility for crimes falling within the jurisdiction of the proposed Special Tribunal shall be forwarded to the Special Prosecutor of the International Criminal Court. The Special Prosecutor shall be requested to analyze the seriousness of the information received with a view to proceeding with an investigation and prosecuting such suspected persons."

5 Kenya: Signature and ratification and implementation status. http://www.icc-cpi.int/Menus/ASP/states+parties/African+States/Kenya.htm.

6 See Articles 11 (2) and 12 (2) of the Rome Statute, *supra* note 1.

7 Decision pursuant to Article 15 of the Rome Statute on the Authorization of an Investigation into the Situation in the Republic of Kenya, ICC-01/09, online at: http://www.icc-cpi.int/iccdocs/doc/doc854287.pdf.

8 Prosecutor's Application Pursuant to Article 58 as to William Samoei Ruto, Henry Kiprono Kosgey and Joshua Arap Sang, December 15, 2010, ICC-01/09, online at: http://www.legal-tools.org/uploads/tx_ltpdb/doc985613_03.pdf and Prosecutor's Application Pursuant to Article 58 as to Francis Kirimi Muthaura, Uhuru Muigai Kenyatta and Mohammed Hussein Ali, December 15, 2010, ICC-01/09, online at: http://www.legal-tools.org/uploads/tx_ltpdb/doc985621_03.pdf.

violence that erupted in various parts of Kenya following the general elections in the country on December 27, 2007, marked one of the key moments in Kenya. The six Kenyans are: Mr. Francis Kirimi Muthaura, former Secretary to the Cabinet and Head of the Civil Service of Kenya, Mr. Uhuru Muigai Kenyatta, then Deputy Prime Minister and now President of Kenya, and Mr. Mohamed Hussein Ali, then Police Commissioner of the Kenya Police Service (suspects in the Kenya I case); and Mr. William Samoei Ruto, then Minister for Agriculture and now Deputy President of Kenya, Henry Kosgei, and Joshua arap Sange, journalist and former head of Kass FM (suspects in Kenya II case).

These confirmation of charges decisions absolved two of the individuals (Mohamed Hussein Ali and Henry Kosgey) from criminal responsibility. The judges of the Pre-Trial Chamber held that they could not find "substantial grounds" to believe that they were responsible for various crimes in the criminal charge sheet. The legal standard of 'substantial grounds' to believe that a suspect is criminally responsible is a higher threshold than the 'reasonable grounds' standard that judges at the ICC consider when charges are brought by the ICC Prosecutor against individuals.[9] This was the end of their encounter with the ICC. The decision of the judges for the remaining four suspects marked the beginning of their ordeal at the hands of the ICC. The four were then no longer suspects but accused persons who should stand trial. There was a shift in Kenya's political landscape. It is a known fact that there are no permanent political alliances or subscribed political ideologies that could be ascribed to any Kenyan politician. Following the confirmation of charges decisions, political alliances of the most unlikely of candidates, including two of the accused, emerged. Media frames began to shift from ethnic group targets to political formation targets.

The filing of the notice to withdraw criminal charges against Francis Kirimi Muthaura came at yet another turning point in Kenya's history. It was less than a month to the first elections following the 2007/2008 post-election violence (further: PEV). By then, the political formations that stood the greatest chance of victory at the March 2013 elections were the Jubilee Alliance made up of,

---

9 The gravity threshold for criminal responsibility is thus: a finding by the judges that 'reasonable grounds' exist to believe that a person could be criminally responsible for crimes within the jurisdiction of the ICC. This finding allows the Prosecutor to then proceed with framing of the charges for the confirmation of charges hearing; a finding by the judges that 'substantial grounds' exist to believe that a suspect is criminally responsible for crimes within the jurisdiction of the court is required to confirm the charges brought by the Prosecutor; a finding by the judges that crimes were committed 'beyond reasonable doubt' is the standard required for a guilty verdict.

among others, Uhuru Kenyatta's National Alliance Party (TNA) and William Ruto's United Republican Party – Kenya (URP) (both are accused persons at the ICC); and the Coalition for Reforms and Democracy (CORD) made up of former Prime Minister Raila Odinga's ODM, former Deputy President Kalonzo Musyoka's Wiper Movement and Moses Wetangula's Forum for the Restoration of Democracy – Kenya (FORD Kenya). The narrative at the time was that the ICC was interfering with the internal politics of the country as Kenyans were being warned not to elect accused persons to lead them. The withdrawal of charges against Uhuru Kenyatta's co-accused just before the elections was used by the Jubilee Alliance as fodder to sway the electorate from any threats that they may have been under from the international community against electing the two accused persons to the highest political positions in the country.

Finally, the decision relating to the non-cooperation of Kenya with the ICC Prosecutor and her subsequent filing of a notice to withdraw the criminal charges against Uhuru Muigai Kenyatta was a final decisive point of the ICC intervention in Kenya. This decision and notice form the basis of the media analysis in this Chapter.

It was widely reported in Kenya that the Prosecutor had no case against the President of Kenya. These reports were countered by the Prosecutor who asserted that the Kenyan government had failed to provide certain key information to allow the Prosecutor to sustain a case that would demonstrate beyond reasonable doubt that Uhuru Kenyatta committed the crimes he was charged with. Prior to this decision and withdrawal of charges, there was a massive campaign launched by the President and his deputy to discredit the ICC politically through the Kenya's influence in the African Union and the United Nations, using so-called shuttle diplomacy missions, while simultaneously using the state organs charged with legal advice and affairs as well as privately hired international criminal defence lawyers to challenge the ICC process.

Background to the Kenya Case II at the ICC

The two cases before the ICC are *The Prosecutor v. Uhuru Muigai Kenyatta*[10] *and The Prosecutor v. William Samoei Ruto and Joshua arap Sang*. While this chapter will address the decision in Kenya Case II, there are references to Kenya Case I, especially because there have been narratives generated by the selected media that relate to both cases and that have an overall application to the ICC intervention in Kenya.

---

10 *The Prosecutor v. Uhuru Muigai Kenyatta* ICC-01/09-02/11.

A brief background to the case is that the accused, Mr. Uhuru Muigai Kenyatta, was accused of the following crimes against humanity: murder, deportation or forcible transfer, rape, persecution, and other inhumane acts. In January 2008, the Mungiki, a sect made up of young men sworn to keep the traditions of the Agikuyu ethnic majority in Kenya, carried out widespread and systematic attacks against non-Kikuyus who were in support of the ODM and living in Naivasha and Nakuru towns in the then Rift Valley Province of Kenya. It was alleged that Mr. Kenyatta and members of the Mungiki created a common plan to carry out killings, displacement of thousands of people, rape, severe physical injuries, mental suffering, and destruction of property. The plan involved the Mungiki carrying out these attacks against the supporters of ODM in order for the PNU, the party that Mr. Kenyatta was a part of, to remain in government. Mr. Kenyatta was instrumental in the common plan in that he offered institutional support as a key member of the PNU and allegedly financed the plan in order to achieve the goal. The charges aganst Mr. Kenyatta and similar charges against his then co-accused Mr. Francis Kirimi Muthaura were confirmed on January 23, 2011, with the judges committing the case to trial. The judges of the Trial Chamber found that there were substantial grounds to believe that Mr. Kenyatta and Mr. Muthaura were responsible for the crimes as alleged in the charge sheet. Two years later, the criminal charges against Mr. Muthaura were withdrawn by the ICC Prosecutor on the grounds that she could no longer sustain the case against him as certain critical witnesses and testimony that they could profer to the judges were no longer available. These witnesses were either killed or voluntarily withdrew their testimony. While Mr. Kenyatta's trial was to commence on February 5, 2014, the Trial Chamber vacated this date upon the ICC Prosecutor's citing of difficulty in obtaining the necessary cooperation from the Kenyan government to obtain evidence in Kenya that would support the prosecution's case beyond a reasonable doubt. The Trial Chamber further vacated the start of Mr. Kenyatta's trial, which was provisionally set to commence on October 5, 2014. On the December 3, 2014, the Trial Chamber rejected the Prosecutor's request for further adjournment and directed the Prosecutor to either withdraw charges against Mr. Kenyatta or indicate readiness to proceed to trial. The matter finally came to an end on December 5, 2014, when the Prosecutor filed a notice to withdraw all the charges against Mr. Kenyatta.

This chapter shall evaluate narratives in the Kenyan media following the decision of Trial Chamber V(b) on December 3, 2014 directing the prosecutor to indicate whether the trial of Mr. Kenyatta would proceed or whether the charges against him would be withdrawn. This decision has by far had the most impact in Kenya and marked the finality of the case against the Kenyan President. While the case began in 2011, when Mr. Kenyatta was not president of the country, he subsequently took office as President in 2013. Certain events that occurred in September 2013 involving a terrorist attack at Westgate Mall in Nairobi shifted a part of Mr. Kenyatta's defence (and that of his deputy who is also on trial at the ICC) from attending to his trial based on his overriding duties to attend to matters of national security. The terrorist attacks in Kenya by the Al-Shabaab militants became a singular focus and rightly or wrongly shifted the debate on the appearance of a head of state at trial while there was need in the country for the head of state to attend to matters of national security.

At the beginning of the decision, the judges in Trial Chamber V(B) commenced by specifying the legal provisions of the Rome Statute system that form the basis of the decision. Notably, the provision in the Rome Statute Article 21 on the applicable law before the ICC was cited with emphasis on sub-article 3, wherein the "application and interpretation of law...must be consistent with internationally recognized Human Rights...".[11] The judges in this instance were making reference to the international Human Rights guarantees of a fair trial afforded to an accused person. This we find enshrined in Article 14(3) of the International Covenant of Civil and Political Rights.[12] This is supported by Article 64 of the Rome Statute on the functions and powers of the Trial Chamber, which the judges cite as the

---

11 Article 21(3) Rome Statute.

12 Article 14(3) of the International Covenant on Civil and Political Rights (1966) provides: In the determination of any criminal charge against him, everyone shall be entitled to the following minimum guarantees, in full equality:

(a) To be informed promptly and in detail in a language which he understands of the nature and cause of the charge against him;
(b) To have adequate time and facilities for the preparation of his defence and to communicate with counsel of his own choosing;
(c) To be tried without undue delay;
(d) To be tried in his presence, and to defend himself in person or through legal assistance of his own choosing; to be informed, if he does not have legal assistance, of this right; and to have legal assistance assigned to him, in any case where the interests of justice so require, and without payment by him in any such case if he does not have sufficient means to pay for it;
(e) To examine, or have examined, the witnesses against him and to obtain the attendance and examination of witnesses on his behalf under the same conditions as witnesses against him;
(f) To have the free assistance of an interpreter if he cannot understand or speak the language used in court;
(g) Not to be compelled to testify against himself or to confess guilt.

basis for their decision. Sub-article two(2) provides that "[T]he Trial Chamber shall ensure that a trial is fair and expeditious and is conducted with full respect for the rights of the accused…"[13]

The Role and Significance of the Media

It is incontrovertible that the media have a significant role in shaping public opinion in all forms of discourse in every country. The media occupy a central and uncontested position in influencing decision making at various levels in society.

Kenya has been home to the regular print media since the early 1900s with the African Standard, today known as The Standard (Kenya) founded in 1902. The Standard (Kenya) has a thirty per cent market share in Kenya. The Daily Nation was started in 1958 and is the most influential daily in Kenya with a circulation of 180,000 copies but a much larger readership as each copy is read by several people. While these are not the only daily newspapers in Kenya, they enjoy a large readership and may inform us of the shifts in media frames relating to the International Criminal Court interventions in Kenya. Other daily newspapers and periodicals include: *The Star, The People, Business Daily, Taifa Leo (Swahili version of The Daily Nation), The East African.*

Print media in Kenya have enjoyed a measure of independence from the state in Kenya. The Daily Nation and The Standard, which maintain the highest readership in the country, trace their origin to colonial times. While they have at times not been under the ownership of the state, they have unfortunately played into the political agenda of the independence and succeeding governments and opposition political parties.

During the era of one-party rule, the Kenya African National Union (KANU) used the media as an important tool to send out messages to the Kenyan public even in the remotest of locales. The state-owned and controlled broadcast media was instrumental in maintaining the status quo of the government of the day and in reigning in any errant or rebellious segments of society. It is for this reason that the organizers of the attempted coup d'etat in 1982 invaded and took over the national broadcaster, the Voice of Kenya radio station to perpetuate their message of takeover (although foiled) of the government of Kenya.[14] With the proliferation of political parties and acceptance of a plurality of political and social opinions in the early 1990s, private media houses began to mushroom, although their

---

13 Article 64 (2) Rome Statute.

14 Branch, D. (2011). *Kenya Between Hope and Despair, 1963–2011.* New Haven, CT: Yale University Press, pp. 154–155.

influence was mainly felt in the urban and peri-urban areas of Kenya. The state maintained de facto control of the mass communication infrastructure through ownership of the only media that broadcasted nationally, the Voice of Kenya, which later was renamed Kenya Broadcasting Corporation, and de jure through the Communications Board established by the Communications Act of Kenya, The Board maintains oversight responsibility today for all media houses.

This analysis of the history and influence of the state and political parties on Kenyan media is vital in understanding the role that the media played in the run-up to the general elections in 2007.

Before the December 3, 2014 decision on cooperation and the December 5, 2014 notice of withdrawal of the charges against Uhuru Muigai Kenyatta, there was concern in Kenya as to the fate of the accused persons Ruto and Sang in Kenya I case as compared to the fate of Kenyatta in the Kenya II case. At the time, while the trials of Ruto and Sang in the Kenya I case had been proceeding for slightly over one year, Kenyatta's trial had not commenced. The ICC Prosecutor had asked to postpone the start of the Kenyatta trial twice, in September 2013 and again in February 2014, each time a few days before the trial was set to commence. The ICC Prosecutor cited that she and her team were facing severe challenges in obtaining evidence from the Kenya government to support the claims that they had made at the confirmation of charges hearings and further claimed that there was severe prosecution witness interference. Crucial witnesses were said to have either recanted their testimony, been intimidated, or died under mysterious circumstances.

After the decision and notification of December 3 and 5, 2014, respectively, there was a shift in the frames as presented by The Star and The Daily Nation. It must be recalled that following the decision and notification, there was erroneous reporting in the Kenyan media about the ICC allegedly acquitting Uhuru Kenyatta. The withdrawal of charges does not equal an acquittal. The Prosecutor explained in her notification the circumstances that led to the withdrawal of charges and that the withdrawal was without prejudice. This means that in the unlikely event that circumstances change in the future to allow the ICC Prosecutor to investigate and obtain the necessary cooperation and evidence from the Kenya government, she may choose to bring further charges against Uhuru Kenyatta.

Unconfirmed reports at the time indicate that there was some disquiet among those allied with the deputy President Ruto because the Kenyan government wasn't directing a similar effort towards ending the Ruto and Sang case as towards preventing the Kenyatta trial from commencing. A closer look at print media in Kenya indicates that this discontent in the ruling political elite was brewing and in some instances, these sentiments began taking root among the two ethnic groups that have produced Kenya's presidents since independence: Uhuru Kenyatta's Kikuyu ethnic group and William Ruto's Kalenjin ethnic group. The Star Newspaper, which has a readership of 15,000–20,000 of the 320,000 daily newspaper readers in Kenya anecdotally referred to the "lesson on forgiveness" from the late Nelson Mandela, former President of South Africa as one that Kenyans need to embrace concerning the PEV.[15] This particular piece was written in the wake of Mandela's death and exhorted the magnanimous character that he was. The writer began by emphasizing that "we'll never see another Mandela in our life time" and that "Mandela took peace and reconciliation to another level and it is one thing warring factions and countries in conflict must embrace."[16] The writer was quick to point out "how badly [the embrace among warring factions is] needed here in Kenya, especially given the recent conflicts and even ongoing ICC cases against the President and his deputy."[17] The emphasis of this article was that Kenyans must accept that the PEV happened and move on seven years after the incident.

A month later, the Star reported on "Movers and Shakers: Why 2014 is the Real Year of The Hague."[18] The piece is apt in its analysis of how Uhuru Kenyatta and William Ruto, the dynamic duo, were the most unlikely of politicians in Kenya to form a political alliance. This is especially the case when one looks at the division of the Kenya cases. Kenya I case involving the deputy President is reflective of the political formation the ODM, while Kenya II case involving President Kenyatta is reflective of the political formation PNU – the two political parties around which the PEV revolves. The division of the cases was also an attempt on the part of then Prosecutor Louis Moreno Ocampo to equally target both sides of the conflict.

In this article in The Star, we are introduced to the concept of "the tyranny of numbers," which worked in favour of the dynamic duo to clinch the presidency of the country in 2013. In a nutshell, the "tyranny of numbers" represents the traditional voting lines that Kenyans have adopted in past elections – voting along ethnic lines. There is the belief that politicians enjoy an almost absolute and blind-like support from members of their ethnic group. This is especially the case of those vying for national positions such as the presidency. The practice has de facto seen candidates from the same ethnic group competing for these national

---

15 'Mandela's Lesson on Forgiveness'. *The Star Newspaper*, December 21, 2013, online at: http://www.the-star.co.ke/news/mandelas-lesson-forgiveness.

16 Ibid, paragraphs 1 and 14.

17 Ibid, paragraph 15.

18 'Movers and Shakers: Why 2014 is the Real Year of The Hague'. *The Star Newspaper*, December 28, 2013, online at: http://www.the-star.co.ke/news/movers-shakers-why-2014-real-year-hague.

positions either concede to one candidate and support this candidate or battle it out in different political parties. It follows therefore that the electorate will also vote en masse for a candidate who comes from their ethinc group. A combination of Uhuru Kenyatta's Kikuyu ethnic group and William Ruto's Kalenjin ethnic group had the potential of surpassing the constitutional requirement in Kenya that in an election, the president and his running mate must muster a total of at least 25 per cent of the votes in each of the regions in Kenya.

While this article in The Star bemoans the quality of the prosecution investigation and evidence against Uhuru Kenyatta, the crux of the article, which is indicative of a frame that the media was developing, is that:

> "What a collapse of the Kenyatta case at the ICC and a continuation of Ruto and Sang's would entail judicially, politically and in terms of continuing cohesion inside the Jubilee administration remains an imponderable at this point in time but the auguries are grim indeed."[19]

The article also noted the unrest that deputy President Ruto's side of the Jubillee Alliance felt concerning presidential appointments that sidelined Ruto's URP members in favour of Kenyatta's TNA members.

This frame began to drive the campaign against the ICC intervention as a whole. While President Kenyatta used the state apparatus to fight his case from a legal and political perspective, the onslaught at the ICC and the international community of Deputy President Ruto's ongoing case was being prepared. The narrative that there would be a recurrence to violence should the Kenya I case proceed, which according to the accused persons was weak and consisted of trumped up charges, was emerging. Perhaps a softer angle to this frame is that the dropping of charges in the Kenyatta case and a continuation of the Ruto and Sang case would hamper peace and reconciliation efforts in Kenya.

This latter point is clearly articulated in The Star's article "Kenya No Longer at Ease" in which it is stated that "(…) if Uhuru's case is dropped and Ruto's chugs on, there will be a high political cost. There is much to fear should anything destabilize the grounds for the alliance."[20] The Star invoked a dilemma that is well-known from the context of the ICTY's role in the Balkans and back then was labelled

---

19 'Movers and Shakers'. *The Star Newspaper* (2013).

20 'Kenya No Longer At Ease'. *The Star Newspaper*, January 11, 2014, online at: http://www.the-star.co.ke/news/kenya-no-longer-ease.

the "justice versus peace – dilemma":[21] "there cannot be justice [per ICC] in the absence of peace and political tranquility."[22]

There was a bag of mixed reactions from The Star following the events at the ICC in December 2014. The editorial pieces were emboldened to castigate the Prosecution for taking as long as it did to finally 'admit' that it did not have a case against President Kenyatta. In an article on January 17, 2015, entitled "The ICC Cases That Never Were," the author levels scathing attacks against the Prosecutor. accusing her of not being at the top of her game.[23]

The allegations against the ICC Prosecutor were that the "ICC is using 'cooked-up' Bensouda evidence to provoke chaos."[24] This came in the wake of a redacted brief by the ICC Prosecutor that was filed after the notification to withdraw the charges against Uhuru Kenyatta and upon the request of judges following an application by the legal representative of victims in the Kenyatta case.

The Star claimed that the continuation of the Ruto case had the potential to hamper peace in Kenya. In its article "ICC Pursuit of Ruto Hurts Peace Efforts" of January 26, 2015, the author crystallized the campaign to scuttle the Ruto case in the months to come. In this piece, the frame that the ICC cases are about ethnic conflicts and targeting of entire ethnic communities as opposed to individual criminal responsibility is captured:

> "(…) when the ICC dropped charges against the technocrats and left only the politicians (and Sang), it unknowingly changed the dynamics of what each person represented. The

---

21 With regard to the ICTY, this dilemma is usually invoked the other way round – in order to describe the ICTY's battle not to be sidelined by diplomacy during the negotiations leading to the Dayton peace conference and to avoid the inclusion of amnesty in the Dayton Peace Agreement. Most authors argue that there was a danger of "justice" being dominated by "peace", taking the side of the ICTY and the fight against impunity. In Kenya, the argument seems to be different: here authors invoking the "peace versus justice – dilemma" usually support impunity in the name of peace, claiming that "doing justice" (or rather: letting the ICC do it) equals "disturbing the peace process."

22 'ICC Should Drop Kenyan Cases for Lack of Evidence'. *The Star Newspaper*, September 29, 2014, online at: http://www.the-star.co.ke/news/article-192113/icc-should-drop-kenyan-cases-lack-evidence.

23 'The ICC Cases That Never Were'. *The Star Newspaper*, January 17, 2015, online at: http://www.the-star.co.ke/news/icc-cases-never-were.

24 'ICC Is Using 'Cooked-Up' Bensouda Evidence to Provoke Chaos'. *The Star Newspaper*, January 21, 2015, online at: http://www.the-star.co.ke/news/icc-using-cooked-bensouda-evidence-provoke-chaos-juja-mp-munyua-0.

'organisations' were no longer the PNU and ODM political structures, but the Kikuyu and Kalenjin ethnic communities."[25]

The greatest concern with this narrative is that it is one that was framed at the beginning of the ICC intervention in Kenya when information on how the ICC works was not as widespread as it is today. Then, it was misunderstood that entire ethnic communities were the targets of the court. Bearing in mind the voting patterns in Kenya which are mostly along ethnic lines, the very fact that the ICC was intervening in matters related to the election process in Kenya in 2007 and its aftermath was misconstrued and in some cases abused by political opportunists to inform the public that the ICC was targeting certain ethnic communities.

But Kenya is far from being the only country, where ethnic categorization is imputed to a tribunal in order to discredit its actions against individual political figures. The same could be observed in the former Yugoslavia and with respect to every ethnic community whose members were accused of crimes. Such individual accusations were immediately turned into collective ones allegedly directed against the whole nation, be it Serbian, Croatian, Bosniak or Kosovo-Albanian. This took place to the extent that it inclined Chief Prosecutor Carla Del Ponte to state explicitly at the beginning of the trial against Slobodan Milošević, that he was accused as an individual and that neither Serbs nor Serbia were indicted. This did not prevent Milošević and his followers from claiming otherwise.

In the above-mentioned article from The Star,[26] the opening of the preliminary investigation by the ICC Prosecutor into the situation in Palestine and the reaction from the United States of America were invoked, claiming that the US castigated any move to attack Israel and rejected the ICC intervention in the name of peaceful negotiations between the Israelis and Palestinians. The author juxtaposed the situation in the Middle East with the conflict between ethnic communities in Kenya. One would assume that he was referring to the Kikuyu and Kalenjin ethnic communities although it is doubtful whether these two communities were at war at the time to merit the kind of negotiations that the author claimed were advocated by the Americans in the Middle East. In addition, the author perilously and rather carelessly stated that "(…) the case against 'the Kikuyu' has collapsed while the one against 'the Kalenjin' continues… Continuing to pursue a unilateral

25 'ICC Pursuit of Ruto Hurts Peace Efforts'. *The Star Newspaper*, January 26, 2015, online at: http://www.the-star.co.ke/news/icc-pursuit-ruto-hurts-peace-efforts.

26 *The Star*, January 26, 2015.

action against Ruto after dropping the case against Uhuru is counterproductive to the cause of peace in Kenya."[27]

Interestingly, and a dead give-away of the next move by the Kenyan government in its agenda to end the Ruto and Sang case, the author advocated that political instability in Kenya would affect the entire African continent and that the African Union (AU) should then use this as its platform to send its message concerning the remaining Kenyan case at the ICC. Here the continuing case of Ruto and Sang did not only hamper peace efforts, which incidentally were never defined, but become a continent-wide concern. At the concluded 24th AU Summit in Addis Ababa, Ethiopia, the Kenyan Foreign Affairs Cabinet Secretary Amina Mohamed repeated the same opinion about a threat to peace caused by the continuation of the ICC case against Ruto.[28]

Both The Star and the The Daily Nation were shifting the focus of the perceived effects of the Ruto and Sang case in Kenyan society onto the continent. The Star report that "the Collapse of Uhuru ICC case is a victory for Africa" on January 30, 2015 was a reminder that the AU remained discontented by the ICC intervention not only in Kenya but on the entire continent.[29] Outgoing AU chairperson and President of Mauritania, Mohamed Ould Abdel Aziz praised Kenya for its efforts in the past six years in attempting to amend the Rome Statute to reflect 'African realities'. He said, "and because these efforts have not succeeded, Kenya has indicated that it will associate itself with the new initiative to establish an African international justice mechanism that handles African challenges from an African perspective."[30] The AU heads of state and government met in Malabo, Equatorial Guinea, in June 2014 and adopted an amended protocol to the African Charter on Human and Peoples Rights establishing an African Court of Justice and Human and Peoples Rights. The Protocol has yet to receive the 14 ratifications required for it to come into force, but the AU Summit in Addis Ababa, Ethiopia,

27 'ICC Pursuit of Ruto Hurts Peace Efforts'. *The Star Newspaper*, par. 7 and 9.

28 'ICC Case against Ruto is a threat to Peace'. *The Star Newspaper*, January 28, 2015, online at: http://www.the-star.co.ke/news/icc-case-against-ruto-threat-peace-foreign-affairs-cs-amina-mohamed-has-told-au-summit.

29 'Collapse of the Uhuru ICC Case is a Victory for Africa – AU'. *The Star Newspaper*, January 30, 2015, online at: http://www.the-star.co.ke/news/collapse-uhuru-icc-case-victory-africa-au.

30 'Collapse of the Uhuru ICC Case is a Win for Africa – AU'. *The Star Newspaper*, para. 6.

indicated that there is an tendency among at least 11 Member States of the AU to ratify the treaty.[31]

The Daily Nation took a different perspective in its editorial pieces prior to the December 3, 2014, decision on non-cooperation and December 5 notification of withdrawal of the Kenyatta charges. In an article on October 23, 2013, "AU cites war on terror as plea for deferral," we begin to see the dividends of the international political campaign by the Kenyan government.[32] Kenya had been involved in sending its top-ranking officials to the capitals of African and European states seeking support for their cause to end the trials of the President and Deputy President.[33] The AU needed little convincing by the government of Kenya to support calls for the ICC to drop the Kenyan cases. It is no secret that the AU and the ICC have enjoyed a frosty relationship since the indictment by the ICC of President Omar al-Bashir of Sudan and later other heads of state such as Muammar Gaddafi and Uhuru Kenyatta.

The AU requested a deferral by the UNSC of the Kenya cases at the ICC because the UNSC has been given special powers under Article 16 of the Rome Statute of the ICC to make a request to the Court for a deferral of a situation or the cessation of a case for a period of 12 months.[34] The request for deferral by the AU also came in the wake of the deadly terrorist attacks that Kenya had been experiencing, especially the attack in September 2013 at the Westgate Mall in Nairobi. In the Daily Nation article, Kenya has the status of "a frontline state in the fight against terrorism." In addition, the head of state and his deputy would be required as a matter of national concern, security, and interest to be fully present

---

31 'Uhuru to Tell AU Summit of ICC Non-Cooperation in PEV Cases'. *The Star Newspaper,* January 30, 2015, online at: http://www.the-star.co.ke/news/uhuru-tell-au-summit-iccs-non-cooperation-pev-cases.

32 'AU Cites War on Terror as Plea for Deferral'. *The Daily Nation,* October 23, 2013, online at: http://www.nation.co.ke/news/AU-cites-war-on-terror-in-plea-for-Kenya-deferral/-/1056/2043676/-/htouw0z/-/index.html.

33 Since the ICC Prosecutor applied to the judges to authorize the investigation of the situation in Kenya, the government of Kenya had filed admissibility challenges at the ICC in accordance with Article 19 of the Rome Statute, arguing that Kenya was able and willing to deal with the crimes that emanated from the PEV in 2007/2008.

34 Article 16 Rome Statute provides: No investigation or prosecution may be commenced or proceeded with under this Statute for a period of 12 months after the Security Council, in a resolution adopted under Chapter VII of the Charter of the United Nations, has requested the Court to that effect; that request may be renewed by the Council under the same conditions.

physically and otherwise to attend to their duties without the looming ICC trials hanging over them.

The AU also declared that the proceedings at the ICC "may pose a threat to the ongoing efforts in the promotion of peace, national healing, and reconciliation as well as the rule of law and stability in Kenya and the region."[35] Here we see a similar claim as above where peace, national healing and reconciliation are invoked as greater values than justice. The only distinction here is that the AU is seeking a deferral, which lasts only 12 months but is renewable and that the interests being considered are regional and national relating to counterterrorism.

In a Daily Nation article on the same day, October 23, 2013, entitled "African states step up push to put off Kenya cases," it is reported that the AU Chairperson Nkosazana Dlamini-Zuma and the AU Council of Ministers Chairman Tedros Adhanom would be leading a delegation of seven top AU representatives from the continent to meet with the UNSC seeking a deferral of the trials of President Kenyatta and Deputy President Ruto "(…) until they are out of office."[36] It can get quite confusing to keep track of the various efforts and avenues that the Kenyan government employs to scuttle the cases at the ICC. In this article, we are introduced to a "Contact Group of the Executive Council" that has been given a mandate by the AU Special Summit to discuss the ICC and Africa, to engage in diplomatic visits to the permanent members of the UNSC in a bid to gain favour and seek a deferral of the cases. The AU Special Summit outcome was a scathing attack on the ICC and repeated calls by some AU Member States to withdraw en masse from the treaty that created the ICC.

There was some relief for William Ruto when the Trial Chamber decided that considering the responsibilities he had as deputy President of Kenya and the need for him to address counterterrorism strategies in Kenya, he could be excused from personally attending his trial. The arguments forwarded by the Ruto defence was that the lawyers were in constant touch with their client and that there was no need for him to be seated in court while he could be attending to pressing state business in Kenya. In support of this, Mr. Ruto had waived his right to be present during his trial, a right that is guaranteed in the Rome Statute as part of the fair trial rights of an accused.

---

35 Supra note 25, paragraph 2.

36 'African states step up push to put off Kenya cases'. *The Daily Nation*, October 23, 2013, online at: http://www.nation.co.ke/news/politics/African-states-step-up-push-to-put-off-Kenya-cases-/-/1064/2044868/-/9aqkm0/-/index.html.

The Daily Nation in its October 25, 2013 article "UN now last hope for deferral" detailed the blow dealt to Ruto by the Appeals Chamber that reversed the Trial Chamber's decision excusing him from trial. The Appeals Chamber found that

> "The Trial Chamber provided Mr Ruto with what amounts to a blanket excusal before the trial had even commenced, effectively making his absence the general rule and his presence an exception."[37]

Whereas the article explained the finding of the judges of appeal that Ruto must attend his trial and not be excused unless the merits of a particular circumstance make it necessary for his excusal, the underlying message was that the investigations and conduct of the Prosecutor in the Ruto and Sang case were terrible and that there was an abuse of the court process in the entire case making it necessary for the UNSC to request the ICC to defer the matter. This decision is said to have "anger[ed] Members of Parliament," and especially that the Appeals Chamber was "insensitive to President Kenyatta and his deputy William Ruto."[38]

The Daily Nation heralded December 5, 2014 as an important date in the foreign policy of Kenya. In an article entitled "How ICC and Security Influenced Foreign Policy", it claimed "Kenya's resolutely Africa-centred and assertive foreign policy ideologically were undergirded by a strong nationalist and pan-African orientation."[39] This is particularly important to note ahead of the 24th AU Summit in Addis Ababa, Ethiopia, where Kenya took to the stage and became the "first country to sign the protocol [to the African Court of Justice and Human and Peoples Rights] because we have always said we believe in Africans solving African problems. We also believe that if we have our own court, we'll have our own way of solving our problems," Ms. Amina Mohamed, Kenyan cabinet secretary for foreign affairs said.[40]

---

37 'UN Now Last Hope for Deferral'. *The Daily Nation,* October 25, 2013, online at: http://mobile.nation.co.ke/News/ICC-Appeals-Chamber-William-Ruto/-/1950946/2047544/-/format/xhtml/-/uef5di/-/index.html.

38 'ICC Decision Angers Mps'. *The Daily Nation*, October 25, 2013, online at: http://mobile.nation.co.ke/news/ICC-decision-angers-MPs/-/1950946/2047552/-/format/xhtml/-/j7cgbb/-/index.html.

39 'How ICC and Security Influenced Foreign Policy'. *The Daily Nation*, December 31, 2014, online at: http://www.nation.co.ke/oped/Opinion/ICC-Cases-Kenya-Uhuru-Kenyatta-William-Ruto/-/440808/2574922/-/12ajdx7/-/index.html.

40 'Kenya Launches Anti-ICC Push'. *The Daily Nation*, January 29, 2015, online at: http://www.nation.co.ke/news/politics/Kenya-launches-anti-ICC-push/-/1064/2606868/-/n61fbs/-/index.html.

Patrycja Grzebyk

International Tribunals' Selective Justice Towards African States

Introduction

States emerging from armed conflicts or crises face numerous political and economic obstacles as well as obstacles of a legal nature. Paramount among the legal issues essential for rebuilding a democratic, united, peaceful society respecting the rule of law is the question of accountability of those who committed international crimes like genocide, crimes against humanity, and war crimes. In some instances, states seek aid from the international community. This is especially the case when their own judicial system is unable to address those crimes (e.g., in case of Rwanda of 1994). In other instances, the international community feels obliged to intervene in order to punish the perpetrators of atrocities, even against the will of the state's authorities (e.g., in the case of Darfur – Sudan). The question thus arises whether international criminal tribunals, i.e. the International Criminal Court (ICC) and the International Criminal Tribunal for Rwanda (ICTR), are effective in supporting African states emerging from conflicts in dealing with international crimes and in fostering the development of the kind of environment necessary to establish the rule of law in those states. This question is crucial especially in light of the recently tense relations between the African states gathered in the African Union and the International Criminal Court.

The International Criminal Court was established in 1998 (its statute entered into force in 2002), and it has issued its first judgments, not counting numerous decisions. All cases dealt with by the Court concern African states. The other international tribunal concerned with crimes committed in Africa, i.e. the International Criminal Tribunal for Rwanda (ICTR), was established in 1994. The work of the ICTR is now coming to an end, but it is worthwhile investigating its role in Rwanda and other African states because its practice inspired the creators of the ICC.[1]

1 Schabas, W. A. (2007). *An Introduction to the International Criminal Court.* Third Edition. Cambridge: Cambridge University Press, p. 13. It can be noticed that there was a practice of regular meetings during which representatives of tribunals *ad hoc* and the ICC exchanged their experience.

The first part of this paper discusses the practice of the ICTR, its relations (mainly) with Rwanda, and the accusations that the ICTR was in fact an instrument of victor's justice. The second part concerns the ICC's practice with regard to African states, with a special focus on the allegations of bias against African states. The third part addresses the question of whether international criminal tribunals are a useful tool to support those states emerging from conflicts in the exercise and administration of justice taking into account their selectiveness.

The International Criminal Tribunal for Rwanda – one-sided justice?

The ICTR was established with the initial support of Rwanda, which at the time sought help in dealing with the mass crimes. Rwanda's judicial system was nonfunctional and largely non-existent in the aftermath of the genocide of 1994.[2] The international community was blamed for the lack of reaction towards the genocide[3], and decided to establish an international tribunal, a sister institution to the International Criminal Tribunal for the former Yugoslavia, the *ad hoc* tribunal affiliated with the Security Council (UNSC).[4] The Security Council seemed convinced that the ICTR would support the Rwandan judiciary in establishing the rule of law and would *contribute to the process of national reconciliation and to the restoration and maintenance of peace.*[5] In the final vote in the Security Council,

2 On establishment of the ICTR see e.g., Boed, R. (2008). 'The International Criminal Tribunal for Rwanda.' In: Bassiouni, M. Ch. (1999) (ed). *International Criminal Law, Volume III International Enforcement*, Third Edition, Leiden: Martinus Nijhoff Publishers, pp. 103–110; Johnson, L. D. (1999). *The International Criminal Tribunal for Rwanda.* In: Bassiouni, M. Ch. (1999) (ed). *International Criminal Law, Volume III Enforcement*, Second Edition, Ardsley: Transnational Publishers, pp. 549–560; Shraga, D., Zacklin, R. (1996). 'The International Criminal Tribunal for Rwanda.' *European Journal of International Law* 7, no. 4, pp. 501–518.

3 Concerning the role of Western countries in non-prevention, acquiescence, or even provoking genocide, see Melvern, L. (2000). *A People Betrayed. The Role of the West in Rwanda's Genocide.* London: Zed Books (See especially chapter 14 "The Secret Meetings of the Security Council"); Grünfeld, F., Huijboom, A. (2007). *The Failure to Prevent Genocide in Rwanda: The Role of Bystanders.* Leiden and Boston: Martinus Nijhoff Publishers, pp. 95–100.

4 S/RES/955 of November 8, 1994.

5 See preamble of the UNSC res. 955. It is worth to emphasize that the budget of two tribunals *ad hoc* amounted to about one seventh of regular UN budget. Wipman, D. (2006). 'The Costs of International Justice'. *American Journal of International Law*, 100, no. 4, p. 861. This can be interpreted as a proof that UNSC considered work of

Rwanda (as a non-permanent member) voted against the resolution creating the ICTR in order to protest against the limitation of the tribunal's temporal jurisdiction, the exclusion of the death penalty, the lack of a separate appeals chamber, the inclusion of violations of common Article 3 of the Geneva Conventions of 1949 and II Additional Protocol of 1997 in the tribunal's material jurisdiction, the possible inclusion of judges from states the Rwandan government regarded as supporters of the *génocidaires* (popular label in Rwanda for participants in the 1994 genocide), and, last but not least, against locating the ICTR in Arusha, Tanzania.[6] Rwanda would have preferred the temporary jurisdiction to cover the period from October 1, 1990 till July 17, 1994 in order to include the alleged preparation of the genocide and to bolster academic and political claims about a conspiracy leading up to the genocide.[7] It also would have liked the ICTR to apply capital punishment, which, at the time of establishing the ICTR, was in use (and legal) in Rwanda and many other African countries. The Rwandan government also rejected the idea of merging the appeals chambers of the ICTY (which had already been established) and the ICTR and would have preferred more trial chambers (which actually were established later on the basis of additional UNSC resolutions) to judge the anticipated vast number of perpetrators. Rwanda also wanted the ICTR to concentrate on genocide rather than on war crimes for political, legal, and practical reasons: in order to strengthen the political and moral benefits the Rwandan government could extract out of the genocide label for its foreign policy and its international standing; in order to prevent the ICTR from investigating mass crimes other than those committed by the Habyarimana entourage, the transitional government installed in April 1994 and the military junta around Théoneste Bagosora; and

---

both tribunals as essential to build a stable and peaceful relations in e.g. Rwanda and in neighbor states.

6 An analysis of the Rwandan approach to the establishment of the ICTR, see Akhavan, P. (1996). 'The International Criminal Tribunal for Rwanda: The Politics and Pragmatics of Punishment.' *American Journal of International Law*, 90, no. 3, pp. 505–508.

7 The 'conspiracy hypothesis' was supported by DesForges, A. (1999) in her book *Leave none to tell the story. Genocide in Rwanda*. New York: Human Rights Watch, and by Melvern (2000). In *The prosecutor v. Bagosora at al.*, the trial chamber found (and the appeals chamber did not refute it), that all evidence induced during the trial and bolstering the conspiracy thesis could also point to an unintended escalation of a political power struggle that went out of control. The judgment caused outrage among Rwandan politicians and victims organizations. See: Bachmann, K., Sparrow-Botero, T., Lambertz, P. (2013). *When Justice Meets Politics. Independence and Autonomy of Ad Hoc International Criminal Tribunals*. Frankfurt/Main: Peter Lang International, pp. 174–180.

in order to prevent the ICTR prosecution from wasting its energy and resources on minor war crimes, such as pillaging, looting, and wanton destruction of civilian buildings, which had taken place on an enormous scale and were unlikely to be ever investigated fully. The objection against some Western judges was the result of the lasting and ferocious dispute between Rwanda and France about the French intervention "Opération Turquoise", and France's alleged role in sheltering *génocidaires* from the new (RPF-led) Rwandan government. Despite its doubts concerning specific provisions regarding the functioning of the ICTR, Rwanda decided to cooperate with the tribunal.

Rwandan authorities stress that there was only one genocide, committed mainly by the Hutu against the Tutsi.[8] Any suggestions that Tutsi are also guilty of mass crimes (not even considering the stigma of genocide) against Hutu, especially in July 1994, can be punished as crimes of genocide ideology according to Rwandan law.[9] In light of these facts, the Rwandan government's hostility towards any attempts to investigate the crimes committed by the Tutsi against the Hutu is understandable.

When in 1999 Carla del Ponte, then a newly appointed prosecutor of both *ad hoc* tribunals, concluded special investigations concerning the crimes committed

8 This interpretation is reflected in the current (post-2006) discourse in Rwanda about "the genocide against the Tutsi", which does not explicitely mention the ethnic affiliation of the perpetrators, but now (in contrast to the situation during the 1990s) uses an ethnic label for the victims. Before the shift to "the genocide against the Tutsi" the official label was "the Rwandan genocide". See also S/Res/2150 of April 16, 2015, which states: "Recalling that the Appeals Chamber of the ICTR issued, on 16 June 2006, a judicial notice (ICTR-98-44-AR73(C)) concluding that it was a 'fact of common knowledge' that 'between 6 April and 17 July 1994, there was a genocide in Rwanda against the Tutsi ethnic group', further recalling that more than a million people were killed during the genocide, including Hutu and others who opposed it, and noting with concern any form of denial of that genocide."

9 Human Rights Watch emphasizes that even mentioning in a debate crimes committed by the Rwandan Patriotic Front can be met with charges of genocide denial, genocide ideology or divisionism (inciting ethnic divisions). Human Rights Watch, *Rwanda: Justice after Genocide – 20 Years On*, March 28, 2014, online at: http://www.hrw.org/news/2014/03/28/rwanda-justice-after-genocide-20-years#_ftn25 See also Jansen Y.-O. (2014). 'Denying Genocide or Denying Free Speech? A Case Study of the Application of Rwanda's Genocide Denial Laws'. *Northwestern Journal of International Human Rights*, 12, no. 2, online at: http://scholarlycommons.law.northwestern.edu/cgi/viewcontent.cgi?article=1172&context=njihr.

by Tutsi,[10] cooperation with Rwanda's authorities gradually deteriorated. It must be emphasized that the special investigations team was composed only of three persons looking into three well-known incidents: the massacre in Butare, the executions in Kabgayi, and the killings in Giti.[11] Given that the crimes against Hutu were confirmed by several reports,[12] it would be sensible to assume that there was no reason to attempt to ignore them. However, there was no willingness on the part of Rwanda to help in these investigations, and Rwanda's cooperation would have been essential to capture the perpetrators.[13] The members of the special investigations team were forced to flee Rwanda and Kigali started to obstruct the proceeding before the ICTR in other cases as well. Under the pretext of bad treatment of Rwandan witnesses before the ICTR, Kigali forbade them to leave Rwanda to participate in the proceedings before the ICTR.[14] When pressure on del Ponte – not only from Rwanda, but also from the US[15] – failed to result in the

---

10 It is sometimes emphasized that good cooperation between Kigali and Louise Arbour was an expression of appreciation of her unwillingness in investigating crimes committed by Tutsi, see Essoungou, A.-M. (2006). *Justice à Arusha. Un tribunal international politiquement encadré face au genocide rwandais. Paris:* L'Harmattan, p. 174. However, Thierry Cruvellier notes that it was in fact Arbour who started special investigations in February 1999, see Cruvellier T. (2006), *Le Tribunal des vaincus. Un Nuremberg pour le Rwanda?* Paris: Calmann-Lévy, p. 240.

11 Cruvellier (2006), 241.

12 See e.g., Gersony, R., *Summary of UNHCR presentation before Commission of Experts, Prospects for Early Repatriation of Rwandan Refugees Currently in Burundi, Tanzania and Zaire*, October 10, 1994, online at http://www.friendsofthecongo.org/pdf/gersony_report.pdf (accessed August 20, 2015); Organization of African Unity (The International Panel of Eminent Personalities to Investigate the 1994 Genocide in Rwanda and the Surrounding Events), *Rwanda: The Preventable Genocide*, July 2000, Chapter 22, online at: http://www.refworld.org/docid/4d1da8752.html. See also e.g., Human Rights Watch (written by Alison Des Forges) (1999). *Leave None to Tell the Story*, online at http://www.hrw.org/reports/1999/03/01/leave-none-tell-story. Amnesty International, Rwanda: Reports of killings and abductions by the Rwandese Patriotic Army, April-August 1994, October 19, 1994, online at: http://www.amnesty.org/en/library/info/AFR47/016/1994).

13 Essoungou (2006), 187.

14 Cruvellier (2006), 194, 241–242. See also an extensive analysis of the crisis in cooperation between Rwanda and ICTR in: Peskin, V. (2008), *International Justice in Rwanda and the Balkans. Virtual Trials and the Struggle for State Cooperation*, Cambridge: Cambridge University Press, pp. 186–206.

15 Del Ponte, C. (2009). *Madame Prosecutor: Confrontations with Humanity's Worst Criminals and the Culture of Impunity. A Memoir.* New York: Other Press, pp. 223–241 (Chapter: *Confronting Kigali 2002 and 2003*).

closure of special investigations, Kigali successfully engaged in efforts to remove del Ponte from the ICTR. The Security Council decided to split the prosecution into two separate offices, the Office of the Prosecutor at the ICTY and the Office of the Prosecutor for the ICTR.[16] Carla del Ponte was appointed Prosecutor at the ICTY, despite the fact that she preferred to work for the ICTR.[17] Her successor, Hassan Bubacar Jallow, did not bring any cases concerning crimes committed by the Rwandan Patriotic Front (RPF – created by the Tutsi) before the ICTR.[18] One case (concerning an execution of 15 civilians, the so-called Kabgayi case) investigated by the office of the ICTR's prosecutor was transferred to a Rwandan court that in 2008 acquitted the two senior officers on trial and sentenced the two lower-ranking ones to eight years' imprisonment. This sentence was appealed and further reduced to five years' imprisonment (2009), thus matching other Rwandan courts' lenient judgments concerning the crimes of the RPF.[19]

The fact that no RPF representative has never been judged before the ICTR for crimes committed against Hutu resulted in allegations that this tribunal represents victor's justice,[20] is dependent on Kigali,[21] and follows the Nuremberg paradigm.[22] However, it must be stressed that not only the lack of cooperation with Rwandan state authorities prevented the ICTR from judging those responsible for crimes on behalf of the RPF (such as in the above mentioned cases); the major problem was the question of limitation of the tribunal's jurisdiction. The ICTR's temporal jurisdiction[23] excluded the investigation of crimes committed during the offensive

16 S/RES/1503 of August 28, 2003.

17 Del Ponte, C. (2009), 238; Reydams L. (2005). 'The ICTR Ten Years On. Back to the Nuremberg Paradigm?' *Journal of International Criminal Justice*, 3, p. 978.

18 See Human Rights Watch. 'Letter to ICTR Chief Prosecutor Hassan Jallow in Response to His Letter on the Prosecution of RPF Crimes.' August 14, 2009, online at: http://www.hrw.org/news/2009/08/14/letter-ictr-chief-prosecutor-hassan-jallow-response-his-letter-prosecution-rpf-crime.

19 Human Rights Watch (2014).

20 It is interesting that Rwanda supported the establishment of an international tribunal in order to avoid accusations of execution of 'vengeful justice', see Akhavan (1996), 504.

21 Lugan L. (2007). *Rwanda. Contre-enquête sur le genocide.* Toulouse: Editions Privat, p. 271.

22 Reydams (2005), 977–979.

23 See Article 1 of the ICTR statute (Competence of the International Tribunal for Rwanda): The International Tribunal for Rwanda shall have the power to prosecute persons responsible for serious violations of international humanitarian law committed in the territory of Rwanda and Rwandan citizens responsible for such violations committed in the territory of neighbouring States between January 1, 1994 and December 31,

of the RPF in 1990, considered by some the beginning of the atrocities which led to the 1994 genocide.[24] Moreover, personal jurisdiction covered the crimes committed in the territory of neighbouring states, but only by citizens of Rwanda, so it largely excluded the Tutsi diaspora e.g. in Uganda and therefor also commanders of the Rwandan Patriotic Army and RPF responsible for crimes in 1990 and in 1994 in Rwanda.[25] In consequence, it is impossible to investigate e.g. the engagement of Ugandans, including Yoveri Museveni (president of Uganda), in supporting military actions of Tutsi in the region[26] who were not necessarily citizens of Rwanda. In result, the majority of Tutsi potential suspects of mass crimes are exempted from the jurisdiction of the ICTR.[27]

Leaving aside the discussion of whether there was a genocide against the Hutu in 1994, it can be stated without any doubt that the crimes committed against the Hutu at that time can be qualified as war crimes or even as crimes against humanity (taking into account their scale and regularity). Thus, these crimes were covered by the jurisdiction of the ICTR.[28] Certainly every international prosecutor having limited resources must be selective in taking on particular cases and pick the most serious ones (where the number of victims or the position of the perpetrator might be a decisive indicator). It may be invoked in the tribunal's defence that the

---

1994, in accordance with the provisions of the present Statute. Compare also with the Article 7 of the Statute.

24 Othman M. C. (2005). *Accountability for International Humanitarian Law Violations: The Case of Rwanda and East Timor.* Berlin: Springer, pp. 10–11.

25 Othman (2005), 10–11.

26 Mahmood Mamdani claims that interference the Rwandan government in the neighboring states is a result of a feeling of responsibility for the safety of all the Tutsi. See Mamdani M. (2001), *When Victims become killers. Colonialism, Nativism, and the Genocide in Rwanda.* Princeton: Princeton University Press, pp. 234–250.

27 Ngirabatware A. (2006). *Rwanda. Le faîte du mensonge et de l'injustice.* Lille: Editions Sources du Nil, pp. 463–470. It must be stressed that Ngirabatware served as Minister of Planning in the Rwandan government in 1994 and on December 20, 2012. Trial Chamber II of the International Criminal Tribunal for Rwanda convicted him of direct and public incitement to commit genocide based on his speech at a roadblock in Nyamyumba Commune on February 22, 1994. It also found him guilty of instigating and aiding and abetting genocide based on his role in distributing weapons and his statements at two roadblocks in Nyamyumba Commune on April 7, 1994. The Trial Chamber also convicted Ngirabatware, under the extended form of joint criminal enterprise, of rape as a crime against humanity (reversed by the Appeals Chamber). It sentenced him to 35 years of imprisonment. The sentence was reduced to 30 years' imprisonment by the Mechanism for International Criminal Tribunals Appeals Chamber on December 18, 2014.

28 See Articles 3 and 4 of the ICTR statute.

number of Tutsi victims (estimates range from 500,000 to 1,200,000) is far greater than that of Hutu victims (estimations differ from 20,000 to 45,000), taking into account only the period covered by the tribunal's jurisdiction.[29] However, the fact that only the crimes committed by one of the parties to the conflict are judged by the ICTR certainly undermines the faith in the impartiality of the tribunal.

The International Criminal Court and the African Union

The International Criminal Court functions according to different principles than the *ad hoc* tribunals. Those principles were not imposed by the Security Council (as in case of the ICTY and the ICTR statutes) but were negotiated by the participants of the Rome conference in 1998. However, it must be stressed that the final shape of the Rome Statute was largely influenced by permanent members of the UNSC, especially by the US, which had one of the biggest delegation during the conference. Still, the majority of the permanent members of the UNSC, i.e. the US, Russia and China, is not party to the Rome Statute. It is remarkable in this context that e.g. Americans form a large part of the ICC staff.

The ICC complements national jurisdiction (Preamble and Article 1 of the Rome Statute), which means that a case is admissible only if the state which has jurisdiction over the crime is unwilling or unable to carry out the investigation or prosecution (Article 17). In the case of the ICTR, the tribunal always had priority over national courts. The ICC can exercise its jurisdiction only if crimes were committed on the territory of a state which is party to the Rome Statute (or the crime was committed on board of its vessels or aircraft), or the person accused of crimes is a national of a state that is party to the Rome Statute (Article 12 (2)). In addition, a state which is not party to the Rome Statute can accept the jurisdiction of the Court (Article 12 (3)) and – what is more important as it contradicts the principle that treaties bind only parties – and the Security Council can also refer a situation to the Court even if it concerns crimes committed on the territory of a non-party to the Rome Statute and crimes are committed by nationals of that kind of state (Article 13).

Currently (in August 2015) the ICC is exclusively investigating situations concerning territories of African states: the Democratic Republic of the Congo (DRC), Uganda, the Central African Republic (CAR I – crimes committed since 2002 and CAR II – crimes committed since 2012), Sudan – Darfur, Kenya, Libya, Côte d'Ivoire, and Mali. At first glance it could be assumed that the ICC is biased against

29 Concerning estimates on number of Tutsi and Hutu victims, see e.g. DesForges (1999).

Africa (some prefer to describe the ICC as an instrument of apartheid,[30] a witch hunt, or even race-hunting.[31]) The fact is that even if there were/are preliminary examinations analysing alleged crimes committed in other parts of the world (e.g. in Afghanistan, Colombia, Georgia, Honduras, Iraq, Ukraine), none of them have resulted in the opening of an investigation so far. However, the picture is not so black and white. It must be emphasized that among the nine situations currently under investigation, over half of them were referred by those African states which are parties to the Rome Statute (DRC,[32] Uganda,[33] CAR,[34] Mali[35]) or those who issued a declaration under article 12 (3) of the Rome Statute in which they accepted the jurisdiction of the Court (Cote d'Ivoire[36]). The prosecutor opened the investigation *proprio motu* only in one situation (Kenya[37]), and two situations (Sudan[38] and Libya[39]) were referred by the UN Security Council. Yet those investigations raise the greatest controversies on the part of African states. In consequence, the argument that the ICC is biased as it deals only with African states is misconceived: investigations were opened in most cases at the request of African states themselves. It is also remarkable that gestures such as the choice of a venue of the review conference of the Rome Statute (Kampala, Uganda, 2010) or the election of Africans for the position of prosecutor of the ICC (Fatou Bensouda from Gambia),

---

30 Gallois, P. M., Vergès, J. (2002). *L'apartheid judiciaire: le Tribunal pénal international, arme de guerre*, Lousanne: L'Age d'Homme, p. 11.

31 'African Union accuses ICC of 'hunting' Africans'. *BBC News Africa*, May 27, 2013, online at: http://www.bbc.com/news/world-africa-22681894; Kersten M. (2012). 'Is the ICC Racist?' *Justice in Conflict*, online at: http://justiceinconflict.org/2012/02/22/is-the-icc-racist/.

32 ICC-OTP-20040419-50, April 19, 2004. Decision to open investigation was made on June 23, 2004.

33 ICC-20040129-44, 29 January 2004. Decision to open investigation was made on July 29, 2004.

34 ICC-OTP-20050107-86, 7 January 2005. Decision to open investigation was made on May 22, 2007.

35 ICC-01/12, (Referral Letter) 13 July 2012. Decision to open investigation was made on January 16, 2013.

36 ICC-02/11, (Declaration under article 12–3 of the Rome Statute) April 18, 2003 and (Letter reconfirming the acceptance of the ICC jurisdiction) December 14, 2010. Authorization to open an investigation, October 3, 2011.

37 ICC-01/09-19. Decision to open investigation was made on May 22, 2007.

38 ICC-02/05, (Referral) March 31, 2005. Decision to open investigation was made on June 6, 2005.

39 ICC-01/11, (Referral) February 26, 2011. Decision to open investigation was made on March 3, 2011.

president of the Assembly of States Parties (Sidiki Kaba from Senegal), or judges (as of 2015, 5 out of the 18 judges will be African) have no effect on the negative perception of the Court by the majority of African states.

However, the Court could be criticized for its selection of the situations being investigated. These include the accusation of the instrumentalization of the Court by the Security Council (in particular by the five permanent members). This could be observed in the case of Libya, when the Security Council referred the situation to the ICC as a follow-up to the authorization of the use of force by Western powers against Gaddafi's regime.[40] Also, in the case of referral of situation in Darfur to the ICC, it could be clearly observed that the Security Council obviously wanted to use (or rather abuse) the Court. Referral of the situation in Darfur was supposed to prove the UNSC's concern about the situation in the region. The problem was that the referral was not followed by a decision on the adoption of any measures which would force Sudan to cooperate with the Court. The UNSC's support was essential in bringing criminals to justice as Sudan is not a party to the Rome Statute and the Court does not have any instruments to force Sudan to cooperate. Not surprisingly, after years of struggling with the al-Bashir regime, the Office of the Prosecutor in December 2014 notified the Security Council that it was stopping its investigations in Sudan due to the "council's lack of foresight on what should happen in Darfur."[41]

In addition, the fact that the Security Council (of which three permanent members are not parties to the Rome Statute) refers situations to the ICC and then in violation of the Rome Statute does not bear the costs of the proceedings[42] certainly must raise objections. It is hard to accept that the US, Russia, and China in practice decide about referring situations in African states to the ICC, yet the costs of these decisions are shared by African states (those which are state parties) but not by these superpowers.

However, it seems that the main problem lies somewhere else. States (as well as the Security Council) refer situations and not particular cases, and thus cannot limit the jurisdiction of the Court to particular persons.[43] In consequence, states' authorities which turn to the ICC in order to prosecute crimes of the opposition

40 Kersten, M. (2011). 'Used and Abandoned: Libya, the UN Security Council and the ICC.' *Justice in Conflict,* online at: http://justiceinconflict.org/2011/08/31/used-and-abandoned-libya-the-un-security-council-and-the-icc/.

41 http://www.un.org/apps/news/story.asp?NewsID=49591#.Vdb1rvnl8o8 (accessed August 20, 2015).

42 Article 115 of the Rome Statute, 2187 U.N.T.S. 90.

43 Articles 13 and 14 of the Rome Statute.

can be surprised by charges against themselves. In addition, as the ICC's jurisdiction covers crimes committed on the territory of states that are parties to the Rome Statute, citizens of those states which do not support the Court and are not parties to its statute still might be surprised by arrest warrants against them.[44] These aspects of the functioning of the Court reinforce the fear of the Court. Certainly, states' authorities are concerned as they can observe that the ICC's prosecutor targets the highest officials, including heads of states. As a result, they take actions to guarantee impunity for themselves.

The African states organized in the African Union protested against the proceedings against incumbent heads of states and senior officials. They even considered adopting a resolution calling on those African states which are parties to the Rome Statute to withdraw from it. Eventually, the AU did not adopt the resolution, which came under heavy criticism (e.g., by Desmond Tutu, who considered the attempt equivalent to looking for a license to kill).[45] However, it adopted a resolution in which states agreed that they would fully respect the immunity of heads of states and not surrender them to the ICC.[46] African states also supported Kenya in its efforts to convince the Security Council to use its powers enshrined in Article 16 of the Rome Statute to defer prosecution against Uhuru Kenyatta, the president of Kenya. To the disappointment of African states, the draft resolution did not achieve a sufficient number of votes among the members of the UNSC.[47]

The African Union is not a monolith, but it is remarkable that the 34 African states that are currently (August 2015) parties to the Rome Statute[48] are not willing

---

44 Article 12 (2) of the Rome Statute.

45 Tutu, D. (2013). 'In Africa, Seeking a License to Kill', *The New York Times,* October 10, 2013.

46 'African Union urges ICC to defer Uhuru Kenyatta case.' *BBC News Africa,* October 12, 2013, online at: http://www.bbc.com/news/world-africa-24506006.

47 Only seven Security Council members (Azerbaijan, China, Morocco, Pakistan, Russia, Rwanda, Togo) voted in favour of the draft resolution S/2013/660 of November 15, 2013. All other members (Argentina, Australia, France, Guatemala, Luxembourg, Republic of Korea, UK, US) abstained from voting thus the draft did not receive the required majority of votes.

48 African states parties to the Rome Statute are (in order of ratification/acceptance of the Statute): Senegal (February 2, 1999), Ghana (December 20, 1999), Mali (August 16, 2000), Lesotho (September 6, 2000), Botswana (September 8, 2000), Sierra Leone (September 15, 2000), Gabon (September 20, 2000), South Africa (November 27, 2000), Nigeria (September 27, 2001), Central African Republic (October 3, 2001), Benin (January 22, 2002), Mauritius (March 5, 2002), DRC (April 11, 2002), Niger (April 11, 2002), Uganda (June 14, 2002), Namibia (June 25, 2002), Gambia (June 28, 2002), United Republic of Tanzania

to defend the idea (grounded in the article 27 of the Rome Statute) that no perpetrators, including those in the highest positions, should be exempt from criminal responsibility. Apparently Kenya and Sudan (with the support of other dictators) are influential enough to convince others that only impunity of high representatives of states might guarantee peaceful relations and – what is perhaps more important – economic growth.[49] The consecutive decisions of the African Union (such as granting immunity from prosecution to all African heads of state and "senior officials" at the African Court of Justice and Human Rights[50] or coordination of actions within the Assembly of States Parties to the Rome Statute[51]) only confirmed the will to protect state authorities from the jurisdiction of any international court.

(August 20, 2002), Malawi (September 19, 2002), Djibouti (November 5, 2002), Zambia (November 13, 2002), Guinea (July 14, 2003), Burkina Faso (April 16, 2004), Congo (May 3, 2004), Burundi (September 21, 2004), Liberia (September 22, 2004), Kenya (March 15, 2005), Comoros (November 1, 2006), Chad (January 1, 2007), Madagascar (March 14, 2008), Seychelles (August 10, 2010), Tunisia (June 24, 2011), Cape Verde (October 10, 2011), Côte d'Ivoire (February 15, 2013).

49 E.g., states parties to the Rome Statute such as Uganda, Burundi and DRC are dependent on Kenyan infrastructure for their import and export.

50 Decision taken on African Union Summit in Equatorial Guinea on June 26 and 27, 2014 according to which the following amendment to the Article 46A bis of the Protocol on the Statute of the African Court of Justice and Human Rights should be introduced: "No charges shall be commenced or continued before the Court against any serving African Union Head of State or Government, or anybody acting or entitled to act in such capacity, or other senior state officials based on their functions, during their tenure of office." See comments: Mark, M. (2014). 'African leaders vote themselves immunity from new human rights court.' *The Guardian,* July 3, 2014, online at http://www.theguardian.com/global-development/2014/jul/03/african-leaders-vote-immunity-human-rights-court (accessed December 22, 2014); and Amnesty International, *Open letter to Heads of State and Government of the African Union: Article 46A bis of the Draft Protocol on Amendments to the Protocol on the Statute of the African Court of Justice and Human Rights,* June 20, 2014, online at: http://www.amnesty.org/en/library/info/AFR01/012/2014/en.

51 It concerns decisions according to which: "(i) African states parties should comply with African Union Decisions on the ICC and continue to speak with one voice to ensure that the African proposals for amendments to Articles 16 and 27 of the Rome Statute of the ICC are considered by the ASP working Group on amendments as well as by the forthcoming sessions of the Assembly of States Parties (ASP) to the Rome Statute; (ii) There is an imperative need for all member states to ensure that they adhere to and articulate commonly agreed positions in line with their obligations under the Constitutive Act of the African Union; (iii) The group of African states parties in New York and the African members of the bureau of ASP should follow-up on the implementation of

Commentators on the current tensions between the African Union and the ICC should, however, be very cautious in condemning African states and their non-cooperation in arresting the incumbent head of state of Sudan.[52] Even if the International Court of Justice confirmed that incumbent heads of states (and other high officials) do not enjoy immunity before international courts, it did state that other states must respect their immunity.[53] The statements of African states just confirm the opinion – not rejected in international jurisprudence and literature – that the obligation of states to respect the immunity of high-ranking state officials has priority over the obligation to prosecute international crimes.[54] It should also be noted that in the case of officials of states that are not parties to the Rome Statute, the statute expressly states that: "The Court may not proceed with a request for surrender or assistance which would require the requested State to act inconsistently with its obligations under international law with respect to the State or diplomatic immunity of a person (…) (article 98 (1))." This means that Article 98 of the Rome Statute permits denying the surrender of a person to the ICC if this would mean a violation of obligations towards a third state. Therefore, the ICC was not authorized to issue to states parties a request for surrender of the President of Sudan and by doing this the Court acted *ultra vires.*[55] Moreover, there has been no precedence in international tribunals' practice in judging incumbent heads of states (there were just a few instances in which former heads of states were prosecuted, e.g. Karl Dönitz, Slobodan Milošević, Charles Taylor). The prosecution of Jean Kambanda as a former head of the Rwandan government can to be added to the list of high-ranking officials judged for international crimes. African authorities might also rightly emphasize that no

---

various Decisions of the Assembly on ICC, in collaboration with the Commission and ensure that the African proposals and concerns are properly considered/addressed by the ASP and report to the Assembly through the Commission on actions taken regularly". See 22nd Ordinary Session of the African Union Assembly concludes: A summary of key decisions, January 31, 2014, online at: http://summits.au.int/en/22ndsummit/events/22nd-ordinary-session-african-union-assembly-concludes-summary-key-decisions-0 (accessed August 20, 2015).

52 See Tladi, D. (2013). 'The ICC Decisions on Chad and Malawi. On Cooperation, Immunities, and Article 98', *Journal of International Criminal Justice*, 11, p. 199.

53 International Court of Justice, *Arrest Warrant of 11 April 2000 (Democratic Republic of the Congo v. Belgium),* Judgment, February 14, 2002, para. 59.

54 See Jia B. B. (2012). 'The Immunity of State Officials for International Crimes Revisited'. *Journal of International Criminal Justice,* 10, pp. 1303–1325.

55 Gaeta, P. (2009). 'Does President Al Bashir Enjoy Immunity from Arrest?' *Journal of International Criminal Justice*, 7, p. 329.

incumbent or former senior official from a Western country, despite accusations of commission of core international crimes, has ever had to face charges before any international tribunal.

International Tribunals' Selectiveness and Its Impact on Post-Conflict Situations

Whenever a state must deal with past abuses, as a UN Secretary-General's report rightly stated, the international community must address "a lack of political will for reform, a lack of institutional independence within the justice sector, a lack of domestic technical capacity, a lack of material and financial resources, a lack of public confidence in Government, a lack of official respect for Human Rights and, more generally, a lack of peace and security."[56] The choice presenting itself to the international community is not between, on the one hand, accepting complete or partial impunity in the form of granting amnesty (e.g., in the cases of Mozambique in 1992 or Algeria in 2005[57]) and, on the other hand, criminal prosecution of every perpetrator. Firstly, the prosecution of crimes does not have to be the only way of addressing past abuses and achieving national reconciliation.[58] Secondly, in the case of criminal proceedings before international tribunals, the choice is rather between impunity and (always) selective justice. All international tribunals are forced to be selective because of a lack of financial and human resources and political constraints.[59] In addition, international tribunals are inherently heavily dependent on the cooperation of states, because perpetrators, victims, witnesses, and all evidence are on the territory of sovereign states. Good cooperation is necessary at every stage of the proceedings, starting from the decision on opening an investigation as the problem of concurrent jurisdictions may arise, and then at all stages of collecting evidence during investigation (as the state must relinquish its prerogative to conduct an investigation in its own its territory), the

56 Report of the Secretary-General, 'The rule of law and transitional justice in conflict and post-conflict societies', August 23, 2004, S/2004/616.

57 Hazan, P. (2006). 'Measuring the impact of punishment and forgiveness: a framework for evaluating transitional justice'. *International Review of the Red Cross*, 88, no. 861, p. 23.

58 Nouwen, S. M. H., Werner, W. G. (2014). 'Monopolising Global Justice. International Criminal Law as Challenge to Human Diversity'. *Journal of International Criminal Justice*, 12, pp. 157–176.

59 See more in Schabas, W. (2009–2010). 'Victor's Justice: Selecting "Situations" at the International Criminal Court'. *The John Marshall Law Review*, 43, p. 542.

surrender of the accused, the delivery of evidence during trial such as the transfer of documents, delivery of warrants, bringing witnesses, and finally enforcement of sentences. At each of these stages a conflict between the international tribunal and the state can occur, especially if we remember that criminal jurisdiction is considered one of the basic attributes of sovereignty.[60] In result, international tribunals are able to act only to the extent to which states are willing to cooperate. In light thereof, it is understandable why some of the ICTR's prosecutors preferred to not deal with special investigations on crimes committed by the RPF, as this would stop any cooperation with Rwanda. Apparently, the choice they had was either to judge some of those guilty of core crimes (including genocide), or to judge none of them. It must further be underscored that nobody claims that those crimes which had been investigated were not worth investigating.[61]

The problem is whether the selective prosecution of crimes can help in building the rule of law in states in post-conflict situations by impressing the idea that perpetrators of crimes will always be punished and by furthering a process of national catharsis in order to channel emotions related to past abuses.[62] Embracing the suffering and victims of one group while ignoring the casualties and hardship endured by another group will hardly contribute to inter-group reconciliation. During the discussion on the adoption of Resolution 955 in the Security Council on November 8, 1994, the Rwandan ambassador declared: "The Tribunal will help national reconciliation and the construction of a new society based on social justice and respect for the fundamental rights of the human person, all of which will be possible only if those responsible for the Rwandese tragedy are brought to justice." It is deplorable that Rwandan authorities could not see that judging crimes committed by the RPF is a condition of reconciliation and lies in the interest of the whole Rwandan nation. Omissions of the ICTR can be in theory corrected by the ICC, who can prosecute members of the RPF who committed crimes against Hutu e.g. on the territory of the DRC (a state party to the Rome Statute). This

60 Kwiecień R. (2004). *Suwerenność państwa. Rekonstrukcja i znaczenie idei w prawie międzynarodowym*, Zakamycze: Kantor Wydawniczy Zakamycze, pp. 54, 148.

61 As Abdul Tejan-Cole wrote: "And while it is true that the ICC can be lambasted for inconsistent case selection, there is not a single case before the Court that one could dismiss as being frivolous or vexatious. They might all be African but they are also all legitimate. It is farcical that we can equate the trial of 25 accused with the trial of an entire continent." See Global Policy Forum, *Is Africa on trial?*, online at: https://www.globalpolicy.org/international-justice/the-international-criminal-court/general-documents-analysis-and-articles-on-the-icc/51455-is-afriica-on-trial.html.

62 Hazan (2006), 25.

holds true at least to some extent, as the Court's jurisdiction is for example limited to a specific time period (in the case of the DRC it is after July 1, 2002, the date of entry into force of the Rome Statute). Yet the case of Bosco Ntaganda (Tutsi) at the ICC[63] can at least prove that there are no groups which are immune from the Court's jurisdiction.[64]

Opening proceedings against incumbent senior officials might be seen as sending a signal that no criminal will escape justice, no matter what kind of position he or she has held. However, the deterrent effect of the penalization of international crimes cannot be proven (or disproven). Thus statements made by former prosecutor of the ICC Luis Moreno Ocampo and others that the "ICC changed the game" by issuing Kenyatta's indictment and ensured that the violence of the 2007 election was not repeated in the 2013 election[65] must be treated as a pure speculation. Current problems with the execution of the arrest warrant issued against Omar al-Bashir[66] or conducting proceedings against Uhuru Kenyatta (president of Kenya)[67] show that the ICC achieved nothing while it lost the support of African states. In addition, it must be taken into account that the persons in the highest positions, when facing criminal proceeding, do not differ in their behaviour from any other criminals. They will use all possible means to avoid responsibility and it must be remembered that they have a great number of government agencies at their disposal to achieve the aim of complete impunity.

---

63 He is accused of war crimes and crimes against humanity.

64 It should be stressed that in 2012 Paul Kagame was warned by the US that he could face prosecution for arming groups that carried out atrocities in DRC. See McGreal Ch. (2012). 'Rwanda's Paul Kagame warned he may be charged with aiding war crimes.' *The Guardian*, July 25, 2012, online at: http://www.theguardian.com/world/2012/jul/25/rwanda-paul-kagame-war-crimes. In case of Ntaganda, he decided to surrender himself in the Embassy of the US in Rwanda. Both states smoothly surrendered him to the ICC.

65 'ICC charges against Uhuru Kenyatta defended by Ocampo'. *BBC*, December 16, 2014, online at: http://www.bbc.com/news/world-africa-30498266 (accessed August 20, 2015).

66 The first warrant of arrest was issued on March 4, 2009. The second warrant of arrest was issued on July 12, 2010. Al-Bashir is accused of crimes against humanity, war crimes, and genocide.

67 The trial was postponed several times at the request of the prosecutor due to lack of evidence (e.g., loss of witnesses) and finally when on December 3, 2014, the Judges of Trial Chamber declined to further adjourn the trial of Uhuru Muigai Kenyatta, the Prosecutor decided to withdraw the charges against him. It should be stressed that charges against Kenyatta were confirmed in 2011, before he held the position of the President of Kenya in 2013. It can be presumed that the proceedings before the ICC only helped him gain power.

The selectiveness of international criminal tribunals can also be used by governments in order to oppress the opposition. The fact that the majority of the accused comes from a specific ethnic group or organization can be an argument that is used to discredit all members of the group. In consequence, the aim to attribute responsibility for crimes to individuals in order to avoid placing blame on a whole nation, ethnicity or other, and thus avoid tensions[68] is contradicted.

Conclusions

The ICC and the ICTR are doomed to be selective and thus they cannot adequately address all abuses suffered by the society of each particular state. The problem is that the choice of cases is based not only on the gravity of the crime or the position of the perpetrators as the Rome Statute requires,[69] but rather that it depends on the possibility of cooperation with the states. If a state is not willing to address all crimes, the international tribunals are even less able to do it if they cannot count on the support of the international community in general, and the Security Council in particular. It is remarkable that the UNSC is willing to refer situations to the ICC or to establish, as it has in previous years, international or internationalized tribunals, but then is not interested in lending effective support to those courts. Because of these constraints, even the ICC cannot avoid the stigma of victor's justice, as it can judge only those defeated.[70] In order to avoid this stigma, the ICC is apparently willing to engage in proceedings against incumbent high officials. However, in the case of *proprio motu* investigations, the prosecutor should sufficiently justify the choice of the situation examined, i.e. explain why a particular situation merits more attention than others. In the case of Kenya, the absence of convincing explanation led to significant controversy.

Selectiveness is also a key feature of (not only) African governments' approach to justice. They support judging criminals as long as these criminals are representatives

---

68 Harroff-Travel M. (2003). 'Do wars ever end? The work of the International Committee of the Red Cross when the guns full silent'. *International Review of the Red Cross*, no. 851, p. 484; Sassòli M., Bouvier A. A. (2003). *Un droit dans la guerre?* Genève: CICR, p. 304.

69 See Article 1 of the Rome Statute which stresses that the Court shall exercise its jurisdiction "for the most serious crimes of international concern". See also Article 17 (1) (d) which states that the case is inadmissible where "the case is not of sufficient gravity to justify further action by the Court". See also Article 8 (1) of the Rome Statute which states: "the Court shall have jurisdiction in respect of war crimes in particular when committed as part of a plan or policy or as part of a large-scale commission of such crimes". Compare also with the Article 53 (1) (b) of the Rome Statute.

70 Schabas (2009–2010), 541.

of their opponents. They support international institutions as long as they are useful in combating their opposition.[71] Rwanda is a case in point: it initiated the work on the establishment of the ICTR and then obstructed cooperation with it as the ICTR's prosecutor could start proceedings against senior officers of the RPF. What is perhaps more striking, Rwanda did not become a party to the Rome Statute of the ICC, thus revealing its real stance towards the fight against impunity.

71 Kersten, M. (2014). 'What Gives? African Union Head of State Immunity.' *Justice in Conflict,* online at: http://justiceinconflict.org/2014/07/07/what-gives-african-union-head-of-state-immunity/#more-5440.

Part III: The International Community and the Prevention of Mass Atrocities

Isabelle Tallec

The Role of International Criminal Justice in French Foreign Policy

On July 17, 1998 the Rome Statute establishing the International Criminal Court (ICC) was adopted by 120 states. For the first time in the history of mankind, states decided to accept the jurisdiction of a permanent international criminal court for the prosecution of the most serious crimes – war crimes, crimes against humanity, genocide, and the crime of aggression – committed in their territories or by their nationals.[1] As a preamble to the Rome Statute, which defines and regulates the powers of the Court, the States Parties declared that crimes, which "threaten the peace, security and well-being of the world [...] must not go unpunished" and assigned the Court with the ambitious goal of "putting an end to impunity for the perpetrators" to "thus contribute to the prevention of such crimes."

Only four years after the founding treaty was signed and successfully ratified and after the Prosecutor had received a substantial number of communications, the Court quickly became confrontedwith a number of legal and political challenges during its early investigations. Its early years were thus marked by a rather mixed record, with discreet investigations, low international visibility, and a controversial indictment policy, in which the majority of the accused, such as Thomas Lubanga, were described as "small fish". The court's exclusive focus on the African continent (with regard to arrest warrants and investigations) and its mixed reception by the local people presented additional problems. Its activities also gave rise to suspicion about the ICC's role in internal political conflicts – most referrals from African states to the ICC came from governments, which wanted to use the ICC as a means to check their internal opposition. Their move toward the ICC was often a means to weaken political opponents, neutralize rebel areas or serve as leverage in peace negotiations rather than fight impunity and protect Human Rights. In many cases, those governments' Human Rights record was hardly any better than that of their adversaries under investigation by the ICC prosecutor. Lastly, another

1 The Rome Statute entered into force on July 1, 2002.

big problem quickly emerged: some states' lack of cooperation with regard to ICC arrest warrants.[2]

The Court has since gained an international stature that it certainly did not have in its infancy. The UN Security Council referrals in the cases of Darfur and Libya, the arrest of Jean-Pierre Bemba and especially that of Laurent Gbagbo have given it greater visibility on the international stage. However, some of the criticism that marked the first investigations of the Court remains, and questions that have arisen concerning its effectiveness and relevance.

Criticism of the ICC is usually levelled either at the court's internal functioning (its policies and politics, the methods of investigation, the length of its procedures) or at its role in the international environment (its relations with states, international organizations, the Security Council). The latter perspective relates to the tension between the autonomy of the institution and state sovereignty. Indeed, unlike the *ad hoc* tribunals created by Security Council resolutions, the Court is primarily an international organization, the product of a treaty between states and of a delicate balance between state sovereignty and prerogatives assigned to a supranational court. Part of the difficulties encountered by the Court are linked to the compromises that had to be made to allow its birth: between the protection of individual rights and state rights, and between state responsibilities and state sovereignty, whose protection was a key issue in the negotiations leading to the creation of the Court. States therefore remain an important player in the Court's activities. To fulfil the objectives assigned to it, the Court has broad authority that is strictly regulated and highly dependent on the signatory states, notably in terms of budgetary and operational management. It has no coercive forces at its disposal and is entirely dependent on the willingness of states to allow ICC investigations on their territory and to execute ICC arrest warrants.

The ICC as an Autonomous Actor on the International Scene?

Does the ICC encounter the aforementioned difficulties because it is not a fully fledged actor in international relations? In response to these questions, the academic community tried to apply several theoretical approaches: from the classical realist versus neo-liberal institutionalist debate, to the use of more innovative approaches such as constructivism. Even if all these theories are useful for understanding the existence and functioning of the ICC as well as the state position

2 See Tallec, I. (2010). 'L'arrestation des criminels: 'le talon d'Achille de la Cour pénale internationale'. *Jeune République*, Institut d'Etudes Politiques de Paris, no. 4, online at: http://issuu.com/jeunerepublique/docs/jr4.

and the role of motivations and interests, the answers they provide are incomplete. Some lock up the reflection in a normative and/or utilitarian debate that seeks to measure the usefulness of the institution, its advantage, its ability to fulfil its tasks. As Caroline Fehl writes, "most contributions discuss – often from a very normative perspective – how much an international court can generally contribute to bringing perpetrators to justice and deterring future atrocities, and how effective the ICC will be in performing these tasks given its specific institutional design".[3]

Yet the ICC is not an international organization like any other. It is also an international jurisdiction, with a distinct innovative institutional design combining supranational and intergovernmental features, and results from the profound changes that have affected the international scene since the end of the Cold War. We thus suggest using another perspective that focuses on the proper autonomy of the ICC in the light of its interactions with the other actors in the international arena, based on the concepts and methods drawn not only from the political sociology of International Relations, but also from the theoretical approaches that are often used in order to assess the ICC's actorness.

As another way of understanding international relations, which emerged in the 1990s alongside traditional schools or theories of international relations, the political sociology of international relations is an alternative approach that is more of a method than a paradigm. It is based on the empirical analysis of actors and processes that make up the international order, and opens international relations to sociology and political science, whose methods and questions are transposed at the international level.[4] The discipline focuses on the actors of international relations, their social and institutional trajectories, their practices and their integration in a relatively institutionalized and binding international environment. It also uses a relational approach that pays attention to interdependencies as well as interactions[5] between those actors and thinks of international relations in terms

---

3 Fehl, C. (2004). 'Explaining the International Criminal Court: A "Pratice Test" for Rationalist and Constructivist Approaches.' *European Journal of International Relations*, 10, no. 3, p. 358.

4 See 'Les relations internationales en France: regard sur une discipline', interview with Smouts, M.-C. (2002). *Revue internationale et stratégique*, 3, no. 47, pp. 83–89.

5 Relations of "interaction" are such that changing the behaviour of an actor entails changing the whole relation. Relations of "interdependence" are those where the actors make choices that individually are marginal, but which cumulatively are likely to change the overall relation. Source: Devin, G. (2002). *Sociologie des relations internationales*, Paris: La Découverte, p. 5.

of practices rather than norms, values or interests and rational choices, in terms of processes rather than outcomes.

This emphasis on the actors of international relations and the results produced by the social interactions between them as well as the changes that have affected the post-Westphalian world from the end of the Cold War and the effects of globalization, were also the starting point for theories of actorness, as they were notably applied to the analysis of the role and place of the European Union on the international scene, and defined as the "ability to function actively and deliberately in relation to other actors in the international system".[6]

Traditional international relations approaches often tend to confuse actorness with statehood and sovereignty. Yet globalisation and new modes of global governance emerging in the aftermath of the Cold War have allowed for an expansion of actorness beyond the traditional state-centric model. Conceptions of sovereignty are changing, as are conceptions of actorness.

Based, among others, on the work of Joseph Jupille and James Caporaso,[7] these approaches put forward interesting definitions of actorness that complement the approach proposed by the political sociology of international relations and propose alternative measurements, such as autonomy, which reflect the institutional distinctiveness and independence of an actor from other actors – meaning that a supranational or international institution can operate relatively independently from individual Member States in making its own decisions.

---

6 See Groenleer, M. L. P., Van Schalk, L. G. (2007). 'United We Stand? The European Union's International Actorness in the Cases of the International Criminal Court and the Kyoto Protocol'. *Journal of Common Market Studies*, 45, no. 5, pp. 969–998; Altunisik, M. B. (2008). 'EU Foreign Policy and the Israeli Palestinian Conflict: How much of an Actor?' *European Security*, 17, no. 1, pp. 105–121; Toje, A. (2008). 'The European Union as a Small Power, or Conceptualizing Europe's Strategic Actorness'. *European Integration*, 30, no. 2, pp. 199–215; Wunderlich, U. (2008). 'The EU – A Post-Westphalian Actor in a Neo-Westphalian World?' Paper for presentation at the UACES Annual/ Research Conference, University of Edinburgh, September 1–3, 2008; Kissack, R. (2008). 'EU Actorness in the International Labour Organization: Comparing Declaratory and Voting Cohesion'. *Global Society*, 22, no. 4, pp. 469–489; Greiçevivci, L. (2011). 'EU Actorness in International Affairs: The Case of EULEX Mission in Kosovo.' *Perspectives on European Politics and Society*, 12, no. 3, pp. 283–303.

7 Jupille, J.; Caporaso, J. A. (1998). 'States, Agency and Rules: The European Union in Global Environmental Politics'. In: Rhodes, C. (1998) (ed). *The European Union in the World Community.* London: Lynne Rienner, pp. 213–229.

Actorness is also frequently associated with another dimension, namely that of "international presence", which seems particularly relevant in the context of the ICC. International presence is defined not only as the capacity to actively influence the external environment, but also to shape the perceptions and expectations of other actors. This presence is, however, variable and multi-dimensional, which means that it can play an active role in some areas of international interactions and a less active one in others. It is intimately linked, in many cases, to 'recognition', the way actorness is perceived by other international actors, and the capacity to act is a function of its recognition by others.

Finally, these theories are also interested in actorness as "a complex set of interacting processes", meaning as the result of social interaction between the studied institutions and their Member States, amending those states' policies through processes such as learning, socialization, and the development of informal practices and routines.

Based on these various sociology-based approaches, our purpose is thus to focus not on the ability of the ICC to meet its stated objectives, but on its will to be an autonomous actor and fulfil entirely new functions in the international arena. In measuring the autonomy of the Court by focusing solely on its powers of decision and its operational expertise, we run the risk of making a comparison with a state's capacity for action, which would necessarily place the Court at a disadvantage. Rather than that, it serves to see if, in areas where it has autonomous powers – that is to say using its power of initiative and all means at its disposal to act independently from states –, it is able to radically change the traditional diplomatic practices by opening up new domains for international action.

The analysis will focus on the impact of the institutional presence of the Court and its procedures concerning state foreign policy, with France as a case study; an impact that will be analysed with the aim of proposing elements contributing to validating two sets of assumptions: international criminal justice as a new instrument of foreign policy and diplomatic practice, and as a resource of influence for French diplomacy.

France was chosen for this study according to several criteria. It was a driving power in the negotiations of the Rome Statute; it is a member state of the European Union which supports the ICC on the basis of several framework decisions urging member states to assist the court and promote its mission. France is also one of the two permanent UN Security Council members to also be state parties to the Rome Statute. This chapter is mainly based on interviews with senior French officials and members of the Court as well as on France's official statements in national and international fora.

From Functional Support to Active Promotion: International Criminal Justice as a New Instrument and Evolving Diplomatic Practice

In an article on the relations between France and the international tribunals, Jean-Marc Sorel identifies three principal stances successively adopted by France towards these institutions: boldness, reluctance, and submission.[8] First, France worked to promote these jurisdictions as a natural extension of a Human Rights-related rhetoric conform with its self-image; then a certain cautiousness or, in some cases, a form of retraction appeared at the time when the ICC statute was being negotiated; this was followed by a reluctance consistent with fears of a middle power and a more classical approach to foreign policy; and finally, a return to reality set in, which entailed a search for a balance between constraints and the desire to promote, which induced what Sorel calls a "compromise or median posture."

Early on, France claimed authorship for the international courts, *ad hoc* tribunals, and the International Criminal Court in particular, to be a "jewel of French combat for international criminal justice for individuals", which put France "at the forefront of the moralization of international relations."[9] It emphasized its particular role in the development of the Rome Statute and its influence on its procedural aspects. During the negotiations at the Rome Conference, France strongly supported various, sometimes bold, proposals, some of which were suggested with the aim of attaining as much influence as possible on the Court: the adoption of a dual legal system combining elements of Anglo-Saxon common law and inquisitorial elements from the civil law system; the creation of a Pre-Trial Chamber as a control mechanism on the *ex officio* powers of the Prosecutor; the unprecedented role afforded to the victims; the concentration on the core crimes, or the complementarity with domestic courts.[10]

Regarding the jurisdiction *ratione materiae* of the Court, France was far from the avant-garde states, which it joined only in the final hours of the negotiations. Opposed to the proposed system (consent of the state of territory or the state of

8 Sorel, J.-M. (2007). 'La France et les juridictions internationales ou la dialectique de l'audace, des réticences et de la soumission'. In: Cahin, G., Poirat, F. and Szurek, S.(2007) (eds.). *La France et le droit international.* Paris: Pedone, pp. 279–337.

9 Sorel (2007), 285.

10 Sorel (2007), 279–337.

nationality) and more closely involved with the US approach,[11] it acquiesced to these provisions in exchange for a temporary exemption (article 124) which allows states to not recognize the jurisdiction of the Court during the seven years following its entry into force for the category of war crimes. This moratorium has long been the focus of criticism against the French government, which feared – under pressure from its highest Defence authorities – the prosecution of its military deployed in international operations. As Foreign affairs Minister Hubert Védrine indeed declared before the Senate in February 1998: "France will vote [at the Rome Conference] for the most effective solutions and the most respectful of its interests; it will ensure that appropriate provisions are taken to prevent abusive complaints for the sole purpose of challenging its external action and the role of the Security Council."[12]

It also seems that this transitional period had been used to check the functioning of the guarantees included in the Statute and to avoid abusive complaints for war crimes that might, unlike other crimes in the Statute, involve an isolated act. The non-renewal of this exemption in 2008 corresponds, according to Jean-Marc Sorel, to a period when France "begins to separate from its ancestral fears towards certain international instruments like the Geneva Conventions and its Additional Protocols. It also means adopting an attitude more in keeping with the image that France now wants to reflect."[13]

Beyond the precaution embodied in article 124, France showed a variable distrust during the functioning of international courts, starting with a reluctance to cooperate with the *ad hoc* tribunals, particularly with regard to the delicate problem of the arrest of wanted criminals by French troops enlisted within the NATO forces. The tone notably escalated between the ICTY and France in December 1997, when Chief Prosecutor Louise Arbour hinted that Serb criminals could find shelter in the area controlled by French forces. Carla Del Ponte herself, in her autobiography, recalls the difficulties she encountered negotiating with the French authorities.[14] Over time, however, and probably due to media pressure launched by Arbour, the reluctance faded away, and France committed itself to "a subdued but effective submission" to the decisions of international criminal courts, "according

---

11 See in particular former US Ambassador-at-Large for War Crimes Issues David Schaeffer's recollection in: Schaeffer, D. (2012). *All the missing souls. A personal history of the war crimes tribunals.* Princeton, Oxford: Princeton University Press, pp. 163–226.

12 Quoted in Sorel (2007), 299.

13 Sorel (2007), 300.

14 Del Ponte, C. (2009). *La traque, les criminels de guerre et moi: autobiographie.* Paris: Ed. Héloïse d'Ormesson.

to the image it wishes to give of a state concerned with the respect of international law."[15] For example, after having vehemently criticized the attitude of the ICTY in relation to French military in the former Yugoslavia, the French government appeared to submit to the requirements of the Prosecutor, signing two agreements with the ICTY and the ICTR to strengthen this cooperation.

After an observation period marked by a certain reserve, France, gradually began to support the ICC This support was both functional (financial participation and judicial cooperation) and political (referrals and diplomatic activism in favour of the Court), in order to make international criminal justice a new norm of instrument and an evolving diplomatic practice in the context of the reformulation of its post-Cold War foreign policy. Beyond a growing interest in the role and place of international criminal justice in the international arena, this position reflects both a renewed support for multilateralism and international law and a new approach to conflict management, peace and reconstruction on the part of France.

A Cautious but Steady Functional Support

France, as a State Party, participates in the budgetary and operational management of the Court, which takes place as part of the Assembly of States Parties (ASP).[16] As the fourth largest contributor to the budget of the Court, with almost ten million euros in 2012, France is very watchful of how the ICC is managed and how it works, sometimes being critical with regard to both the cost of the institution and its management methods. In its official statements to the ASP, the French government expressed its expectations for financial efficiency and "return on investment", a message that also stands out clearly in interviews with French officials. In December 2011, at the 10th session of the ASP in New York, France was thus among the countries that opposed any growth of the ICC budget, leading with UK the "zero growth policy group" that has raised considerable controversy, among NGOs in particular.

15 Sorel (2007), 324.

16 The Assembly of States Parties is the management and legislative body of the ICC. It is composed of representatives of the states that have ratified the Rome Statute. It meets at least once a year, at the headquarters of the Court in The Hague or at the headquarters of the United Nations in New York. It sets the general policies for the administration of the Court and reviews its activities and all issues relevant to the ICC. During those meetings, the States Parties discuss new projects, adopt normative texts and the ICC's annual budget, elect the judges, the Prosecutor, and the Deputy Prosecutor(s).

Martin Briens, Deputy Permanent Representative of France to the United Nations, declared in this respect: "The support of France in the investigation and prosecution of the Court, the core of its activities, is indisputable. We are the 4th contributor to the ICC. It is [...] one of our priorities. But this support is accompanied by a requirement of good governance and management. The financial crisis affects every state and every individual. Budgetary discipline is imperative and we expect the Court to make the same efforts as those made by our fellow citizens - to combine legal action and effectiveness in the use of budgetary resources allocated to it."

When it comes to the cooperation with the Court,[17] all requests and responses by the official authorities remain largely confidential. While some interviews mention France's relatively good record in this respect, thanks to the presence of French military bases in Africa, others stress its the reluctance to disclose sensitive or protected information. Several strong initiatives are nevertheless to be credited to the French authorities: the transfer of Thomas Lubanga to The Hague on board of a French military aircraft, the highly publicized arrest, in October 2010, of Rwandan Callixte Mbarushimana, General Secretary of the Democratic Forces for the Liberation of Rwanda (FDLR), who had sought refuge in France since 2003 and was arrested by the French police in execution of an arrest warrant issued by the ICC, and especially the support of the French Force Licorne in the arrest of Laurent Gbagbo in Côte d'Ivoire.

Another mode of direct participation in the functioning of the ICC is the presence of French nationals among the staff of the Court. In this area, however, France has shown some weakness, with poor representation of judges and French officials.[18] Already in February 2003, at the time the Court was established and

---

17 Provisions of article 86 of the Rome Statute entitled "General obligation to cooperate" specify that "States Parties shall cooperate fully with the Court in the investigation and prosecution of crimes within its jurisdiction." Requests for cooperation may target the identification, arrest and surrender of persons, gathering of evidence or examination of prosecuted persons, permission to transit through the state's territory for a person surrendered to the Court, temporary transfer of a prisoner to obtain his testimony, and any other logistic aid or information transfer.

18 Pursuant to article 36.4 (a) of the Rome Statute: "Nominations of candidates for election to the Court may be made by any State Party to this Statute, and shall be made either: (i) By the procedure for the nomination of candidates for appointment to the highest judicial offices in the State in question; or (ii) By the procedure provided for the nomination of candidates for the International Court of Justice in the Statute of that Court." The French nominee is selected by the French authorities after a national selection procedure conducted by the National Group of the Permanent Court of Arbitration

the first judges were elected, France had taken a somewhat ambiguous attitude. Shortly before the closing date for nominations at the end of November 2003, the French government had not yet presented any candidate. In reality, the French political authorities wanted to promote a former adviser to President Chirac, Jean-Claude Antonetti, Chamber President at the Paris Court of Appeal, who lacked the required qualities. Finally, the appointment of Claude Jorda, at the time president of the ICTY, as a French candidate was a relief, "but France almost came to demonstrate, once again, that its ideals hardly complied with contingencies of a less noble policy."[19]

Yet when six new judges were elected at the Assembly of States Parties held at the headquarters of the United Nations in New York between December 12 and December 21, 2011, and as the mandate of sitting French judge Bruno Cotte was bound to expire,[20] it was the Briton Howard Morrison, then an ICTY judge, who was finally elected to the fifteenth round, after a bitter battle against the second European candidate, French Bruno Cathala, a former Registrar at the ICC. Similarly, France's influence seemed to gradually decline within the Office of the Prosecutor (OTP), in which it held key positions for a few years. Some French officials even deplored an "Anglo-Saxon takeover" of the OTP, regretting that the field was abandoned by French-speaking people, as outlined by a report of the *Commission nationale consultative des droits de l'homme* (CNCDH) in October 2012: "The contrast is striking between the initial position of the Court – with a French judge and Registrar, and French high-level officials within the Office of the Prosecutor – and the current eclipse of the French presence in the wake of the recent election of judges by the ASP."[21]

Of this area, Frederic Charillon has said that "the classical structural handicaps of France […] are still considerable: lack of visibility on job vacancies over the

(PCA), which makes its selection according to preset criteria, followed by hearings of the candidates. The candidate shall then "be available to campaign in New York and The Hague", as indicated on the website of the French Ministry of Justice.

19 Sorel (2007), 292.

20 Bruno Cotte had replaced Claude Jorda, who resigned before the end of his mandate in 2007.

21 The *Commission nationale consultative des droits de l'homme* (CNCDH) is an independent French administrative authority established in 1947 to inform the work of the government and Parliament in the field of Human Rights and fundamental freedoms. Its opinion may be requested by either the Prime Minister or any other member of the government, or by self-referral. It thus took up the issue of the position of France towards the International Criminal Court and issued a report in October 2012, online at: http://www.cncdh.fr/fr/publications/avis-sur-la-cour-penale-internationale.

medium term, targeting senior positions [...], lack of overall management or anticipatory diplomacy of influence in this matter, low culture of *coalition building,* inadequate belief in the importance of investing into networks of influence or norms."[22]

However, France has in recent years multiplied new activities to display French expertise in this area. Thus, in cooperation with the Jurisdiction, Complementarity and Cooperation Division (JCCD) from the Office of the Prosecutor, the Foreign Affairs Ministry has organized a series of regional conferences – in December 2009 in Dakar (Senegal), in October 2010 in Yaoundé (Cameroon) – bringing together officials from the Ministries of Foreign Affairs and Justice from several African countries, lawyers, judges and members of civil society, with the aim of helping these groups tackle the challenges and address the opportunities of international criminal justice. In November 2009 and November 2010, the Ministry also partnered with the International Relations Institute of Cameroon (IRIC) to organize regional seminars with the aim of conducting training and outreach activities on issues of transitional justice.

A Promotional Discourse

At the time of the creation of the ICC, France announced what role it would be playing in this "important international advance", but subsequently adopted a wait-and-see approach, a cautious policy, with few notable interventions during the early years of the Court. However, from 2005 on – the date of referral of the situation in Darfur to the Court – things changed, and France, at the initiative of this referral, increased the number of statements in favour of the Court. Adhering to the communication and the galvanizing strategy promoted by the Court, France now stands out by maintaining a relatively regular and promotional discourse about the importance and benefits of international criminal justice, its role in the fight against impunity and building peace, the mission of the International Criminal Court, and the importance of the universal ratification of the Rome Statute.

This discourse is essentially delivered by the main actors responsible for advancing France's message and its position in foreign policy: the President of the Republic, the Minister of Foreign Affairs and the Permanent Representative of France at the UN. It is spread in a number of multilateral fora, including those which have an institutional or political linkage with the ICC: the UN Security Council, the UN General Assembly, the Assembly of States Parties, and the Council of the European

---

22 Charillon, F. (2011). *La politique étrangère de la France de la fin de la guerre froide au printemps arabe.* Paris: La Documentation Française, p. 157.

Union. But it is also present at the national level, notably within the framework of the Conference of Ambassadors, a major event of the French diplomacy which has brought together ministers and state secretaries of the Foreign Affairs, all 181 heads of diplomatic missions and French officials of the central administration every year since 1993.

Many of these are official statements on the occurrence of dramatic situations or the extension of certain conflicts (Democratic Republic of Congo, Ivory Coast, Sudan, Libya), but not only. In some other cases, the purpose is to promote international criminal justice through the preventive or curative effects it is supposed to have on other global issues: peacebuilding in Africa, protection of civilians in armed conflict, responsibility to protect, child soldiers, promoting and strengthening the rule of law, safety of women and sexual violence. Justice and the fight against impunity are seen as instruments of prevention or conflict management, as "a tool in the promotion of a global order"[23] that is used for the purpose of obtaining a cessation of violence, and inseparable from the peace and post-conflict reconstruction for which they are considered as preconditions.

In this context, the ICC is presented as "one of the most fundamental advances in the history of humanity, a humanity aware of the dangers its own demons expose it to."[24] It has found, in the case of Libya, "once more a justification of its existence", because "today, facing the atrocities we are witnessing, impunity is no longer an option."[25] "France has repeatedly stated: [it supports] without reserve the Prosecutor of the International Criminal Court and its work"[26] and "calls upon all States to adhere to the Rome Statute and to cooperate with the International Criminal Court."[27] More recently, François Hollande, current President of the French Republic, declared in August 2012: "Bashar al-Assad must go. There's no political solution with him. He is a threat, he's continuing with unbelievable violence to massacre the people, destroy cities and kill women and children – we've had evidence of this again in the past few days. It is intolerable for the human

---

23 Danner, A. Simmons, B. A. (2010). 'Credible commitments and the International Criminal Court'. *International Organization*, 64, no. 2, p. 244.

24 Speech by Kouchner, B. (2010) 65th Session of the UN General Assembly, General Debate, September 27, 2010.

25 Speech by Araud, G. (2011) before the UN Security Council, February 26, 2011, S/PV.6491.

26 Speech by Le Frapper du Hellen, B. before the UN Security Council, June 29, 2010, S/PV.6347.

27 Speech by Ripert, J.-M. (2009) before the UN Security Council, November 11, 2009, S/PV.6216.

conscience, unacceptable for the region's security and stability. The matter should be referred to the International Criminal Court so that those responsible for these atrocities one day stand trial. I want to be clear: France shoulders all her responsibilities and spares no effort in order for the Syrian people to gain their freedom and security".[28]

This discourse of reiterated support and "total commitment" has been put into practice within the Security Council twice. In cooperation with the UK, France initiated the Council's referral of the situations in Darfur (2005) and Libya (2011) to the Court, showing in both cases diplomatic activism: it took two months to obtain a vote of the Council in the case of Darfur, with four abstentions, including those of China and the United States; a fortnight in the case of Libya, when a text was unanimously voted. France also remained mindful, – following the arrest warrant against Omar al-Bashir and despite some "failures"[29] – of avoiding the presence of a French representative alongside the Sudanese president at official events.

France has recently tried to address this issue specifically, in order to establish whether a UNSC referral to the ICC under Chapter VII of the UN Charter has a binding force for all Member States of the UN, whether they are Parties to the Rome Statute or not. These assumptions have recently been challenged in the debate surrounding the arrest warrant against al-Bashir, when several African Union members expressed their doubts on whether obligations to serve UNSC resolutions urging to cooperate with the ICC enjoyed priority over obligations to recognize a sitting head of state's diplomatic immunity under international law. French diplomats have also initiated a process of reflection, seeking to lay the foundations for a unified doctrine in the area of international justice. A significant initiative has been, under the supervision of the Ministry of Foreign Affairs, the organization of a seminar entitled "International and transitional justice: elements for a French diplomatic doctrine" in 2011.[30]

---

28 Hollande's speech can be retrieved from the website of the French Embassy at the UN: http://www.franceonu.org/Syria-8699.

29 The presence of Omar al-Bashir, unveiled in the last minute, at the inauguration of President Guelleh of Djibouti on May 8 and 9, 2011, was particularly embarrassing for the French government, criticized for having been represented by the Minister of Cooperation, Henri de Raincourt.

30 Fox, H.; Webb, P. (2013). *The Law of State Immunity*. Oxford: Oxford University Press, p. 538; Williams, S., Sherif, L. (2009). 'The Arrest Warrant for President al-Bashir: Immunities of Incumbent Heads of State and the International Criminal Court.' *Journal of Conflict and Security Law, 14, no. 1, pp. 71–92; Du Plessis, M. and Gevers, C. (2011), ISS Paper 225, online at: https://www.issafrica.org/uploads/Paper225.pdf; and for the most*

This seminar, spread out over two years and bringing together diplomats, researchers, members of NGOs and practitioners of international criminal justice, aimed to highlight the issues and challenges of international and transitional justice, and to suggest guidelines for the formation of a coherent doctrine. This initiative is particularly noteworthy considering that France never wished to frame the principles of its external action into a particular doctrine.

Conclusion

The question of ICC autonomy is a key issue for its legitimacy and effectiveness, its existence and recognition as a fully-fledged actor in international relations. Indeed, as Benjamin Schiff writes, the ICC is "the institutional expression of a maximum international consensus over implementation of international criminal law. It must therefore operate among the imperatives of justice and politics, manage sovereign sensitivities of states, and gain legitimacy through judicial probity and organizational efficiency"[31]. It shows a dependence on the states which created it, which not only affects its functioning, but also its image in the international arena.

The sociological approach, which studies the Court in its interactions with other actors in the international arena, nevertheless shows that, despite the criticisms and "multiple dilemmas"[32] standing in its way, the Court has in a slow but perceptible movement built an evolving and universally recognized "institutional presence", which is part of the international political landscape. This hypothesis can partly be verified by the marked evolution that characterizes the attitude of France towards the ICC, both in the construction of its external legal policy[33] and

---

recent developments around the ICC and Al Bashir in South Africa: Allison, S. (2015). 'Think again: Bashir visits SA – and brings a constitutional crisis with him.' *ISS Today*, Institute for Security Studies, June 15, 2015, online at: https://www.issafrica.org/iss-today/think-again-bashir-visits-sa-and-brings-a-constitutional-crisis-with-him.

31 Schiff, B. N. (2008). 'Managing Multiple Dilemmas: Politics, Justice, Law and Administration at the International Criminal Court'. *International Studies Association Papers*, p. 28; online at: http://citation.allacademic.com/meta/p_mla_apa_research_citation/2/5/0/9/9/p250992_index.html?phpsessid=nf7e6fil7p8clu8h99egsh00o4

32 Schiff (2008), 28.

33 As defined by former French diplomat Guy de Lacharrière and taken up in Fernandez (2010), p. 14: "External legal policy should be understood as 'a policy towards the law and not necessarily determined by the law'. It is therefore to analyze the international norms states are trying to promote or to which they oppose, the explanations they offer to support their positions and techniques they use for this purpose."

in the impact of the existence and activities of the Court on its foreign policy. This finding requires several comments.

Even is France has from the start supported the establishment of the Court with a Human Rights position conform to the image it wants to reflect, it has not avoided in practice displaying reluctance following the humanist momentum caused by the creation of the Court. This was partly based on the fact that state political interests – or considerations relating to international peace and security – and legal requirements do not always coincide.[34]

The position of France, however, is that it has a growing interest to respect and promote these fundamental norms, because in the end, its position entails advantages and constraints that balance each other out, the latter being the "price to pay" for the international influence of a middle power. This intermediate position seems to create "conflicting postures that do not know major powers or, conversely, smaller states [...] The 'big' states can afford some resistance at a lower price [...] and 'small' states have, in contrast, little alternative"[35].

Its support for international criminal justice can be explained by the circumstance that it is forced to reformulate its foreign policy to maintain its place in the contemporary international order. For a middle power like France, which now has moderate military and economic means but continues to have global ambition, this growing interest in international criminal justice could still be seen through its discourse and public posture as an alternative, even a substitute, for hard power on the international scene, as a strengthening of "soft power" through new, promotional rhetoric. But it can also be seen as a new international political practice, a new diplomatic resource that allows France to position itself as a force of proposal and influence, notably within the Security Council.

The evolution of France's position towards the ICC is indeed part of a broader evolution of French foreign policy and its attempts at reformulation since the end of the Cold War. The ICC may thus be associated with the "new international political practices" described by Frédéric Charillon: France must include them in its actions if it "wants to continue to exist as a force structuring the world to come". "To get a place in the post-bipolar international order, it must rely more on its ability to frame issues, devise new rules and tell the real world, than on its military, economic and demographic powers that are now put into perspective"[36].

---

34 Sorel (2007), 336.

35 Sorel (2007), 337.

36 Charillon, F. (2010). *La France peut-elle encore agir sur le monde?* Paris: Armand Colin, p. 9.

France, writes French historian Maurice Vaisse, has to become "a force of proposal and not a protesting one", to move to a "culture of influence and partnership"[37], to transform itself into a project initiator that is able to aggregate around its proposals, as in the case of the Darfour and Libya referrals. This change would primarily be based not only on an active presence in the world, but also on a role in the development of international norms and participation in international expertise. International criminal justice may thus allow a mid-sized power like France, with global ambition, to pursue a fairly independent and strong policy, particularly within the Security Council, which in this context provides a unique playing field.

These new norms of discourse and public posture on international criminal justice still take into account political realities. They do not prevent selectivity in action, nor a critical reading of the Court's activities and choices. As discussed above, the French position was first marked by a cautious wait-and-see policy, before proceeding from formal support to a more active promotion. It is possible to trace real shift in French rhetoric and basic cooperation with the ICC. It is, however, necessary to make a distinction between rhetoric and actions, between discourse and practice. Foreign policy towards international criminal justice is in itself a strand of foreign policy, with its limitations, constraints, strategies and interests to be defended. Justice plays a smaller or larger part in this, depending on the particular circumstances.

Projecting the image of an international actor fighting for Human Rights and justice, France may indeed also sometimes follow its own foreign policy interests, as shown by its position during the negotiations for the Rome Statute or its financial demands within the Assembly of State Parties. Moreover France's attitude cannot be separated from the strategic options adopted in its traditional geographic spheres of influence, French-speaking Africa in particular, but especially from its position as a permanent member of the Security Council. Thus, after the Review Conference of the Rome Statute, which was held in Kampala in June 2010, France did not approve of the text on the crime of aggression, saying that "this draft text [...] disregards the relevant provisions of the Charter of the United Nations enshrined in article 5 of the Rome Statute. In article 15 *bis*, paragraph 8, the text restricts the role of the United Nations Security Council and contravenes the Charter of the United Nations under the terms of which the Security Council alone shall determine the existence of an act of aggression. Under these conditions, France cannot depart from its position

37 Vaisse, M. (2009). *La puissance ou l'influence? La France dans le monde depuis 1958.* Paris: Fayard, pp. 571–572.

of principle"[38]. Furthermore, even if France played a role in referring the Darfur case to the ICC, it has since then be criticized as a Security Council permanent member for failing to increase cooperation with the Court and putting pressure on the Sudanese government, despite the repeated calls from the Prosecutor.

There is no doubt, however, that international criminal justice is not only becoming a new diplomatic device, but also a source of influence for France on the international stage, as evidenced by the key issues it now raises for diplomats – such as the role of law in foreign policy and international relations in general, the use of mechanisms like the ICC, what they allow and do not allow, the proper time to activate them, the consequences of their implementation –, as also evidenced by the strong activism France has been deploying towards the situation in Syria, whose further developments will undoubtedly throw new light on this analysis.

38 Statements by States Parties in explanation of position after the adoption of resolution RC/Res. 6 on the crime of aggression (with which were also associated the United States, observer member of the ASP).

Agnieszka Bieńczyk-Missala

Early Warning and the Prevention of Atrocity Crimes: the Role of the United Nations

The idea of preventing mass atrocities became part of the international order after World War II. Yet it was not until the 1990s that the actual debate about the practical aspects of prevention began. At the time, the international community realized that it had not been able to respond effectively to mass violations of Human Rights, and that it should be more focused on prevention. This chapter first outlines the emergence of the idea of prevention in the context of the development of the UN system of Human Rights protection. The system is largely a consequence of World War II and a product of the Cold War era. It has a clear preventive dimension, especially if it is coupled with monitoring the Human Rights situation as well as promotion and education in this regard. This chapter describes the main reasons behind the decision of the UN General Assembly to adopt "R2P" in 2005 and then presents the preventive instruments that are available to and used by the UN.

The United Nations Human Rights protection system

The preventive idea is enshrined in the Charter of the United Nations of June 26, 1945. Bearing in mind past wars, the states undertook to "save succeeding generations from the scourge of war" and to "reaffirm faith in fundamental Human Rights, in the dignity and worth of the human person."[1]

In the spirit of these words, the Convention on the Prevention and Punishment of the Crime of Genocide (further "the Convention") was adopted relatively soon thereafter, on December 9, 1948. The states confirmed genocide, whether committed in time of peace or in time of war, to be a crime under international law that had to be prevented. Under Article 8 of the Convention, any Contracting Party "may call upon the competent organs of the United Nations to take such action under the Charter of the United Nations as they consider appropriate for the prevention."[2]

At the time of drafting of the Convention, no clear concept existed as to the form prevention was to take, nor had any mechanisms of prevention been developed.

1 Charter of the United Nations, preamble.

2 Convention on the Prevention and Punishment of the Crime of Genocide, Articles 1, 8.

The convention failed to specify the meaning, content, and scope of the obligation to prevent. The focus of the Convention was on the punishment of genocide, and punishment as such was perceived as an instrument of prevention. This approach corresponded to the ideas of Raphael (Rafał) Lemkin, who coined the term 'genocide' and who had been one of the champions of the Convention. In his book *Axis Rule in Occupied Europe*, he argued that punishing the perpetrators of the crimes committed during World War II would help prevent such crimes from being committed again in the future.[3] Prevention had no priority for the UN during the Cold War. The Genocide Convention was not invoked to prevent atrocities in any place such as Tibet, Iraq, Iran, Paraguay, Argentina, East Timor, Cambodia, Uganda, and many others, where mass crimes took place.[4]

At the same time as work progressed on the Genocide Convention, the UN Human Rights protection system was being developed. Debates on the prevention of gross Human Rights violations tend to disregard the role of international aspects of Human Rights protection. Yet the efforts to implement these rights undertaken by intergovernmental and non-governmental institutions as well as states (as part of their foreign policy), have a very significant preventive aspect that is individual rather than collective. The system of international Human Rights protection which developed after 1945 had its precursors already in international humanitarian law. Conventions adopted in The Hague and Geneva were based on the principle to protect non-belligerents (inter alia: wounded soldiers, prisoners of war, and non-combatant civilians) from the dangers of war, though without criminalizing war per se. This motivation was humanitarian and essentially idealistic; it preferred the welfare and fate of the individual person above almost all other values.[5] Monitoring of Human Rights situations in UN member states was developed pursuant to article 1 of the UN Charter as well as articles 55 and 56, which include UN members commitments to promote the universal respect for, and observance of, Human Rights and fundamental freedoms for all without

3 Lemkin, R. (1944). *Axis Rule in Occupied Europe: Laws of Occupation – Analysis of Government – Proposals for Redress.* Washington, D.C.: Carnegie Endowment for International Peace, pp. 93–94.

4 Ben-Naftali, O. (2009). 'The Obligations to Prevent and to Punish Genocide'. In: Gaeta, P. (2009) (ed). *The UN Genocide Convention. A Commentary.* Oxford: Oxford University Press, pp. 36–44.

5 Henkin, L. (1978). *The Rights of Man Today.* Boulder: Westview Press, p. 95–110; Shelton, D. (2007). 'An Introduction to the History of International Human Rights Law'. *George Washington University Law School Working Paper*, online at: http://scholarship.law.gwu.edu/cgi/viewcontent.cgi?article=2045&context=faculty_publications.

distinction regarding race, sex, language, or religion.[6] Importantly, no state submitted reservations to these articles and the remaining Human Rights clauses in the Charter.[7]

However, UN members were cautious in accepting Human Rights obligations. Until 1989, their focus was on the implementation of standards within the different member states that would not infringe their national sovereignty. Human Rights included in the Universal Declaration of Human Rights of December 10, 1948 were declared "a common standard of achievement for all peoples and all nations."[8] The Human Rights instruments that were adopted later, such as the International Covenant on Civil and Political Rights (ICCPR) and the International Covenant on Economic, Social and Cultural Rights (ICESCR), called on states to create conditions whereby everyone could enjoy civil and political as well as economic, social, and cultural rights.[9] Their implementation was delegated to the legislation of the member states which had ratified the covenants.[10] Prevention was not explicitely mentioned, but some of the enumerated rights could be seen as safeguards against massive Human Rights violations, for example the freedom of religion; the prohibition of hate propaganda; the postulated respect for the rights of ethnic, religious, and linguistic minorities.

In the International Convention on the Elimination of All Forms of Racial Discrimination of December 21, 1965, the signatory states moved beyond the obligation to eradicate racial discrimination. They also included the duty to suppress racism and racist violence,[11] including the dissemination of racist ideas, racial

6 Charter of the United Nations, Articles: 1, 55, 26.

7 Drzewicki, K. (2002). *The United Nations Charter and the Universal Declaration of Human Rights.* In: R. Hanski, R. Suksi, M. (2002) (eds.). *An Introduction to the International Protection of Human Rights*, Second edition, Turku/Åbo: Institute for Human Rights, Åbo Akademi University, pp. 65–76.

8 Universal Declaration of Human Rights, preamble.

9 International Covenant on Civil and Political Rights, preamble, G.A. res. 2200A (XXI), 21 U.N. GAOR Supp. (No. 16) at 52, U.N. Doc. A/6316 (1966), 999 U.N.T.S. 171; *International Covenant on* Economic, Social and Cultural Rights, preamble, G.A. res. 2200A (XXI), 21 U.N. GAOR Supp. (No. 16) at 49, U.N. Doc. A/6316 (1966), 993 U.N.T.S. 3.

10 M. Nowak, M. (1993). *UN Covenant on Civil and Political Rights: CCPR Commentary*, Kehl: Engel Publishers.

11 International Convention on the Elimination of All Forms of Racial Discrimination, Article 3 *et seq.*

hatred and financial support to racist organisations. Organizations that promote and incite racial discrimination were to be declared illegal and prohibited.[12]

In 1946, the United Nations Commission on Human Rights (UNCHR) was founded. In 1970, the United Nations authorized the UNCHR to examine individual complaints, which may be referred to the Commission by persons and non-governmental organizations when gross violations of Human Rights occur. Since 2006, the Human Rights Council also has the additional prerogative of universal periodic review, allowing it to examine the Human Rights situation in all United Nations states. The Human Rights Council, like its predecessor, can appoint special rapporteurs and engage in fact-finding missions. It cooperates with the United Nations High Commissioner for Human Rights, who is responsible for responding to Human Rights violations and for the promotion of Human Rights.[13]

Today, individuals have unprecedented rights. They can lodge complaints with UN treaty bodies and with the Human Rights Council, or they may choose to complain to regional courts of Human Rights like the ones established by the Council of Europe, the Organization of American States, and the African Union (previously the Organization of African Unity). While these systems of Human Rights protection differ in terms of obligations of their members and the efficacy of their enforcement mechanisms, they all play an important role in monitoring the Human Rights situation among their member states and promote Human Rights.

There still is a gap between the adopted standards and their implementation, which is due to the tension that exists between individual rights states grant to their citizens and the principle of sovereignty that shelters states from interference by other states (principle of non-interference).[14] Many states have interpreted this

---

12 About the Convention see also: Lérner, L. (1980). *The U.N. Convention on the Elimination of All Forms of Racial Discrimination.* Alphen aan den Rijn: Sijthoff & Noordhoff International; Meron, T. (1985). 'The Meaning and the Reach of the International Convention on the Elimination of All Forms of Racial Discrimination'. *American Journal of International Law*, 79, pp. 283–319.

13 Gerber, P. (2009). *Prevention is Better than Cure, The UN and Human Rights Education.* Research Project for the Geneva Academy of International Humanitarian Law and Human Rights, June 2009, online at: https://www.academia.edu/200434/Prevention_is_Better_than_Cure_The_UN_and_Human_Rights_Education Ramcharan, B. (2010). *Preventive Human Rights Strategies.* London, New York: Routledge.

14 On the subject of Human Rights and sovereignty, see Reus-Smit, C. (2001). 'Human Rights and the Social Construction of Sovereignty'. *Review of International Studies*, 27, pp. 519–538; Aceves, W. J. (2002). 'Relative Normativity: Challenging the Sovereignty Norm Through Human Rights Litigation'. *Hastings International and Comparative Law Review*, 25, pp. 261–280.

principle as contradictory to external criticism of their treatment of their own citizen. During the Cold War, the Soviet Union regarded interference from outside as a threat to peace (and the principle of non-interference as a cornerstone of peace between nations). The United States, with its long tradition of respect for Human Rights, promoted an understanding according to which Human Rights enjoyed priority over the authority of governments. They supported the development of an international system of Human Rights protection, but at the same time did everything in their power to prevent the US from external interference in Human Rights issues. Until today, they are not a signatory state to the Inter-American Court of Human Rights.

In 1977, US president Jimmy Carter decided to incorporate Human Rights into the foreign policy of the United States.[15] He also included Human Rights and fundamental freedoms in the Declaration on Principles Guiding Relations between Participating States adopted by the states from both sides of the Iron Curtain at the summit in Helsinki on August 1, 1975. It was the first time in history that Human Rights were mentioned alongside the principle of non-interference. At the 1991 Moscow meeting of the Conference on the Human Dimension of the CSCE, the the participating states declared "categorically and irrevocably […] that the commitments undertaken in the field of the human dimension of the CSCE are matters of direct and legitimate concern to all participating States and do not belong exclusively to the internal affairs of the State concerned."[16] The Vienna Declaration, adopted by the World Conference on Human Rights in Vienna in 1993, included a similar wording: "the promotion and protection of all Human Rights is a legitimate concern of the international community".[17] These declarations were declaratory and not legally binding. Nonetheless, they had a strong impact on the Human Rights work of the United Nations in subsequent years, including the progress made with regard to prevention.

---

15 See in particular: Forsythe,D. P. (1989). *Human Rights and U.S. Foreign Policy: Congress Reconsidered.* Gainesville: University of Florida Press; Dobriansky; P. J. (1989). 'Human Rights and U.S. Foreign Policy'. *The Washington Quarterly*, pp. 153–156.

16 CSCE (2001). 'Document of the Moscow Meeting of the Conference on the Human Dimension of the CSCE, 3 October 1991'. In: *OSCE Human Dimension Commitments, A Reference Guide.* Warsaw, p. 241.

17 Vienna Declaration and Programme of Action, para. 4.

From Response to Prevention

In the first half of the 1990s, the United Nations focused primarily on responding to Human Right violations. When the Cold War ended and the wave of democratization swept through Central and Eastern Europe, the future of Human Rights seemed bright. After a period of 'silence', the Security Council started to address these issues in its resolutions, balancing respect for Human Rights and international peace and security.

The first example was Resolution 688/1991 on the situation in Northern Iraq (during the fights between Kurdish *Peshmerga* and the central government under Saddam Hussein). In the resolution, the Security Council appealed to all Member States and to all humanitarian organizations to contribute to the humanitarian relief efforts, and insisted that Iraq allow immediate access by international humanitarian organizations to all those in need of assistance in all parts of Iraq and to make available all necessary facilities for their operations. In 1992, the Security Council for the first time ever authorized a humanitarian intervention in Somalia (Resolution 794/1992), and then in Bosnia and Herzegovina (Resolution 816/1993), where atrocities were taking place.[18]

However, on other occasions the United Nations were less active, for example in Sri Lanka, where the conflict between the Sinhalese and the Tamils caused 90,000 casualties.[19] In Rwanda, UN member states withdrew troops and reduced the powerful Blue Helmets to the size of a toothless monitoring mission after the massacres had started in April 1994.[20] In Srebrenica, the United Nations failed

---

18 Lillich, R. B. (1994). 'The Role of the UN Security Council in Protecting Human Rights in Crisis Situations: UN Humanitarian Intervention in the Post-Cold War World'. *Tulane Journal of International and Comparative Law*, 3, pp. 5–11.

19 Report of the Secretary-General's Panel of Experts on Accountability in Sri Lanka, March 31, 2011, online at: http://www.un.org/News/dh/infocus/Sri_Lanka/POE_Report_Full.pdf.

20 According to the later assessment of the military commander of the UN mission UNAMIR in Rwanda, Romeo Dallaire, the original mission had had the required capabilities to prevent or stop the genocide which unfolded in April 1994. But at its very beginning, members of the presidential guard had disarmed and killed a small Belgian paratrooper commando whose members had tried to protect the Prime Minister of the country, Agathe Uwilingiyimana. Afterwards, the Belgian government withdrew its troops and inclined other troop-providing UN members to do the same. See: Report of the Independent Inquiry into the actions of the United Nations during the 1994 genocide in Rwanda, December 15, 1999, S/1999/1257, online at: http://reliefweb.int/report/rwanda/report-independent-inquiry-actions-united-nations-during-1994-genocide-rwanda and

completely when in the Security Council-declared safe area, with peacekeeping troops present, 7,000 Bosnian Muslims were massacred.

In 1999, NATO launched a large-scale bombing campaign in the former Yugoslavia (on the territories of Serbia and Montenegro) as a response to massive Human Rights abuses of Serb forces against the civilian population in Kosovo. This took place without the necessary UNSC mandate as the UNSC was divided over the issue. The intervention itself also was very controversial because of the large number of civilian casualties, the use of banned weapons, and the deliberate targeting of civilian premises like the Belgrade TV tower and passenger trains.[21] These cases show the problems the UN used to have with adequate responses to massive Human Rights violations: the organization can only act if the necessary consensus is reached in the UNSC, if member states commit enough resources (financial, diplomatic, and military) to an intervention, if the mandate is robust and the conditions favourable to carrying out the intervention. Some authors, pointing to the fact that prevention is less expensive than reaction, suggest the UN redirect its work towards the prevention of crimes such as genocide, crimes against humanity and war crimes.[22] But prevention at the UN level struggles with the same paradox as in national criminal jurisdictions: it addresses a problem that does not even come into being if prevention is successful. When the police prevents a crime, it neither shows up in the crime statistics, nor in the statistic of solved cases and arrests made – and thus hardly ever bolsters the police's prestige in the public. The same is true for the UN: ending a massacre will bring prestige and acclaim to the countries that committed forces for intervening, whereas preventing

---

Dallaire, R. (2003). Shake Hands with the Devil. The Failure of Humanity in Rwanda. Toronto: Random House Canada; Anyidoho, H. K. (1997). *Guns over Kigali: The Rwandese Civil War – 1994 (A Personal Account).* Collana: Spear Books Imprint. More details about Rwanda's genocide can be found in Allan Rutambo Ngari's chapter about the Great Lakes and Patrycja Grzebyk's chapter concerning the lessons learnt from the ICTR and the ICC in Africa, both in this book.

21 Domagala, A. (2004). 'Humanitarian Intervention: The Utopia of Just War? The NATO intervention in Kosovo and the restraints of Humanitarian Intervention'. *Sussex European Institute Working Paper,* no. 76, online at: https://www.sussex.ac.uk/webteam/gateway/file.php?name=sei-working-paper-no-76.pdf&site=266 Massa, A.-S.: 'NATO's Intervention in Kosovo and the Decision of the Prosecutor of the International Criminal Tribunal for the Former Yugoslavia Not to Investigate: An Abusive Exercise of Prosecutorial Discretion?' *Berkeley Journal of International Law,* February 24, 1996, pp. 610–649.

22 Reisman, M. (2007–2008). 'Acting Before Victims Become Victims: Preventing and Arresting Mass Murder'. *Case Western Reserve Journal of International Law,* 40, pp. 68–72.

a massacre will only come with a reward for those who intervene when the threat was absolutely imminent and obvious to the public.

Nevertheless, in 1998, the Secretary-General of the United Nations Kofi Annan declared at the UNCHR that the next century would become the century of prevention.[23] He continued to elaborate on this concept in his subsequent reports. Speaking on the 10th anniversary of the 1994 genocide in Rwanda, he announced the appointment of a Special Advisor on Genocide Prevention and launched an Action Plan to Prevent Genocide. The Five Point Action Plan included 1) preventing armed conflict which usually provides the context for genocide, 2) protection of civilians in armed conflict including a mandate for UN peacekeepers to protect civilians, 3) ending impunity through judicial action in both national and international courts, 4) information gathering and early warning through a UN Special Advisor for Genocide Prevention making recommendations to the UN Security Council on actions to prevent or halt genocide, and 5) swift and decisive action along a continuum of steps, including military action.[24]

The actions of the Secretary-General corresponded with the conclusions from the report *Responsibility to Protect*, dated December 2001.[25] The report was produced by renowned experts of the International Commission on Intervention and State Sovereignty working under the auspices of Canada. It addressed the question of how and when the international community should respond to mass atrocities. Prevention was listed as the topmost responsibility. The responsibility to react, involving the need to resort to military action in extreme cases, should be an exception. The energy of the states should be directed primarily at prevention.[26]

The final document of the 2005 UN world summit in September 2005 declared states to have the duty to cooperate in the field of Human Rights, and to respect, protect and promote Human Rights. It also called upon states to prevent Human

---

23 Statement by Secretary-General Kofi Annan at the opening of the fifty-fourth session of the Commission on Human Rights, March 18, 1998, Press Release SG/SM/6487 HR/4355.

24 Secretary-General Kofi Annan, *Action Plan to Prevent Genocide*, Address in Geneva at tenth Anniversary of 1994 Genocide in Rwanda, April 7, 2004, http://www.preventgenocide.org/prevent/UNdocs/KofiAnnansActionPlantoPreventGenocide7Apr2004.htm.

25 *Report of the International Commission on Intervention and State Sovereignty, The Responsibility to Protect*, December 2001, http://responsibilitytoprotect.org/ICISS%20 Report.pdf.

26 2005 World Summit Outcome, para. 138–139; see also: Kędzia, Z. (2010). 'The Responsibility to Protect: Political Strength versus Legal Fragility'. In: Bieńczyk-Missala, A. Dębski, S. (2010) (eds.). *Rafał Lemkin: a Hero of Humankind.* Warsaw: The Polish Institute of International Affairs, pp. 271–288.

Rights abuses and to expand the UN capabilities for early warning and assessment of possible genocide, war crimes, ethnic cleansing, and crimes against humanity.

Importantly, the responsibility to prevent has been confirmed by the International Court of Justice (ICJ). In the case of Bosnia and Herzegovina, the ICJ decided about a motion for provisional measures against the Federal Republic of Yugoslavia (FRY) with regard to the duty to prevent the genocide in Srebrenica in June 1995. In 2007, the ICJ ruled that the FRY had failed to observe its obligation to prevent and to punish genocide, imposed by Article 1 of the Genocide Convention. The ICJ noted that the duty to prevent rests with all parties, is not territorially limited, and refers to immediate and effective action using all necessary measures to prevent and stop genocide.[27]

The United Nations' Preventive Instruments

The Early Warning System

The first contribution to prevention on the part of the United Nations is the early warning system. Reliable, objective assessment of the situation is crucial for effective action. Reports written in the 1990s after the events of Rwanda and Srebrenica pointed to weaknesses of the information management and of the early warning processes in the UN. With regard to Rwanda, the Independent Inquiry came to the conclusion that the UN was lacking an institution that would shoulder the burden of early warning and risk analysis.[28] The information flow inside the UN and between the UN and the Security Council was also dysfunctional. The report of the Secretary-General on the Srebrenica massacre noted that early warning offers no guarantee for swift effective action, but it does increase the likelihood of more a robust and faster response.[29]

The early warning system now comprises the field offices of the UN, the peacekeeping missions, the High Commissioner for Human Rights, and organizations such as the World Health Organisation, UNICEF, and other UN agencies. They monitor the situation on the ground, identify tensions, and regularly file reports. The member states have a role in early warning, too, but they are often reluctant to share sensitive information with the UN because of differences in interest.

27 International Court of Justice Judgment of February 26, 2007, http://www.icj-cij.org/docket/files/91/13685.pdf (accessed December 15, 2014).

28 Report of the Independent Inquiry into the actions of the United Nations during the 1994 genocide in Rwanda, December 15, 1999, S/1999/1257.

29 Report of the Secretary-General pursuant to General Assembly resolution 53/35. *The Fall of Srebrenica,* A/54/549, para. 474.

Moreover, NGOs, particularly those given consulting status by the Economic and Social Council (ECOSOC) and participating in the work of UN bodies can raise alerts about the likelihood of mass crimes that might occur in the near future.

A relatively new institution is the Office of the Special Adviser on the Prevention of Genocide (OSAPG), founded in 2005. The responsibility of this office is the prevention of genocide, which is defined more comprehensively than in the Rome Statute. The eight factors list of OSAPG includes also the monitoring of elements that are not part of the Rome Statute's genocide definition and some of them even do not in themselves constitute an international crime (e.g., the registration of members of a group). The Office collects information about the likelihood of genocide in a specific situation. The factors on which its assessment is based do not define genocide, but are meant to indicate whether genocide is becoming more or less likely in a given situation.[30]

OSAPG cooperates primarily with the UN institutions in the field and collects and analyses data, using indicators such as: inter-group relations, discrimination, arms transfers, intent to destroy a group, etc. Based on the analyses, it proposes a risk assessment report. If the Office believes there is a risk of genocide, it issues warning appeals and recommendations which are referred to the Secretary-General and the Security Council. The information is also distributed to international organizations, states, and individual persons.

If the OSAPG determines that there is a risk of genocide, it is not able to offer 'good offices' or advisory services to the government. Its role is limited to early warning and mobilizing the United Nations to action. So far, the Office has issued warnings with relation to e.g. Sudan, South Sudan, Syria, the Central-African Republic, and Kenya.

Other important UN bodies involved in early warning are the Department of Political Affairs and Early Warning and the Contingency Planning Section of the Office for the Coordination of Humanitarian Affairs. The United Nations Interagency Framework for Coordination on Preventive Action (the so called "Framework Team") coordinates the 21 UN agencies, departments, funds, and programmes that have access to field information.[31]

In the report on early warning and the responsibility to protect presented to the General Assembly on July 14, 2010, the Secretary-General listed three key

---

30 See Office of the Special Advisor on the Prevention of Genocide (no year). Analysis Framework. New York: UN, available at: http://www.un.org/ar/preventgenocide/adviser/pdf/osapg_analysis_framework.pdf.

31 *Early Warning, Assessment and the Responsibility to Protect*, July 14, 2010, Report of the Secretary-General, A/64/864, p. 3.

issues. Firstly, he noted that there is insufficient information sharing among the UN bodies and actions are often duplicated. Secondly, the existing mechanisms for gathering and assessing information do not include the need for prevention. Thirdly, special focus should be placed on instruments that serve the purpose of careful, adequate, and impartial assessment of the situation on the ground. This is a necessary condition for selecting the optimal response.

Preventive Diplomacy

When there is a risk of mass crimes or escalating conflicts, the United Nations may engage in preventive diplomacy. This applies in particular to the Secretary-General, who can offer 'good services', and to the Security Council, which is able to put its weight behind the preventive diplomacy efforts by officially taking a position.[32] Good cooperation with individual states and with regional organizations is a prerequisite for these efforts to be successful. Mandated by the United Nations, diplomats and public officials are able to act as special envoys and in this capacity may engage in confidential diplomacy. Unofficially, they may make attempts to persuade a government to change its policy. They may also publicly address Human Rights situations and speak about inter-group relations that pose a threat of mass-scale atrocities.

In terms of organizational support, the Department of Political Affairs of the United Nations has a Mediation Support Unit, which offers advice and assistance to envoys, negotiators, and political missions.

Unfortunately, so far the United Nations have not developed a separate procedure that would make preventive diplomacy a measure of preventing atrocity crimes. Most UN bodies focus on preventing armed conflict. In consequence, gross violations of Human Rights tend to be overlooked. The extent to which they are taken into consideration is often dependent on the awareness and involvement of individual actors in the process.

Raising the issue of grave Human Rights violations may cause difficulties in contacts with local authorities and may push them towards a more rigid stance in negotiations. If peace is at stake, UN representatives may feel reluctant to press the Human Rights issue. A timely effort to address this issue should be, on principle, a component of the preventive diplomacy efforts. Until now, it is not.

---

32 For more information on the UN institutional frameworks see: *Preventive Diplomacy: Delivering Results*, Report of the Secretary-General, online at: http://www.un.org/wcm/content/site/undpa/main/issues/preventive_diplomacy/main_preventive.

The Secretary-General's report "Strengthening the role of mediation in the peaceful settlement of disputes, conflict prevention and resolution" was drafted in 2012 in response to Resolution 65/283 of the General Assembly. The report acknowledges the need for an understanding of Human Rights Law and International Humanitarian Law by the persons who serve on preventive diplomacy missions. With regard to UN supported agreements, the report notes that no mediator can support or accept any form of amnesty for perpetrators of genocide, war crimes, crimes against humanity, or gross violations of Human Rights.[33]

Economic instruments

Mass Human Rights violations typically occur in poverty-stricken areas. Therefore, financial instruments are usually considered important. In a broad view, it is reflected in economic aid, either *via* direct financial assistance or *via* granting loans that will boost the local economy and make violence 'unprofitable'. The United Nations operates numerous funds, programmes, and agencies that play various roles in this scope. To increase their effectiveness, on the initiative of the Secretary-General, in 1997 the United Nations Development Group was created. At present, the Group unites the 32 UN funds, programmes, agencies, departments, and offices that play a role in development. It includes the biggest units: United Nations Development Programme, United Nations Children Fund, World Food Programme, World Health Organisations, as well as a host of smaller ones. The UN signs individually drafted United Nations Development Assistance Plans with the states it works with. The plans offer guidelines for the funds and programmes on how to provide assistance. The notions behind the plans are in line with the Millennium Declaration and related Millennium Development Goals (MDGs) as well as the Economic Development and Poverty Reduction Strategy (EDPRS 2).

A predictable, democratic government is a strong factor in support of the disbursement, because it ensures that the funds will not be put to military use and will not eventually be used against the population. To avoid these problems, resources are usually directed towards specific projects. Incidents of Human Rights violations and lacking transparency of local politics are often reasons for withholding aid, as was the case with Rwanda, for example. After the 1994 genocide, international

33 Secretary-General of the UN (2012). *Strengthening the role of mediation in the peaceful settlement of disputes, conflict prevention and resolution, Report of the Secretary-General.* Online at: http://www.peacemaker.un.org/sites/peacemaker.un.org/files/SGReport_StrenghteningtheRoleofMediation_A66811.pdf; see also: Ramcharan, B. (2008). Preventive Diplomacy at the UN. Bloomington: Indiana University Press.

aid resources started flowing into the country. Yet as a result of the accusations of breached standards, the stream of aid has been drying up since 2012.[34]

Moreover, the Security Council under Chapter VIII of the UN Charter is able to impose economic sanctions on undemocratic regimes whose policies are violent or create a risk of violence. The UNSC has used this instrument against the regimes in Southern Rhodesia in 1965–1979 and South Africa in 1986–1994. The efficacy assessment of the sanctions was ambiguous.[35] On the one hand, they mobilized local businesses to put pressure on the government. On the other hand, they also contributed to the impoverishment of those whose rights were in the UN's focus, including the population of neighbouring states.

The entire spectrum of sanctions was applied against the former Yugoslavia during the conflicts in the Balkans in the 1990s. There was an embargo on arms trade and on loans, Yugoslav (and later Serbian) assets abroad were frozen, and eventually an embargo on investments was put in place. Neither of these measures prevented the crimes or stopped crimes that were underway. However, in the long term, the sanctions pushed the conflict parties to sit down at the negotiation table in Dayton, and they drove apart the leadership of the Bosnian Serbs (which was militarily and economically dependent on Serbia, but took a hawkish stance during the negotiations) and the leadership of Yugoslavia under Slobodan Milošević (which was more inclined to compromises because it was more affected by the sanctions).[36]

Military Instruments

When there is a risk of mass atrocities, the UN is also able to use military measures if the UNSC is united and member states commit the necessary resources. The objective of military action is primarily to limit conflict parties' access to weapons in order to prevent large-scale atrocities against civilians. Under Chapter VII of

---

34 International Development Statistics (IDS) online databases, http://www.oecd.org/dac/stats/idsonline.htm.

35 Baehr, P. R. (1996). *The Role of Human Rights in Foreign Policy.* Houndmills, Basingstoke, Hampshire: Macmillan Press; Matthews, R. O.; Pratt, C. (1988) (eds.). *Human Rights in Canadian Foreign Policy.* Ottawa: McGill-Queen's University Press, pp. 18–19; Higgins, R. (1987). 'Human Rights and Foreign Policy'. *Rivista di Studi Politici Internazionali*, pp. 572–574, 578–580.

36 Comras, V. D. (2011). 'Pressuring Milošević: Financial Pressure Against Serbia and Montenegro 1992–1995'. In: Asher, D. L., Comras,V. D., Cronin, P. M. (2011). *Pressure, Coercive Economic Statecraft and U.S. National Security.* Washington, D. C.: Center for a New American Security, pp. 55–74, online at: http://www.cnas.org/files/documents/publications/CNAS_Pressure_AsherComrasCronin_1.pdf.

the UN Charter, the Security Council may use military sanctions to impose an embargo on arms sales to a specific state. In practice, these measures are viewed as ineffective, because the competition on the arms market is fierce and it is relatively easy to find alternative suppliers.[37] The embargo may also generate a situation of imbalance in access to arms between combatants, which may translate into a greater scale of atrocities. This is one of the lessons learned from the conflict in the former Yugoslavia, where, at the beginning, the Bosnian Serb leadership had relatively easy access to weapons once the Yugoslav Army dissolved and left its heavy weapons to the newly formed Bosnian Serb Army units. This was later counterbalanced by arms imports of the other conflict parties, all of which were – under the UN embargo – illegal.[38] Here lies another reason for the limited efficacy of sanctions: they have to be monitored. But often the monitors (like the participants in UN-led military interventions) are part of a dual chain of command – the command structure of the UN and of their own command structure. In the case of conflicting interests between the UNSC and the governments to whose chain of command belong monitors in a specific situation, they may avert their eyes from an arms transport that violates the UN embargo but is consistent with the monitors' government's interest.

Preventive military instruments also include military intervention, a measure that may be used if there is a serious risk of mass Human Rights violations. This reason for intervention was not expressly included in the UN Charter, which only allows for interventions motivated by a threat to peace or breach of peace or by aggression, or in order words – if states' basic interests are violated. Force may only be used for self-defence or in line with the principles specified in Chapter VII of the Charter.

The debate on so-called 'humanitarian intervention' grew in intensity after the end of the Cold War order and the outbursts of violence that followed in Somalia, Rwanda, and the former Yugoslavia. Supporters of humanitarian intervention argued that respect for Human Rights is listed in the UN Charter as one of the goals and objectives of the organization. Moreover, they pointed out that Article 2(4) of the Charter forbids the use of force "against the territorial integrity or political independence of any state." At least in principle, humanitarian intervention is

---

37 Kuźniar, R. (2000). *Prawa człowieka, prawo, instytucje, stosunki międzynarodowe.* Warsaw: Wydawnictwo Naukowe Scholar, pp. 341–342.

38 Croatia obtained modern heavy weapons from Germany and the US, whereas the Bosniak Army was armed through clandestine US-Iranian channels. See: Wiebes, C. (2002). *Intelligence en de oorlog in Bosnie. De rol van de inlichtingen- en veiligheidsdiensten.* Amsterdam: NIOD, pp. 136–224.

targeted neither against territorial integrity nor political independence. Instead, it is intended as an instrument of protecting the population and providing humanitarian aid.[39] The debate was heavily influenced by the notion of "Responsibility to Protect".[40]

The preventive dimension manifested itself in practice in Security Council Resolution 1973 of March 17, 2011. The resolution formed the legal basis for intervention in Libya, where a civil war was raging. Libyan President Muammar Gaddafi used hate speech in his public appearances, threatening anyone considered disloyal to the government forces. The media reported violence perpetrated by these forces against the population (even though some of these reports were unconfirmed). The resolution authorized the use of all necessary measures to protect civilians and civilian populated areas under threat of attack, imposed a no-fly zone over Libya, and escalated the sanctions the Security Council had implemented earlier.

The operation in Libya gave rise to many concerns, mainly due to the absence of proper documentation of mass violations of Human Rights that were used to justify the intervention. It was also controversial because the UNSC mandate only called for protecting the civilian population, but did not cover the use of force in a way that would help one side of the conflict to prevail over the other and finally led to regime change. The absence of clear, well-documented evidence of atrocities is always going to undermine the reasonableness of a preventive intervention designed in the framework of Human Rights protection.[41] But it should also be clear that even the best documentation of Human Rights violations will not trigger international intervention as long as the most important stakeholders (the permanent UNSC members) see intervention as contrary to their interests in foreign policy and the wealthiest UN members are not ready to commit the necessary resources to an intervention. The case of Libya demonstrates how inextricably interlinked foreign policy interests and humanitarian needs are: a humanitarian catastrophe may trigger intervention if it is consistent with the interest of the intervening forces and it may not lead to any interference from the outside, should

39 Lillich, R. B. (1973) (ed.). *Humanitarian Intervention And The United Nations*, Charlottesville: University Press of Virginia.

40 For more information on "R2P", see the chapter by Dorota Heidrich in this book.

41 Kuperman, A. J. (2013). 'A Model Humanitarian Intervention? Reassessing NATO's Libya Campaign'. *International Security*, vol. 38, no. 1, pp. 105–136, online at: http://belfercenter.ksg.harvard.edu/publication/23297/model_humanitarian_intervention_reassessing_natos_libya_campaign.html.
Fermor, C. (2012/13). 'NATO's Decision to intervene in Libya (2011). Realist principles or humanitarian norms?' *Journal of Politics & International Studies*, 8, pp. 328–332.

intervention be contrary to the interest of those who would be able to intervene. A good example for the latter is the situation in Darfur that actually escalated after sanctions were imposed on Sudan and members of the Sudanese leadership were targeted by ICC arrest warrants which were the consequence of an UNSC referral. The conflict is currently ongoing with Khartoum fuelling it by supporting the Janjaweed militias with weapons and political support but without any palpable interference. Syria is another example demonstrating that the best early warning system may not lead to a robust humanitarian intervention if intervention is not in the interest of those who would be able to intervene.

The case of Syria shows that the international community is not always prepared to engage in a military response with the objective of putting an end to international crimes against the civilian population and preventing such crimes from being perpetrated. A proposal to overcome the UN's political and logistic difficulties was made by a group of nongovernmental organisations from Canada. The group proposed to create a United Nations Emergency Peace Service (UNEPS), which would be capable of rapid intervention if mass killings were a risk in a specific situation. The authors of the report claim that the UNEPS is the missing instrument in the much larger toolbox for upholding Human Rights.[42] The ultimate objective is to ensure that in the event of atrocities or a risk thereof, the United Nations would be able to act within 24 hours instead of inclining member states to take action. However, the proposal does not address the root of the UN's inability to respond to international crimes – the conflicts of interest among UN member states and the lack of readiness of member states that are able, but not willing to commit forces to an intervention (e.g., because of conflicting foreign policy interests or strong domestic opposition to such a move).

One of the most recent UN-led interventions shows clearly that the UN's problem consists not so much in dysfunctional procedures, unreliable early warning mechanisms and lack of capabilities, but in the lack of convergence of interests in the UNSC and among member states that are able to take part in military interventions. In 2013, eastern Congolese fighters, who had been integrated into the *Forces Armées de la République Démocratique du Congo* (FARDC) but felt betrayed, withdrew from their units, launched a rebellion, formed the M 23 movement and, in November 2013, sieged Goma, the largest city of the region at the border with Rwanda. The FARDC escaped, leaving the civilian population

---

42 Johansen, R. C. (2006) (ed.). 'A United Nations Emergency Peace Service To Prevent Genocide And Crimes Against Humanity.' Online at: https://www.opendemocracy.net/opensecurity/h-peter-langille/un-emergency-peace-service.

at the mercy of the rebels, who are widely regarded as Rwandan proxy forces that fulfil a twofold task in eastern Congo: they secure access to scarce primary resources and check the remainders of Hutu militias (Forces démocratiques de libération du Rwanda, FDLR) which had fled in 1994 and threaten the security of the Rwandan borderland from their strongholds in Eastern Congo. Faced with the crisis around Goma, the UNSC passed resolution 2098/2013 and subsequently 2147/2014. Especially the latter is important here, as it provides an extraordinarily robust mandate for MONUSCO, which urges MONUSCO to neutralize "armed groups through the Intervention brigade [...] either unilaterally or jointly with the FARDC, in a robust, highly mobile and versatile manner and in strict compliance with international law [...] prevent the expansion of all armed groups, neutralize these groups, and disarm them in order to contribute to the objective of reducing the threat posed by armed groups to state authority and civilian security in eastern DRC and to make space for stabilization activities."[43]

Supported by a strong and well-equipped South African detachment which had relatively modern tanks and combat helicopters at its disposal, the United Nations Intervention Force Brigade drove the M 23 rebels away from Goma throught the Eastern Congolese jungle to the Ugandan border, forcing them to surrender unconditionally. It is worth mentioning that MONUSCO's new mandate also included the disarmament of other militias, including the FDLR, which had often been supported by the FARDC against M 23 [44]and other proxy forces, supported by DRC's neighbours. The M 23 campaign is widely regarded as a successful UN-led peace-making intervention, was possible because there were no major divisions in the UNSC, which was able to give MONUSCO a robust mandate, enabling the Blue Helmets not only (as had been the case in Rwanda and Bosnia) to shoot in self-defence, but in order to achieve and enforce the UNSC's objectives. But it would have failed without the strong commitment of the participating UN member countries South Africa, Tanzania, and Malawi.

The campaign strained bilateral relations between South Africa and Rwanda and triggered domestic problems for the South African government, which struggled to

---

43 UNSC Res. 2147, online at: http://www.un.org/en/ga/search/view_doc.asp?symbol=S/RES/2147%282014%29.

44 M 23 was a rebellious faction of the Congolese Army in the Eastern part of the DRC (bordering with Rwanda), supported by Rwanda, which left the armed forces in protest against the alleged violation of the peace treaty between the Congolese Government and the National Congress for the Defense of the People (signed on March 23, 2009). It then created a militia in the territory around Goma. See also Allan Ngari's chapter about the Great Lakes in this book.

justify why South African soldiers risked their life in such a distant country where no South African interests seemed to be at stake.[45]

Early preventive measures are less expensive, less risky, less time-consuming, and less drastic than military intervention. Despite an awareness of these facts, and despite all past efforts, so far no coherent United Nations system of prevention has been established that would be effective in addressing situations where the risk of mass crimes is imminent.

The notion of the duty to prevent, adopted by the United Nations only in 2005, is relatively young and not yet clearly defined by the Security Council, the General Assembly, and the Secretary-General. The above-listed instruments, at the disposal of the United Nations offer no guarantee of fast and effective action. But the latter does not only depend on a smooth information management that makes sure that the most relevant information reaches the most important stakeholders and institutions, but first and foremost on whether preventive action is congruent with the foreign policy preferences and the domestic interest of those governments that are able to intervene efficiently. Swift and precise early warning is a precondition for prevention, but it will not trigger action if action meets resistance among the permanent UNSC members or if it is contrary to the interest of those who are able to carry out the necessary action. In other words, the UN and its members have to be well-informed about where, when, and what should be prevented, but they also need to be able and willing to prevent.

45 Among foreign policy experts in South Africa, there were rumours pointing to South African interests in the Congolese mining sector that allegedly explained the South African Defense Force's engagement better than humanitarian concerns invoked by diplomats and ministers.

Dorota Heidrich

Responsibility to Protect – An (In)effective Tool for Atrocity Crimes Prevention?

One of the most significant challenges for the international community in over two decades with regard to Human Rights protection and humanitarian issues has been mass atrocity crimes prevention. It is to this purpose that the concept of "Responsibility to Protect" (R2P) was devised.[1] It is rooted in the endeavours to find the right way of reacting to heinous international crimes and – more generally – systematic abuses of Human Rights both in times of peace and during violent conflicts. The issue became especially important after the numerous failures of the international community to avert and halt horrific events in a series of crises around the world during 1990s. There is a stark contrast between the reluctance of the international community to take action in Rwanda 1994 and Srebrenica 1995 on the one hand, and the intervention in Kosovo 1999 and Libya 2011. In all these cases, there was no clear pattern which would have allowed to reconcile the principle of sovereignty with the protection of civilians. As Kofi Annan put it: "If humanitarian intervention is, indeed, an unacceptable assault on sovereignty, how should we respond to a Rwanda, to a Srebrenica – to gross and systematic violations of Human Rights that offend every precept of our common humanity?"[2] In its report of 2000, the International Independent Commission on Kosovo left no doubts that "experience from the NATO intervention in Kosovo suggests the need to close the gap between legality and legitimacy. The Commission believes that the time is now ripe for the presentation of a principled framework for humanitarian intervention which could be used to guide future

---

1 Since the inception of the term as defined in the report *Responsibility to Protect* (ICISS, 2001), the literature explaining R2P's nature and contents has become abundant. The scope of the present analysis is not to repeat what has already been published but rather to concentrate on the analysis of its preventive elements (or as it is called – the first pillar of R2P) both in terms of theory and practice.

2 Annan, K. (2000). *We the Peoples. The Role of the United Nations in the 21st Century.* New York: United Nations, p. 48, online at: http://www.unmillenniumproject.org/documents/wethepeople.pdf.

responses to imminent humanitarian catastrophes and which could be used to assess claims for humanitarian intervention."[3]

In reply to that call, the foreign minister of Canada declared in September 2000 that his government would fund the International Commission on Intervention and State Sovereignty (ICISS), mandated with preparing a report on how to reconcile Human Rights with state sovereignty and non-interference and on whether at all the international community could move on from the rigid interpretation of the UN Charter's provisions about the use of force. The Commission's report entitled *Responsibility to Protect* was published in December 2001.[4]

How much has been done since the release of the ICISS report? Have its recommendations been implemented? At the time of writing, the IRIN agency informed at the beginning of 2015, even though there were over ten thousand troops deployed throughout the Central African Republic, 1.5 million people faced insecurity, 2.7 million were in need of immediate humanitarian assistance.[5] The total number of civilians killed in the fighting between Seleka and Anti-Balaka rebels remains unknown, but there are over four hundred thousand IDPs.[6]

Alarming news and information have been published about the situation in Syria. According to the United Nations Office for the Coordination of Humanitarian Affairs (OCHA), the conflict has claimed 191,369 casualties; 12.2 million people are in need of humanitarian assistance (4.6 million in besieged or remote areas) and 7.6 million have been internally displaced.[7]

Another place where the international community is incapable of protecting the civilian population is the territory controlled by the so-called Islamic State,[8] whose authorities do not abide even by the most basic humanitarian standards.

---

3 International Independent Commission on Kosovo (2000), *The Kosovo Report. Conflict. International Response. Lessons learned.* Oxford: Oxford University Press, p. 10, online at: http://reliefweb.int/sites/reliefweb.int/files/resources/6D26FF88119644CFC1256989005CD392-thekosovoreport.pdf.

4 International Commission on Intervention and State Sovereignty (2012). *The Responsibility to Protect.* Ottawa: IDRC, online at: www.iciss.ca/pdf/Commission-Report.pdf.

5 IRIN (2015). *CAR data – a crisis in numbers.* Online at: http://www.irinnews.org/report/100994/car-data-a-crisis-in-numbers.

6 IRIN (2015).

7 UNOCHA (2015). Online at: http://syria.unocha.org. For evidence about mass atrocities see also: The Independent International Commission of Inquiry on the Syrian Arab Republic, online at: http://www.ohchr.org/EN/HRBodies/HRC/IICISyria/Pages/IndependentInternationalCommission.aspx.

8 Islamic State is also known under the name of the Islamic State of Iraq and Syria/ash-Sham (ISIS) or Islamic State of Iraq and the Levant (ISIL).

The civilian population is targeted indiscriminately; religious, national and ethnic groups are being persecuted. As the Washington Director of Human Rights Watch, Sarah Margon, has put it: the Islamic State's "campaign of killings is remarkably gruesome – they hide nothing, promote their atrocities via social media, and make clear they don't subscribe to the same norms, values, laws, and standards that serve to guide the international community. Instead, ISIS employs an overt strategy of cruelty to sow fear and subdue populations under its control, bolstered by tactics that seem to be a throwback, if you will, to another era."[9] It is estimated that more than five hundred thousand Yazidis and other religious minorities have been driven from their homes.[10] The genocide label has been appearing in the speeches made by both UN officials and world leaders.[11]

Elsewhere, the civilian population of the eastern parts of Ukraine has been under serious direct or indirect military pressure. The Ukrainian government lodged a declaration to the Registrar of the International Criminal Court (ICC) accepting

---

9 Human Rights Watch (2014). 'ISIL's Reign of Terror: Confronting the Growing Humanitarian Crisis in Iraq and Syria', Testimony of Sarah Margon. Senate Foreign Relations Committee, December 9, 2014, online at: http://www.hrw.org/news/2014/12/09/isil-s-reign-terror-confronting-growing-humanitarian-crisis-iraq-and-syria-testimony.

10 Human Rights Watch (2014).

11 United Nations Assistant Secretary-General for Human Rights, Mr. Ivan Šimonović speaking of ISIL crimes against the Yazidis population: http://www.ohchr.org/EN/NewYork/Stories/Pages/IvanSimonovicvisittoIraq.aspx#sthash.1LUwd5zO.dpufhttp://www.ohchr.org/EN/NewYork/Stories/Pages/IvanSimonovicvisittoIraq.aspx; President Barack Obama announcing his decision to authorize airstrikes against the ISIL troops: http://www.whitehouse.gov/the-press-office/2014/08/07/statement-president and speaking of ISIL that is responsible for the killing of Jim Foley: http://www.whitehouse.gov/the-press-office/2014/08/20/statement-president; Secretary of State John Kerry on "warning signs of genocide" against the Yazidis: http://news.sky.com/story/1315089/isis-violence-all-warning-signs-of-genocide or Kurdish leaders speaking in similar words about the persecutions against the Yazidis: http://www.smh.com.au/national/kurdish-leader-calls-for-action-to-prevent-imminent-genocide-20141007-10rje3.html. For more on crimes committed by ISIL see also: *Report on the Protection of Civilians in the Non International Armed Conflict in Iraq: 5 June – 5 July 2014*, OHCHR, UNAMI Human Rights Office, online at: http://www.ohchr.org/Documents/Countries/IQ/UNAMI_OHCHR_POC%20Report_FINAL_18July2014A.pdf; *Report of the Office of the United Nations High Commissioner for Human Rights on the Human Rights situation in Iraq in the light of abuses committed by the so-called Islamic State in Iraq and the Levant and associated groups*, Human Rights Council, March 13, 2015, A/HCR/28/18, online at: http://www.ohchr.org/EN/HRBodies/HRC/SpecialSessions/Session22/Pages/22ndtSpecialSession.aspx.

ICC jurisdiction over alleged crimes committed on its territory from November 21, 2013 to February 22, 2014.[12] However, this self-referral excludes events taking place in the area where military and paramilitary activities are on-going (eastern Ukraine). Another self-referral (Crimea and parts of eastern Ukraine) is currently being discussed in Kiev.[13]

Considering the above examples of recent serious Human Rights abuses which in some of the cases have already or may have already led to the commission of crimes, one needs to pose the question whether, and if at all – to what extent, R2P can be regarded as an effective tool of crimes prevention. In order to reply, it is first of all necessary to analyse the scope, content and character of R2P, then to see what preventive mechanisms are offered within the concept and – last but not least – whether at this point it has been possible to operationalize the preventive elements of R2P.

The Content of R2P and its Legal Character

The ICISS 2001 report's findings are based on the idea of "sovereignty as responsibility", whose roots are most often associated with a Sudanese diplomat, senior fellow at the Brookings Institution and former high UN official, Francis M. Deng. In 1996, Deng co-edited a book entitled *Sovereignty as Responsibility. Conflict*

---

12 Kamiński, Ireneusz C. (2014). 'International Law Aspects of the situation in Ukraine.' In: Bachmann, K., Lyubashenko, I. (2014) (eds). *The Maidan Uprising, Separatism and Foreign Intervention. Ukraine's complex transition*. Frankfurt/M.: Peter Lang Int., pp. 379–404 and Bachmann, K. (2014). 'The Challenges: Political and Economic Transition.' In: Bachmann & Lyubashenko (2014), pp. 405–442.

13 Radio Svoboda (2015). Україна звернеться до «Гаазького трибуналу» щодо злочинів проти людяності на Донбасі, January 15, 2015, online at: http://www.radiosvoboda.org/content/article/26812424.html; see also: 'Voice of America 2015). 'Ukraine wants ICC to probe crimes in Crimea, East.' *The Voice of America*, online at: http://www.voanews.com/content/reu-ukraine-icc-crimea-russia/2723651.html. Ukraine's foreign minister Pavlo Klimkin noted: "We are quite optimistic about more, definitely more, engagement [on the part] of the ICC" and an ICC referral would cover "everything under the [ICC] mandate, including crimes against humanity". Klimkin, speaking of the attack on the strategic port of Mariupol in eastern Ukraine, which killed 30 in January, said that "[t]he shelling killed, in seconds, more than 30 people and heavily wounded 100 people. (…) If you deliberately shell and, I stress, deliberately shell cities, killing civilians, it's a completely different situation (compared to military operations) and we have to engage the ICC".

Management in Africa.[14] Focusing on Africa, the authors of the volume introduced and explained the concept of 'sovereignty as responsibility', according to which sovereign states have a duty to protect their own citizens as they take primary responsibility for them. Moreover, states must not act in whatever way they wish to and expect the international community to refrain from criticism. The erosion of sovereignty in favour of Human Rights protection and humanitarian intervention was more than obvious to the authors of *Sovereignty as Responsibility.*[15] At the same time, they expected states to remain responsible and to be held accountable for the consequences of their policies.[16] However, when people are oppressed, their intrinsic power to hold their governments accountable becomes very limited, and the international community, as the ultimate guarantor of universal standards, needs to act.[17] "It [the international community – DH] has a corresponding responsibility to provide innocent victims of internal conflicts and gross violations of Human Rights with essential protection and assistance."[18] The authors of the volume did not present a brand new approach towards sovereignty.[19] It is worth mentioning that more than a year before the book was published, the Commission on Global Governance presented its findings in the report *Our Global Neighbourhood* (1995), in which it clearly stated that the Westphalian way of understanding state sovereignty had become out-dated and that the power of the sovereign was limited when human security issues were being negatively impacted.[20] Closely reading Boutros Boutros Ghali's *Agenda for Peace* (1992), one can detect a similar idea. Talking about how to bring peace to nations large and small, the former Secretary-General observed: "The time of absolute and exclusive sovereignty (...) has passed; its theory was never matched by reality. It is the task of leaders of States

14 Deng, F. M., Kimaro, S., Lyons, T., Rothchild, D. and Zartman, I. W. (1996). *Sovereignty as Responsibility. Conflict Management in Africa.* Washington, D.C.: The Brookings Institution.

15 Deng, Kimaro, Lyons, Rotchild and Zartman (1996), xv.

16 Deng, Kimaro, Lyons, Rotchild and Zartman (1996), xii.

17 Deng, Kimaro, Lyons, Rotchild and Zartman (1996), xiii.

18 Deng, Kimaro, Lyons, Rotchild and Zartman (1996), xiii.

19 The idea of responsibility of a sovereign for the population was discussed in Thomas Hobbes', John Locke's and Jean-Jacques Rousseau's works. See: Martin, S. (2011). 'Sovereignty and the Responsibility to Protect'. *Griffith Law Review*, 20, no. 1, and Glanville L. (2011). 'On the Meaning of "Responsibility". In: 'The Responsibility to Protect'. *Griffith Law Review* 20, no. 2, pp. 447–69.

20 Report of the Commission on Global Governance (1995). *Our Global Neighbourhood.* Oxford: Oxford University Press.

today to understand this and to find a balance between the needs of good internal governance and the requirements of an ever more interdependent world."[21]

All these ideas formed the basis for the final analyses presented in the 2001 ICISS Report. It claims that the understanding of sovereignty must shift from sovereignty as control to sovereignty as responsibility. Furthermore, state sovereignty implies states' primary responsibility for the protection of their people. Lastly, "where a population is suffering serious harm, as a result of internal war, insurgency, repression or state failure, and the state in question is unwilling or unable to halt or avert it, the principle of non-intervention yields to the international responsibility to protect."[22] R2P, according to the report, does not equal humanitarian intervention,[23] the latter being defined as "action [most often of a military character – DH] taken against a state or its leaders, without its or their consent, for purposes which are claimed to be humanitarian or protective.[24]" According to the authors of the report, the simple fact of changing the language used to describe military action for humanitarian purposes may help forge negative associations. R2P is much broader than humanitarian intervention; not only does it encompass direct reactions to gross violations of Human Rights (where the last resort would be the use of military force), but it covers a whole range of activities under the so-called three pillars of R2P, i.e. the responsibility to prevent, the responsibility to react, and the responsibility to rebuild. The first element/pillar (responsibility to prevent) will be of special interest to the present analysis.

The responsibility to prevent mechanism is supposed "to address both the root causes and direct causes of internal conflict and other man-made crises putting populations at risk."[25] It is quite clear that this part of R2P is of primary importance. If prevention works, there are no further steps necessary; neither turning to responsibility to react, nor moving into the direction of responsibility to rebuild. Had there been effective prevention in the former Yugoslavia, Rwanda, Sierra Leone, and other places struck by mass violations of Human Rights, no crimes would have been committed. At the same time, prevention is one of the most challenging tasks. It is difficult to test the universal effectiveness of preventive measures once they are in force. Any improvements may come only after the testing phase, when

21 Report of the Secretary-General (1992). *An Agenda for Peace. Preventive diplomacy, peace-making and peace-keeping*, A/47/277 – S/24111.

22 ICISS, *The Responsibility to Protect*, xi.

23 The authors of the report purposely use the term intervention for human protection purposes instead of humanitarian intervention.

24 ICISS, *The Responsibility to Protect*, 8.

25 ICISS, *The Responsibility to Protect*, 7.

some elements appear imperfect.[26] However, the more energy and resources are invested in prevention efforts, the more probable it becomes to avoid situations which amount to mass atrocity crimes. An effective strategy for mass atrocity crimes prevention must be a set of flexible mechanisms that can quickly be adapted to various situations; the general capacity for prevention already exists, however it is based on mechanisms and institutions which were established long ago. A well-functioning preventive architecture requires the existence of an early warning system that provides access to information and data, the analysis of which triggers alarms, which in turn lead to action. However, effectiveness of a preventive strategy to a large extent depends on one more factor – political will, which does not result from mere moral or legal obligations, but rather from states' interests.[27] The lack of political will can hamper or impede any preventive strategy, even the most perfect one. As Jennifer Welsh and Serena Sharma put it, the commitment to prevention within the R2P context has so far been rather rhetorical.[28] As it will be argued further on, the current R2P architecture will not be enough to lead to effective prevention.

Understanding the legal character of R2P seems to be crucial as this is what, at least to a certain extent, determines its effectiveness. The ICISS report characterized R2P as *a guiding principle for the international community of states,*[29] *the foundations of which lay in* "obligations inherent in the concept of sovereignty; the responsibility of the Security Council, under Article 24 of the UN Charter, for the maintenance of international peace and security; specific legal obligations under Human Rights and human protection declarations, covenants and treaties, international humanitarian law and national law; the developing practice of states, regional organizations and the Security Council itself."[30]

The Report of the Secretary-General's High Level Panel on Threats, Challenges and Change (*A More Secure World: Our Shared Responsibility*, 2004) endorsed

---

26 More about the issue of prevention and the inherent paradox of prevention can be found in Agnieszka Bieńczyk-Missala's chapter in this book.

27 The role state preferences and interests (also the preference structure of domestic politics) and the importance of UN members ability and readiness to participate in interventions is dealt with in Angieszka Bieńczyk-Missala's chapter in this book, too.

28 Welsh, J. M., Sharma, S. K. (2012). 'Operationalizing the Responsibility to Prevent.' *Oxford Institute for Ethics, Law and Armed Conflict Policy Brief.*

29 ICISS, *The Responsibility to Protect*, xi.

30 ICISS, *The Responsibility to Protect*, p. xi.

R2P as "an emerging norm."[31] And finally, the UN Summit Outcome Document of 2005 confirmed its significance by quoting the R2P concept in the paragraphs 138 and 139.[32]

Regardless of these facts, the concept has not become a legally binding norm as of yet, however it has been regarded as a universally appreciated concept, as representatives of 191 nations approved the 2005 Outcome Document.[33]

---

31 Report of the Secretary-General's High-level Panel on Threats, Challenges and Change (2004), *A More Secure World: Our Shared Responsibility.* New York: United Nations, para. 202–203.

32 The two paragraphs read: "138. Each individual State has the responsibility to protect its populations from genocide, war crimes, ethnic cleansing and crimes against humanity. This responsibility entails the prevention of such crimes, including their incitement, through appropriate and necessary means. We accept that responsibility and will act in accordance with it. The international community should, as appropriate, encourage and help States to exercise this responsibility and support the United Nations in establishing an early warning capability. 139. The international community, through the United Nations, also has the responsibility to use appropriate diplomatic, humanitarian and other peaceful means, in accordance with Chapters VI and VIII of the Charter, to help protect populations from genocide, war crimes, ethnic cleansing and crimes against humanity. In this context, we are prepared to take collective action, in a timely and decisive manner, through the Security Council, in accordance with the Charter, including Chapter VII, on a case-by-case basis and in cooperation with relevant regional organizations as appropriate, should peaceful means be inadequate and national authorities manifestly fail to protect their populations from genocide, war crimes, ethnic cleansing and crimes against humanity. We stress the need for the General Assembly to continue consideration of the responsibility to protect populations from genocide, war crimes, ethnic cleansing and crimes against humanity and its implications, bearing in mind the principles of the Charter and international law. We also intend to commit ourselves, as necessary and appropriate, to helping States build capacity to protect their populations from genocide, war crimes, ethnic cleansing and crimes against humanity and to assisting those which are under stress before crises and conflicts break out." See: *2005 World Summit Outcome Document*, UN Doc. A/RES/60/1, online at: http://www.un.org/womenwatch/ods/A-RES-60-1-E.pdf.

33 For more on understanding the concept of R2P and its legal character, see for example: Anne Orford, A. (2011). *International Authority and the Responsibility to Protect.* Cambridge: Cambridge University Press; and Stahn, C. (2007). 'Responsibility to Protect: Political Rhetoric or Emerging Legal Norm?' *The American Journal of International Law* 101/1, pp. 99–120.

The document limited the scope of R2P to genocide, crimes against humanity, war crimes and ethnic cleansing,[34] and emphasized that each state was obliged to protect their populations from such crimes. Paragraph 138 stressed UN members' acceptance of the responsibility to protect populations from atrocity crimes, which entailed "the prevention of such crimes, including their incitement."

Even though the document spoke about the responsibility of the international community to take collective action to protect endangered populations "in a timely and decisive manner", which ought to be invoked when states fail to live up to their responsibility to protect, the wording of the two paragraphs was a slight disappointment, to say the least, for the supporters of R2P. The UN members failed to solve the principal issue concerning R2P's application, namely who should respond to the commission of atrocity crimes if the Security Council is unable to act (e.g., when blocked by one of its veto powers) and whether the international community bears a legal duty to react to states' deliberate action or acts of omission.

What was interesting in course of the debate about the Outcome Document's paragraphs 138 and 139, not all actors deeply devoted to the protection of and assistance to vulnerable populations and atrocity crimes victims were satisfied with the endorsement of R2P by the UN Summit. The core argument was that the document lacked any detailed directions on how the enforcement element entailed in R2P should be implemented. Some of them opposed any mention of the possibility of imposing military measures for humanitarian protection purposes. One of the principal humanitarian NGOs, *Médecins sans Frontières* (MSF), opted against the concept, especially its coercive element.[35]

The concept of Responsibility to Protect was later developed and clarified by numerous documents, debates and results of academic research. Among these there are six reports of the Secretary-General followed by informal debates in the General Assembly as well as other documents of the UN's organs.[36]

---

34 For the analysis of the atrocity crimes definition see: *Framework of Analysis for Atrocity Crimes. A tool for prevention.* United Nations 2014, online at: http://www.un.org/en/preventgenocide/adviser/pdf/framework%20of%20analysis%20for%20atrocity%20crimes_en.pdf.

35 For more on MSF position, see: Weissman, F. (2010). "'Not In Our Name": Why Médecins Sans Frontières Does Not Support the "Responsibility to Protect". *Criminal Justice Ethics*, vol. 29, no. 2.

36 A comprehensive set of core documents on R2P can be found on the web page of the International Coalition for the Responsibility to Protect (http://www.responsibilitytoprotect.org)

The very fact that the Outcome Document mentioned R2P as a concept raised hopes that it would soon become an international customary norm. Today, little of that optimism remains, especially after the concept was invoked by the UNSC in order to justify the military intervention in Libya in 2011,[37] which went far beyond humanitarian objectives.[38] Currently, the necessary elements of a customary international norm (*opinio iuris sive necessitatis* and state practice) are still lacking.[39] It is uncertain whether this would improve if R2P became legally binding. As Alex Bellamy observed: "R2P's principal role has been to contribute to the establishment of habits of protection among UN member states, through the aligning of protection goals with state interests and identities, and, through that, to influence changes in the international context surrounding the commission of genocide and mass atrocities. In this capacity, R2P helps influence the extent to which calls for action might be translated into positive action, by increasing the likelihood not only that there will be such calls, but also that they will resonate among actors who accept that they have a responsibility to protect foreign populations when they can."[40.]

To some extent, standards, informal codes of conduct or moral obligations in the international community may prove more effective than strict legal norms, especially when the lack of political consensus around new international norms

---

37 Resolution 1973 (2011) adopted by the Security Council at its 6498th meeting, on March 17, 2011, S/RES/1973 (2011), http://www.un.org/en/ga/search/view_doc.asp?symbol=S/RES/1973(2011). The resolution reiterated "the responsibility of the Libyan authorities to protect the Libyan population and reaffirming that parties to armed conflicts bear the primary responsibility to take all feasible steps to ensure the protection of civilians…"

38 About the impact of the intervention in Libya on the discussion about R2P see for example: Bellamy, A. J. (2014). 'From Tripoli to Damascus? Lesson learning and the implementation of the Responsibility to Protect'. *International Politics,* 51, no. 1.

39 For more on the theoretical debate on how the legal character of R2P can be evaluated see: Serrano, M. and Weiss, T. G. (2014) (eds). *The international Politics of Human Rights. Rallying to the R2P cause?* London, New York: Routledge, pp. 14–17 (e-book); and Shawki, N. (2011). 'Responsibility to Protect: The Evolution of an International Norm'. *Global Responsibility to Protect*, 3, no. 2.

40 Bellamy, A. J. (2013). 'The Responsibility to Protect: Added value or hot air?' *Cooperation and Conflict* 48/3, p. 352. A similar opinion was expressed by Edward Luck, who said: "The responsibility to protect is, in many ways, a political project. It will make a difference to the extent that it reflects-and is perceived to reflect- popular sentiments and values, across societies, borders, and regions." Luck, E. (2001). 'The Responsibility to Protect: The First Decade'. *Global Responsibility to Protect* no. 3, p. 7.

renders their implementation simply impossible, or when states' leaders prefer to tacitly abide by standards or codes of conduct rather than be bound by international legal norms.[41] What requires emphasis here is that the core idea of R2P, which is the protection of populations from genocide, crimes against humanity, war crimes, and ethnic cleansing, is "founded upon international legal obligations under Human Rights and human protection declarations, covenants and treaties, international humanitarian and refugee law and national laws that set forth standards of conduct and the means to enforce these standards."[42] Therefore, the issue whether these crimes are punishable under international norms is by no means problematic. Neither is the responsibility of states for protection of individuals under their jurisdiction from these acts.[43]

41 On of the best examples that may be given here is the process of evolution of standards and norms on internally displaced persons (IDPs) protection. *Guiding Principles on Internal Displacement* were put together by a team led by Francis M. Deng in 1998. Today, the notion of IDPs is known to systems of national law of many states (to mention just a few: Angola, Burundi, Colombia, Serbia, Bosnia and Herzegovina, Iraq, or Sierra Leone) as well as to an African Union Convention for the Protection and Assistance of IDPs (2009) and to the Protocol on the Protection and Assistance to Internally Displaced Persons of the International Conference on the Great Lakes Region, which forms part of the Pact on Security, Stability and Development in the Great Lakes Region signed in 2006. The scope here is not to analyse the effectiveness of legal instruments for IDPs protection, but IDPs regulations example is rather used to show how non-binding standards may be transformed to legal regulations. As Erin Mooney observed, "[w]hile R2P and the Guiding Principles [on IDPs] are not binding on states, in a strict legal sense, they are based on existing law that is binding. That they both articulate pre-existing norms in no way diminishes their normative value. To the contrary, it is one of their strengths; the experience in promoting the Guiding Principles attests that this can be tremendously useful towards securing states' acceptance and, ultimately, application of these standards". Mooney, E. D. (2010). 'Something Old, Something New, Something Borrowed … Something Blue? The Protection Potential of a Marriage of Concepts between R2P and IDP Protection'. *Global Responsibility to protect* 2, no. 1–2, p. 69.

42 *A toolkit on the Responsibility to Protect*, ICR2P, http://responsibilitytoprotect.org/ICR2P%20Toolkit%20on%20the%20Responsibility%20to%20Protect%20high%20res.pdf.

43 That attitude of UN members is evident from how they spoke about R2P during the informal debates in the UN General Assembly, available both on UN websites and on the web page of the International Coalition for the Responsibility to Protect (http://www.responsibilitytoprotect.org).

The most debatable part of the R2P concept, as indicated before, is the responsibility of the international community, not only with regard to **what** the international community is responsible for, but also **whom** it is responsible **to** and **to whom** it is accountable for not fulfilling the inherent responsibility.[44] These questions will evidently be subject to further debates and analyses.

For the purpose of this chapter, the key issue is whether the non-binding standards can at all be effective, even if they do not impose legal obligations on states. Would making R2P normative enhance its implementation? As Aidan Hehir observed, "R2P's entire utility is predicated […] on its normative power to mobilize political will."[45] This has been supported by Francis M. Deng who wrote: "perhaps there's nothing new here… It's almost a restatement of resolve and perhaps a rearrangement of our tools or a mobilization of the relevant tools and relevant actors, to be alert to what needs to be done and to be mobilized to do it."[46]

The Preventive Toolbox Offered by R2P

The ICISS report, proposing three significant elements of prevention (early-warning system, preventive toolbox, and political will) offered interesting proposals on the composition of the preventive toolbox in which two groups of tools were mentioned – those which may be used in the so-called "root cause prevention" and those that deal with "direct prevention."

"Root cause prevention" was closely linked to ideas that have for a long time been present within the debate on conflict prevention strategies. However, as the UN Secretary-General observed in his 2013 report on state responsibility and prevention, "conflict prevention and atrocity prevention are closely related but they are not synonymous. Focusing exclusively on conflict prevention would overlook atrocity crimes that occur outside of armed conflict or that are not necessarily related to armed conflict[47]. Therefore, it cannot be assumed that efforts to prevent or resolve conflict will simultaneously reduce the likelihood of mass atrocity crimes.[48] As Jennifer Welsh and Serena Sharma, pointing to differences between conflict prevention strategies and crimes prevention patterns, noted:

44 This draws on Luke Glanville's argumentation presented in: Glanville (2011), passim.

45 Hehir (2011), 1339.

46 Aiden Hehir's interview with Francis Deng, New York, August 20, 2009; quoted in Behir (2011), 1339.

47 Report of the Secretary-General (2013). *Responsibility to Protect: State Responsibility and Prevention,* UN Doc. A/67/929–S/2013/399, paragraphs 12–13.

48 Welsh & Sharma (2012).

- the large majority of episodes of mass killing since 1945 occurred within the context of armed conflict, while a third of the cases did not;
- only one out of every ten reported civilian deaths occurred in the context of armed conflict, with the majority of deaths taking place outside of official combat zones;
- even if mass atrocities happen during an armed conflict, they often have no direct link to the causes of the conflict or its conduct;
- preventing conflicts require limitations to the use of force while preventing mass atrocity crimes may require military means;
- mass atrocity crimes are prohibited by international law while armed conflict is regulated by the ius in bello norms.[49]

With these arguments in mind, the root cause prevention tools offered by the ICISS report remain a valuable idea.

"Direct prevention" is composed of instruments that reflect "the shorter time available in which to make difference." Each of the proposed tools, which ought to be understood as actions and measures that aim to "make it absolutely unnecessary to employ directly coercive measures against the state concerned", may take various forms: "straightforward assistance, positive inducements or, in more difficult cases, the negative form of threatened punishment."

Root cause and direct prevention tools are presented in the table below.

Table 9: Responsibility to prevent – preventive toolbox

Root cause prevention tools	Direct prevention tools
I. *Addressing **political** needs and deficiencies, for example:*	1. ***political and diplomatic**, for example:* *POSITIVE INDUCEMENTS*
1. Democratic institutions and capacity building;	• fact-finding;
2. Constitutional power sharing;	• friends groups
3. Power altering and redistribution arrangements;	• eminent persons commissions • dialogue and mediation through good offices
4. Confidence building measures between different groups and communities;	• international appeals • non-official dialogue
5. Support for freedom of press and the rule of law;	• problem-solving workshops *NEGATIVE INDUCEMENTS*
6. Promotion of civil society;	• political sanctions
7. Other types of initiatives that fit in the human security framework.	• diplomatic isolation

49 Welsh & Sharma (2012).

Root cause prevention tools	Direct prevention tools
II. *tackling* ***economic*** *deprivation and poverty, for example:* 1. development of assistance projects; 2. even distribution of resources; 3. promotion of economic growth and opportunity; 4. better terms of trade for developing countries; 5. encouragement of economic and structural reform; 6. technical assistance for strengthening regulatory mechanisms. III. *strengthening* ***legal*** *protection and institutions, for example:* • strengthening the rule of law; • protection of integrity and independence of the judiciary; • fair law enforcement; • protection od vulnerable groups; • support to local institutions; • Human Rights advancement. IV. *reforms of the* ***military*** *and other security services, for example:* • education and training for military forces; • reintegration of ex-combatants; • strengthening civilian control mechanisms; • accountability of security services; • adherence to arms control, disarmament and non-proliferation regimes.	• suspension in international organizations • travel and asset restrictions on targeted persons • application of "naming and shaming" technique 2. ***economic****, for example:* *POSITIVE INDUCEMENTS* • promises of new funding, investment • wise development and humanitarian assistance *NEGATIVE INDUCEMENTS* • threats of economic and financial sanctions • withdrawal of investment • curtailment of aid [these can have both bilateral and multilateral character] 3. ***legal****, for example:* • offers of mediation, arbitration, adjudication • deployment of Human Rights monitors • establishment of criminal tribunals [or at present – a threat of turning to ICC (referral by a state party, Security Council or by the decision of the Prosecutor), should national institutions be unwilling of unable to prosecute – DH] • application of universal jurisdiction over crimes prohibited by treaties such as the 1949 Geneva Conventions and 1977 Additional Protocols, 1984 Convention Against Torture, 1948 Convention on the Prevention and Suppression of the Crime of Genocide, etc. 4. ***military****, for example:* • consensual preventive deployment of international military forces

Source: ICISS, *The Responsibility to Protect*, p. 19.

The ICISS report, besides proposing the preventive toolbox, noted that there exist serious challenges in regards to effectiveness of prevention, "including: the inherent intrusive character of certain preventive strategies, the lack of funds available for preventive efforts, the dangers exacerbating domestic tensions through increased international involvement, and the difficulty of mobilizing political will before a crisis becomes apparent."[50] These impediments are addressed in the 2013 UN Secretary-General report on *Responsibility to Protect: State Responsibility and Prevention*. Ban Ki-moon puts emphasis on the mobilization of political will as a key factor in prevention: "First and foremost, political will and leadership are required to translate that commitment into practice. It is sometimes difficult to demonstrate the added value of prevention, particularly early preventive action, which may not have immediate, visible outcomes. While such action is most likely to save lives and is less costly and contentious than action taken at a later stage, it can be challenging to secure the political support and resources required to undertake it."[51]

The report, stressing the significance of prevention, proposed concentrating on "developing the necessary national capacity to build societies resilient to atrocity crimes."[52] It is important to identify the so-called risk factors and to mobilize national institutions and the international community to work out effective preventive tools. As Ban Ki-moon has said, prevention "does not mean looking the other way in times of crisis, vainly hoping that things will get better. We have done that too often. Nor can it be just a brief pause while Chapter VII 'enforcement measures' are being prepared. (…) Prevention means proactive, decisive and early action to stop violence before it begins."[53]

The 2013 report devotes space to early warning strategies by proposing to understand and address possible risk factors associated with the commission of atrocity crimes.[54] Even though it is not always possible to draw a direct causal

---

50 Welsh & Sharma (2012).

51 *Responsibility to Protect: State Responsibility and Prevention*, para. 66.

52 Overview of the United Nations Secretary-General Ban Ki-moon's Report on the Responsibility to Protect: *State Responsibility and Prevention,* online at: http://responsibilitytoprotect.org/ICR2P%20Summary%20of%20UNSG%20Report%202013.pdf.

53 Ki-moon, B. (2012). *Address to the Stanley Foundation Conference on Responsibility to Protect, New York, January 18, 2012,* online at: http://www.un.org/apps/news/infocus/sgspeeches/statments_full.asp?statID=1433#.VP9xOMayhSU.

54 This has been elaborated in UN (2014). *Framework of Analysis for Atrocity Crimes. A tool for prevention.* United Nations 2014, online at: http://www.un.org/en/preventgenocide/adviser/pdf/framework%20of%20analysis%20for%20atrocity%20crimes_en.pdf.

relation between the presence of particular risk factors and the occurrence of atrocity crimes, these acts rarely appear in the absence of all or most of the risk factors. This concept has been developed in the UN *Framework of Analysis for Atrocity Crimes.* There are fourteen risk factors presented, eight of them common to all four atrocity crimes and the remaining six characteristic of a specific crime.[55] The framework defines risk factors as "conditions that increase the risk of or susceptibility to negative outcomes."[56] The list is to help "identify warning signs or indicators" informing that crimes might occur.[57] As the authors of the framework point out, "if we understand the root causes and precursors of these crimes, and can identify risk factors that can lead to or enable their commission, it follows that we can also identify measures that can be taken by States and the international community to prevent these crimes." While the framework concentrates on creating a pattern of analysis of possible threats of commission of crimes, the 2013 Secretary-General report attempted to offer policy options for atrocity prevention which are: building national resilience, promoting and protecting Human Rights, adopting targeted measures to prevent atrocity crimes.

How Can the Preventive Element of R2P be Operationalized and Implemented?

Operationalization of prevention as an element of R2P requires more than just naming the risk factors. It requires further analysis in order to understand the stages which usually lead to crimes. If one is not aware of the fact that the commission of mass atrocities does not occur unexpectedly but rather it is a long process, it is difficult to think about effective prevention. Once we identify stages of the process, it is easier to operationalize prevention as tools may be designed to fit

55 The listed risk factors, together with indicators are: 1. risk factors common to all four mass atrocity crimes, situations of armed conflict or other forms of instability; record of serious violations of international Human Rights and humanitarian law; weakness of state structures; motives or incentives; capacity to commit atrocity crimes; absence of mitigating factors; enabling circumstances or preparatory action; triggering factors and 2. specific risk factors: intergroup tensions or patterns of discrimination against protected groups; signs of an intent to destroy in whole or in part a protected group (genocide); signs of a widespread or systematic attack against any civilian population; signs of a plan or policy to attack any civilian population (crimes against humanity); serious threats to those protected under international humanitarian law; serious threats to humanitarian or peacekeeping operations (war crimes). See: UN (2014).

56 UN (2014), 5.

57 UN (2014), 5.

them. Jennifer Welsh and Serena Sharma suggest a temporal view of systematic and temporal prevention:

Graph 1: Temporal view of systematic and targeted prevention.

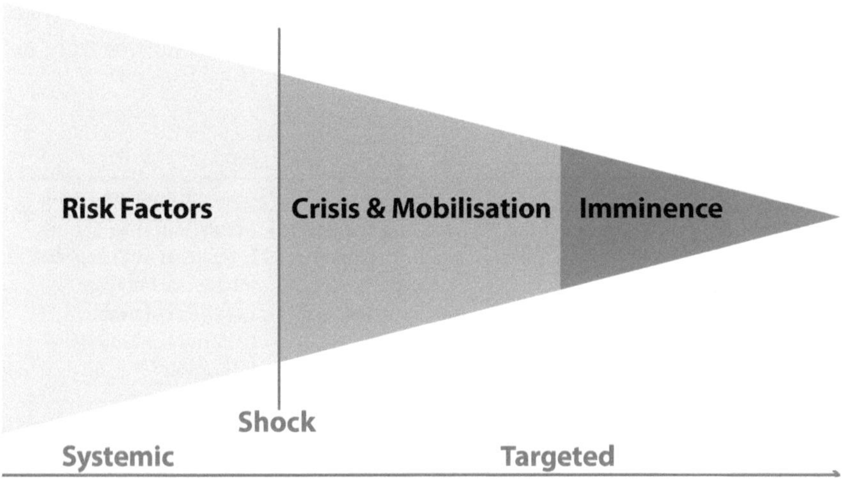

Source: Welsh & Sharma (2012), p. 6.

The three stages of escalation explain why and at which point the probability of crimes becomes so high that it may be difficult to avert it. Therefore national governments and institutions as well as the international community should attempt to apply different preventive strategies at different stages of escalation. The first stage (which requires long-term, systematic prevention strategies) presented in the figure (risk factors) creates a potential for mass atrocity crimes, but they are not inevitable. Crisis and mobilization which follow (this requires targeted preventive measures) is a stage in which "general risk is transformed into likelihood", however "atrocity crimes will not be committed unless there is explicit organization and mobilization", the signs of which may include hate propaganda or organizing and training militia groups[58]. Imminent emergency is the last stage of escalation (this requires targeted preventive measures) in which there are clear indicators of the imminent threat of the commission of crimes. Prevention at the final stage is difficult, if not – at least in some cases – impossible. Welsh and Sharma also propose that: first, any preventive action should be centred around the victims (reducing vulnerability); second, it ought to address the behaviour

58 Welsh & Sharma (2012), 6.

of perpetrator and; third, it should create a less permissive environment for the commission of crimes.[59]

Based on the three stages of crimes prevention division, the following targeted preventive tools that respond to crises and signs of mobilization and to imminent emergency (targeted preventive tools) are offered (in order to change the behaviour of perpetrators, third parties should implement the tools starting from the bottom of the table and moving to the top):

Table 10: Targeted preventive tools.

	Perpetrators	Victims	Situation/ Environment
Imminent Emergency	• Targeted sanctions (asset freezes, travel bans) • Threat of International Criminal Prosecution • Security Council Resolutions naming or warning individuals • Breaking diplomatic Relations or economic ties	• Opening borders to allow refugees to escape • No-fly zones or safe havens • Physical protection of camps • Strengthening victims' capacity to defend themselves • Recognizing opposition groups • Supporting exiles	• Mediation/ negotiations • Satellite surveillance and intelligence sharing • Provision of mobile communications technology • Radio jamming • Spreading of alternative views through UN broadcasts • Emergency summits • Peace operations
Crisis & Mobilization	• Statements of concern (e.g. UN Secretary-General or Human Rights Council) • Travel advisories • Economic incentives to adopt alternative behaviours (trade policy alterations, aid conditionality, debt relief)	• Preventive deployments of military force (consensual or non-consensual) • Deployment of Human Rights monitoring missions • Challenging dangerous speech	• Reducing the availability of weapons (bilateral and multilateral measures) • Ambassador recall • Increased NGO scrutiny • Visible international engagement (e.g., Security Council agenda) • Dissemination of relevant norms and legal obligations

Source: Welsh & Sharma (2012), p. 9.

59 Welsh & Sharma (2012), 7.

Conclusion

To conclude, the proposed concepts of operationalization of R2P preventive pillar is a step forward in the right direction, however we need to keep in mind that crimes in the past have happened even though preventive measures were at the disposal of states and intergovernmental institutions. Today, there are even more tools on the table; international awareness of preventions has been on the rise. It is quite clear how to analyse facts in order to prevent crimes commission. The most serious challenges for the international community seems to be the lack of political will to act where action is needed. Incentives and action must appear first in national states, regardless of what their political, economic or military power is. In the past decades, prevention "has been rhetorically prioritized but in practice largely ignored."[60] As noted by Thomas Weiss: "…logically speaking if you can't even get people mobilized to do something in the midst of a crisis, the idea that somehow even before you have a crisis they're all going to align and put money into it seems to me to be against the nature of human beings and certainly against the nature of the international system[61]".

Responsibility to Protect can be regarded as an input to the process of building a culture of atrocity crimes prevention. However, this chapter argues that its present significance is due to the discussions that its contents and attempts of implementation have provoked, rather than its endorsement.

The preventive architecture and the early warning mechanism that has been set up within the UN and other international institutions are plausible. However, their significance is being tested in reality and still tends to prove the existence of incompatibility of rhetoric and practice. If R2P is to shape future behaviour of states and the wider international community, support for its implementation would need to come from the Security Council. Expecting that the unchanged Council composition (with the veto power of the permanent members (P5)[62]) and mandate could be reconciled with the rallying cry of R2P is a fool's errand. Without a substantial institutional reform of the UN, hope that the R2P's first pillar can be an inventive original instrument of prevention of mass atrocity crimes is futile.

---

60 Hehir (2011), 1336.

61 Talk between Thomas Weiss and Aiden Hehir, quoted in Hehir (2011).

62 One of the concepts proposed is to make the P5 pledge that they will not use their veto power with resolutions dealing with mass atrocity crimes prevention and halting. For more on that see: Blätter, A.; Williams, P. D. (2011). 'The Responsibility Not To Veto' and the polemical response by Levine, D. H. (2011). 'Some Concerns About 'The Responsibility Not to Veto', both in *Global Responsibility to Protect*, no. 3.

The whole concept must work as a preventive measure in itself. And this must mean that it should be given teeth, which has not happened as yet. From what one can observe so far, vital states' interests will shape the character of the Responsibility to Protect in the future. It needs to be stressed, that any action or operationalization that leads to leaving aside the discussion of the use of coercive mechanisms in situations when it is indispensible to protect civilian population from mass atrocity crimes will mean that the international community is actually avoiding engagement and is pushing away the responsibility for the protection of human rights abuses. The current discussion in the UN and other international for a clearly have this characteristic of avoiding debated on coercive action in order to mobilize consent around non-coercive protection measure. As David Chandler rightly observes, "it appears that the more that R2P is disassociated from the […] focus on justifying military intervention, the more confusing the pronouncements of its leading advocates become".[63] He continues by pointing that "[t]oday, the relationship between the R2P and the right of humanitarian intervention appears to be much less clear"[64] which obviously leads to situations when the reactions of the international community, and -predominantly – Western states – are blocked by lack of political consensus over the possibility to use force. Therefore it seems that if the R2P is to work as a fully fledged preventive measure, discussions about the criteria for the use of coercive force must once again be opened. Jennifer Welsh's comment can be quoted here: "There is clearly a need to […] develop noncoercive tools that third parties can wisely employ to address the deep causes of mass atrocity crimes. But there is also an urgent need to elaborate the more targeted and coercive tools that the international community can employ as part of pillar three (the international responsibility to react to R[2]P crimes – whether those tools are being employed preventively (to avoid an imminent catastrophe) or as part of a response to ongoing large – scale atrocities".[65]

63 Chandler, D. (2009). 'Unravelling the Paradox of 'The Responsibility to Protect'. *Irish Studies in International Affairs*, vol. 20, no. 1, p. 32.

64 Chandler (2009), 28.

65 Welsh, J. (2011). 'Civilian Protection in Libya: Putting Coercion and Controvercy Back into RtoP. *Ethics & International Affairs*. 25, no. 3, pp. 260–261.

Bibliography

(Online papers and online-documents and freely available e-books quoted in the footnotes are not included)

Aceves, W. J. (2002). 'Relative Normativity: Challenging the Sovereignty Norm Through Human Rights Litigation'. *Hastings International and Comparative Law Review*, Vol. 25.

Akhavan, P. (1996). 'The International Criminal Tribunal for Rwanda: The Politics and Pragmatics of Punishment.' *American Journal of International Law*, vol. 90, no. 3.

Akhavan, P. (2009). Are International Criminal Tribunals a Disincentive to Peace?: Reconciling Judicial Romanticism with Political Realism. *Human Rights Quarterly, 31.*

Allen, T. (2010). Bitter Roots: The 'Invention' of Acholi Traditional Justice. In: Allen, T. & Vlassenroot, K. (eds). *The Lord's Resistance Army: Myth and Reality.* London/New York: Zed Books, pp. 242–261.

Allen, T. & Vlassenroot, K. (2010) (eds). *The Lord's Resistance Army: Myth and Reality.* London/New York: Zed Books.

Altunisik, M. B. (2008). 'EU Foreign Policy and the Israeli Palestinian Conflict: How much of an Actor?' *European Security*, vol. 17, no. 1.

Ambos, K. Large, J. & Wierda, M. (eds) (2008), *Building a Future on Peace and Justice: Studies on Transitional Justice, Peace and Development.* Heidelberg: Springer.

Annan, K. (2000). *We the Peoples. The Role of the United Nations in the 21st Century.* New York: United Nations.

Anyidoho, H. K. (1997). *Guns over Kigali: The Rwandese Civil War – 1994 (A Personal Account).* Collana: Spear Books Imprint.

Apuuli, K. P. (2008). 'The International Criminal Court & the Lord's Resistance Army Insurgency in Northern Uganda.' In: Nhema, A. & Zezela, P. T. (eds). *The Resolution of African Conflicts: The Management of Conflict Resolution and Post-Conflict Reconstruction.* Addis Ababa: Ossrea.

Bachmann, K. (2011): 'When the court refuses to write history'. *Review of International Affairs.* Vol. 62, 1143.

Bachmann, K. (2014). 'The Challenges: Political and Economic Transition.' In: Bachmann, K.; Lyubashenko, I. (2014) (eds). *The Maidan Uprising, Separatism and Foreign Intervention. Ukraine's complex transition.* Frankfurt/M.: Peter Lang. Int, pp. 405–442.

Bachmann, K.; Lyubashenko, I. (2014) (eds). *The Maidan Uprising, Separatism and Foreign Intervention. Ukraine's complex transition*. Frankfurt/M.: Peter Lang.

Bachmann, K.; Fatić, A. (2015). *The UN International Criminal Tribunals. Transition without Justice?* London, New York: Routledge.

Baehr, P. R. (1996). *The Role of Human Rights in Foreign Policy*, Houndmills, Basingstoke, Hampshire: Macmillan Press.

Bassiouni, M. C. (2011). *Crimes Against Humanity. Historical Evolution and Contemporary Application*. New York: Cambridge University Press.

Bell, Ch. (2009). 'Transitional Justice, Interdisciplinarity and the State of the "Field" or "Non-Field"'. International Journal of Transitional Justice, vol. 3, no. 1.

Bellamy, A. J. (2013). 'The Responsibility to Protect: Added value or hot air?' *Cooperation and Conflict* 48/3.

Bellamy, A. J. (2014). 'From Tripoli to Damascus? Lesson learning and the implementation of the Responsibility to Protect'. *International Politics*, vol. 51, no. 1.

Ben-Naftali, O. (2009). 'The Obligations to Prevent and to Punish Genocide'. In: Gaeta, P. (2009) (ed). *The UN Genocide Convention. A Commentary*. Oxford: Oxford University Press, pp. 36–44.

Boed, R. (2008). 'The International Criminal Tribunal for Rwanda.' In: Bassiouni, M. Ch (ed) (1999). *International Criminal Law, Volume III International Enforcement*, Third Edition. Leiden: Martinus Nijhoff Publishers, pp. 103–110.

Börzel, T. and Risse, T. (2000). 'When Europe Hits Home: Europeanization and Domestic Change'. *European Integration Online Papers*. Vol. 4, no. 15.

Boshoff H. (2010). 'Historical Overview.' In: Boshoff, H. Vrey, W. and Rautenbach, W. (eds) (2010). *The Burundi Peace Process: from civil war to conditional peace*. Pretoria, South Africa: Institute for Security Studies, pp. 3–9.

Boshoff, H. Vrey, W. and Rautenbach, W. (2010) (eds). *The Burundi Peace Process: from civil war to conditional peace*. Pretoria, South Africa: Institute for Security Studies.

Braithwaite, J., Charlesworth, H., Soares, A. (2012). *Networked Governance of Freedom and Tyranny: Peace in Timor-Leste*. Canberra: ANU e-press.

Branch, A. (2007). *The Political Dilemmas of Global Justice: Anti-Civilian Violence and the Violence of Humanitarianism, the Case of Northern Uganda*. PhD Thesis. Columbia University.

Branch, D. (2011). *Kenya Between Hope and Despair, 1963–2011*. New Haven, CT: Yale University Press.

Brennan, F. G. (1998). 'The State of the Judicature'. *Australian Law Journal 72*.

Barahona de Brito, A., Whitehead, L. (2012). *Transitional justice: Reframing the Debate*. In: Popovski, V., Serrano, M. (2012) (eds). *Transitional Justice in Latin America and Eastern Europe*. New York: United Nations University Press, pp. 439–462.

Brooks, P., Gewritz, P. (1998). *Law's stories: Narrative and Rhetoric in the Law*. New Haven, CT: Yale University Press.

Buckley-Zistel, S., Beck, T. K., Braun, Ch., Mieth, F. (2014) (eds). *Transitional Justice Theories*. New York: Routledge.

Bukuluki, P. (2011). *Negotiating Retributive and Restorative Justice in Conflict Transformation Efforts*. Zürich, Berlin: Lit-Verlag.

Cahin, G., Poirat, F. and Szurek, S. (2007) (eds). *La France et le droit international*. Paris: Pedone.

Castel, H. (2013). 'Maximizing Transitional Justice Opportunities: the Case for East Timor's CAVR'. In: Mayersen, D., Pohlman, A. (2013) (eds). *Genocide and Mass Atrocities in Asia. Legacies and Prevention*. London, New York: Routledge, p. 68–85.

Chandler, D. (2009). 'Unravelling the Paradox of 'The Responsibility to Protect'. *Irish Studies in International Affairs*, vol. 20, no. 1.

Charillon, F. (2011). *La politique étrangère de la France de la fin de la guerre froide au printemps arabe*. Paris: La Documentation Française.

Charillon, F. (2010). *La France peut-elle encore agir sur le monde?* Paris: Armand Colin.

Clark, P. (2010): *The Gacaca Courts, Post-Genocide Justice and Reconciliation in Rwanda. Justice without Lawyers*. Cambridge and New York: Cambridge University Press.

Clarke, K. M. (2009). *Fictions of Justice: The International Criminal Court and the Challenge of Legal Pluralism in Sub-Saharan Africa*. Cambridge: Cambridge University Press.

Cohen, S. (2001). *The Elementary Forms of Denial. States of Denial Knowing about Atrocities and Suffering*, Maiden: Blackwell Publishers.

Daalder, I. H. And O'Hanlon, M. E. (2000). *Winning Ugly. NATO's War to Save Kosovo*. Washington D.C.: Brookings Institutions Press.

Dallaire, R. (2003). *Shake Hands with the Devil. The Failure of Humanity in Rwanda*. Toronto: Random House Canada.

Daly, K. (2000). *Restorative justice in Diverse and Unequal Societies*. Flinders University Symposium on Criminal Justice in Diverse Societies, Adelaide, *Law in Context* 17(1).

Danner, A. Simmons, B. A. (2010). 'Credible commitments and the International Criminal Court'. *International Organization*, vol. 64, no. 2.

De Greiff, P., Duthie, R. (2009) (eds). *Transitional Justice and Development. Making Conncetions*. New York: Social Science Research Council.

Del Ponte C. (2009). *Madame Prosecutor: Confrontations with Humanity's Worst Criminals and the Culture of Impunity. A Memoir.* New York: Other Press.

Del Ponte, C. (2009). *La traque, les criminels de guerre et moi: autobiographie.* Paris: Ed. Héloïse d'Ormesson.

DeShaw Rae, J. (2009). *Peacebuilding and Transitional Justice in East Timor.* Boulder: Lynne Rienner Publishers.

Devin, G. (2002). *Sociologie des relations internationales*, Paris: La Découverte.

Doak, J. (2011). 'The Therapeutic Dimensions of Transitional Justice: Emotional repair and victim satisfaction in international trials and truth commissions.' *International Criminal Law Review*, 11.

Dolan, C. (2009). *Social Torture: The Case of Northern Uganda, 1986–2006.* New York and Oxford: Berghahn Books.

Drexler, E. (2009). 'Addressing the Legacies of Mass Violence and Genocide in East Timor and Indonesia'. In: Hinton, A., O'Neill, K. L. (2009) (eds). *Genocide: Truth, Memory and Representation.* Durham: Duke University Press, pp. 219–246.

Drzewicki, K. (2002). *The United Nations Charter and the Universal Declaration of Human Rights.* In: R. Hanski, R. Suksi, M. (2002) (eds.). *An Introduction to the International Protection of Human Rights*, Second edition, Turku/Åbo: Institute for Human Rights, Åbo Akademi University, pp. 65–76.

Du Plessis, M., Ford, J. (2008). Executive Summary. In M. Du Plessis, J. Ford (Eds). *Unable or Unwilling? Studies on Domestic Implementation of the ICC Statute in Selected African Countries.* Pretoria: Institute for Security Studies.

Du Plessis, M., Ford, J. (eds). *Unable or Unwilling? Studies on Domestic Implementation of the ICC Statute in Selected African Countries.* Pretoria: Institute for Security Studies.

Du Toit, F. (2011). *Reconciliation and Transitional Justice: the case of Rwanda's Gacaca Courts.* Cape Town: Institute for Justice and Reconciliation.

Džunuzović, A. (2009). *Lanet Olsun – Zločin nad Bošnjacima istočne Bosn.* Sarajevo: Mladi Muslimani.

Eichstaedt, P. (2009). *First Kill Your Family: Child Soldiers of Uganda and the Lord's Resistance Army,* Chicago: Lawrence Hill Books.

Elster, J. (2004), *Closing the Books. Transitional Justice in Historical Perspective.* Cambridge: Cambridge University Press.

Eltringham, N. (2004): *Accounting for horror. Post-genocide debates in Rwanda.* London: Pluto Press.

Essoungou, A.-M. (2006). *Justice à Arusha. Un tribunal international politiquement encadré face au genocide rwandais.* Paris: L'Harmatta.

Fehl, C. (2004). 'Explaining the International Criminal Court: A "Pratice Test" for Rationalist and Constructivist Approaches.' *European Journal of International Relations*, vol. 10, no. 3.

Femmes Africa Solidarité (2001). *Engendering the Peace Process in Burundi: Women's Best Practices in Africa.* Oxford: New Internationalist Publications Ltd.

Fermor, C. (2012/13). 'NATO's Decision to intervene in Libya (2011). Realist principles or humanitarian norms?' *Journal of Politics & International Studies*, vol. 8.

Finnström, S. (2008). *Living With Bad Surroundings.* Durham/London: Duke University Press.

Finnström, S. (2010). 'Reconciliation Grown Bitter?: War, Retribution, and Ritual Action in Northern Uganda.' In: Shaw, R. & Waldorf, L. (eds). *Localizing Transitional Justice: Interventions and Priorities after Mass Violence.* Stanford: Stanford University Press, pp. 135–156.

Forsythe, D. P. (1989). *Human Rights and U.S. Foreign Policy: Congress Reconsidered.* Gainesville: University of Florida Press.

Fox, H., Webb, P. (2013). *The Law of State Immunity*. Oxford: Oxford University Press.

Gaeta, P. (2009). 'Does President Al Bashir Wnjoy Immunity from Arrest?' *Journal of International Criminal Justice*, vol. 7.

Gaeta, P. (2009) (ed). *The UN Genocide Convention. A Commentary.* Oxford: Oxford University Press.

Gahima, G. (2013). *Transitional Justice in Rwanda. Accountability for Atrocity.* New York: Routledge.

Gallois, P. M., Vergès, J. (2002). *L'apartheid judiciaire: le Tribunal pénal international, arme de guerre.* Lousanne: L'Age d'Homme.

Garcia-Godos, J., Lekha Sriram, C. (2013), 'Introduction'. In: Lekha Sriram, C., Garcia-Godos, J., Herman, J., Martin-Ortega, O. (2013) (eds). *Transitional Justice and Peacebuilding on the Ground. Victims and Ex-combatants.* London, New York: Routledge

Glanville L. (2011). 'On the Meaning of "Responsibility". *The Responsibility to Protect, Griffith Law Review* 20, no. 2.

Glasius, M. (2009). 'What is Global Justice and Who Decides? Civil Society and Victim Responses to the International Criminal Court's First Investigations.' *Human Rights Quarterly,* 31.

Godos, J., Herman, J., Martin-Ortega, O. (2013) (eds). *Transitional Justice and Peacebuilding on the Ground. Victims and Ex-combatants.* London, New York: Routledge.

Gordy, E. (2013). *Guilt, Responsibility, and Denial The Past at Stake in Post-Milošević Serbia.* Philadelphia: University of Pennsylvania Press.

Graydon, C. (2005). 'Local Justice Systems in Timor-Leste: Washed up, or Watch this Space?' *Development Bulletin*, no. 68, pp. 66–70.

Greiçevivci, L. (2011). 'EU Actorness in International Affairs: The Case of EULEX Mission in Kosovo.' *Perspectives on European Politics and Society*, vol. 12, no. 3.

Grenfell, L. (2006). 'Legal Pluralism and the Rule of Law in Timor-Leste'. *Leiden Journal of International Law,* no. 19.

Grenfell, L. (2009). 'Promoting the Rule of Law in Timor-Leste.' *Conflict, Security & Development*, vol. 9, no. 2.

Groenleer, M. L. P., Van Schalk, L. G. (2007). 'United We Stand? The European Union's International Actorness in the Cases of the International Criminal Court and the Kyoto Protocol'. *Journal of Common Market Studies*, vol. 45, no. 5.

Grünfeld, F., Huijboom, A. (2007). *The Failure to Prevent Genocide in Rwanda: The Role of Bystanders.* Leiden and Boston: Martinus Nijhoff Publishers.

Gunn, G. C. (2011). *Historical Dictionary of East Timor.* Plymouth: Scarecrow Press.

Hainsworth, P., McCloskey, S. (2000) (eds). *The East Timor Question. The Struggle for Independence from Indonesia.* New York: I. B. Taurus.

Hamutuk, L. (2003). 'Reviewing the East Timor Commission for Reception, Truth and Reconciliation (CAVR)'. *La'u Hamutuk Bulletin* vol. 4, no. 5.

Hanski, R. Suksi, M. (2002) (eds). *An Introduction to the International Protection of Human Rights*, Second edition, Turku/Åbo: Institute for Human Rights, Åbo Akademi University.

Harris Rimmer, S. (2010). *Gender and Transitional Justice: the Women of East Timor.* London, New York: Routledge.

Harroff-Travel M. (2003). 'Do wars ever end? The work of the International Committee of the Red Cross when the guns full silent'. *International Review of the Red Cross,* vol. 85, issue 851.

Hayner P. (1994). 'Fifteen Truth Commissions (1974–1994), A Comparative Study', *Human Rights Quarterly* 16, 597.

Hayner, P. (2010). *Unspeakable truths. Transitional Justice and the Challenge of Truth Commissions.* London, New York: Routledge.

Hazan, P. (2004). *Justice in a Time of War. The True Story Behind the International Criminal Tribunal for the Former Yugoslavia.* Texas and Paris: Texas A&M University Press.

Hazan, P. (2006). 'Measuring the impact of punishment and forgiveness: a framework for evaluating transitional justice'. *International Review of the Red Cross*, vol. 88.

Henkin, L. (1978). *The Rights of Man Today.* Boulder: Westview Press.

Hinton, A., O'Neill, K. L. (2009) (eds). *Genocide: Truth, Memory and Representation.* Durham: Duke University Press.

Higgins, R. (1987). 'Human Rights and Foreign Policy'. *Rivista di Studi Politici Internazionali* 54/4.

Hoare, M. A. (2010). 'Bosnia-Hercegovina and International Justice: Past Failures and Future Solutions.' *East European Politics and Societies* 24.

Hovil, L. (2012). *A Poisoned Chalice? Local Civil Society and the International Criminal Court's Engagement.* Kampala: International Refugee Rights Initiative.

Hovil, L. & Lomo, Z. (2005). *Whose Justice? Perceptions of Uganda's Amnesty Act 2000: The Potential for Conflict Resolution and long-term Reconciliation.* Kampala: Refugee Law Project.

Howell K. (2004): 'Developing Conceptualisations of Europeanization: Synthesising Methodological Approaches'. *Queen's Paper on Europeanization*, no. 3.

Huyse, L., Salter, M. (eds) (2008). *Traditional Justice and Reconciliation after Violent Conflict: Learning from African Experiences.* Stockholm: International IDEA.

International Center for Transitional Justice and Human Rights Center of the University of Berkeley (2005). *Forgotten Voices: A Population-Based Survey on Attitudes about Peace and Justice in Northern Uganda.* New York: International Center for Transitional Justice.

Jansen Y.-O. (2014). 'Denying Genocide or Denying Free Speech? A Case Study of the Application of Rwanda's Genocide Denial Laws'. *Northwestern Journal of International Human Rights*, vol. 12, no. 2.

Jia B. B. (2012). 'The Immunity of State Officials for International Crimes Revisited'. *Journal of International Criminal Justice*, vol. 10.

Johnson, L. D. (1999). *The International Criminal Tribunal for Rwanda.* In: Bassiouni, M. Ch. (1999) (ed). *International Criminal Law, Volume III Enforcement*, Second Edition, Ardsley: Transnational Publishers, pp. 549–560.

Johntone, G., Van Ness, D. W. (2007) (eds). *Handbook of Restorative Justice.* Portland: Willan Publishing.

Jupille, J.; Caporaso, J. A. (1998). 'States, Agency and Rules: The European Union in Global Environmental Politics'. In: Rhodes, C. (1998) (ed). *The European Union in the World Community.* London: Lynne Rienner, pp. 213–229.

Kamiński, Ireneusz C. (2014). 'International Law Aspects of the situation in Ukraine.' In: Bachmann, K.; Lyubashenko, I. (2014). *The Maidan Uprising, Separatism and Foreign Intervention. Ukraine's Complex Transition.* Frankfurt/M.: Peter Lang, pp. 379–405.

Kędzia, Z. (2010). 'The Responsibility to Protect: Political Strength versus Legal Fragility'. In: Bieńczyk-Missala, A. Dębski, S. (2010) (eds). *Rafał Lemkin: a Hero of Humankind.* Warsaw: The Polish Institute of International Affairs, pp. 271–288.

Kent, L. (2012). *The Dynamics of Transitional Justice. International Models and Local Realities in East Timor.* London, New York: Routledge.

Kevins, J. (2005). *A Not-So-Distant Horror: Mass Violence in East Timor.* Ithaca, New York: Cornell University Press.

Kim, H. & Sikkink, K. (2010). 'Explaining the Deterrence Effect of Human Rights Prosecutions for Transitional Countries.' *International Studies Quarterly,* 54, no. 4.

Kingsbury, D. (2009). *East Timor. The Price of Liberty.* New York: Palgrave MacMillan.

Kissack, R. (2008). 'EU Actorness in the International Labour Organization: Comparing Declaratory and Voting Cohesion'. *Global Society*, vol. 22, no. 4.

Klarin, M. (2009). 'The Impact of the ICTY Trials on Public Opinion in the Former Yugoslavia', *Journal of International Criminal Justice* 7, no. 1.

Komakech, L. & Sheff, A. (2009). *Tradition in Transition: Drawing on The Old to Develop a New Jurisprudence for Dealing with Uganda's Legacy of Violence.* Kampala: Refugee Law Project.

Kühnel, S. M. and Krebs, D. (2010). *Statistik für Sozialwissenschaften.* Reinbeck bei Hamburg: Rowohlt.

Kritz, N. (2009). 'Policy Implications of Empirical Research on Transitional Justice'. In: H. Kuperman, A. J. (2013). 'A Model Humanitarian Intervention? Reassessing NATO's Libya Campaign'. *International Security*, vol. 38, issue 1.

Kuźniar, R. (2000). *Prawa człowieka, prawo, instytucje, stosunki międzynarodowe.* Warsaw: Wydawnictwo Naukowe Scholar.

Kwiecień R. (2004). *Suwerenność państwa. Rekonstrukcja i znaczenie idei w prawie międzynarodowym.* Zakamycze: Kantor Wydawniczy Zakamycze.

Lamony, S. A. (2007). *Approaching National Reconciliation in Uganda: Perspectives on Applicable Justice Systems.* Kampala: Uganda Coalition for the International Criminal Court.

Latigo, J. O. (2008). 'Northern Uganda: Tradition-Based Practices in the Acholi Region.' In: Huyse, L., Salter, M. (eds) (2008). *Traditional Justice and Reconciliation after Violent Conflict: Learning from African Experiences.* Stockholm: International IDEA, pp. 85–120.

Laughland, J. (2007). *Travesty. The Trial of Slobodan Milošević and the Corruption of International Justice.* London, Ann Arbor: Pluto Press.

Lederach, J. P. (1995). *Preparing for Peace: Conflict Transformation across Cultures.* Syracuse, N.Y: Syracuse University Press.

Lekha Sriram, C., Garcia-Godos, J., Herman, J., Martin-Ortega, O. (2013) (eds). *Transitional Justice and Peacebuilding on the Ground. Victims and Ex-combatants.* London, New York: Routledge.

Lemkin, R. (1944). *Axis Rule in Occupied Europe: Laws of Occupation – Analysis of Government – Proposals for Redress.* Washington, D.C.: Carnegie Endowment for International Peace.

Lérner, L. (1980). *The U.N. Convention on the Elimination of All Forms of Racial Discrimination.* Alphen aan den Rijn: Sijthoff & Noordhoff International.

Levine, D. H. (2011). 'Some Concerns About 'The Responsibility Not to Veto'. *Global Responsibility to Protect,* no. 3.

Lillich, R. B. (1973) (ed). *Humanitarian Intervention And The United Nations.* Charlottesville: Charlottesville: University Press of Virginia.

Lillich, R. B. (1994). 'The Role of the UN Security Council in Protecting Human Rights in Crisis Situations: UN Humanitarian Intervention in the Post-Cold War World'. *Tulane Journal of International and Comparative Law*, vol. 3.

Lincoln, J. (2001). *Transitional Justice, Peace and Accountability: Outreach and the role of International Courts After Conflicts.* New York: Routledge.

Lindsey, T. (2008) (ed). *Indonesia. Law and Society.* Toronto, Singapore: Irwin Law (The Federation Press).

Luck, E. (2001). 'The Responsibility to Protect: The First Decade'. *Global Responsibility to Protect,* no. 3.

Lugan L. (2007). *Rwanda. Contre-enquête sur le genocide.* Toulouse: Editions Privat.

Magnarell, P. J. (2000). *Justice in Africa: Rwanda's Genocide, its Courts, and the UN Criminal Tribunal.* Aldershot: Ashgate.

Mamdani M. (2001). *When Victims become killers. Colonialism, Nativism, and the Genocide in Rwanda.* Princeton: Princeton University Press.

Mamdani, M. (1998). *When Does Reconciliation Turn into a Denial of Justice?* Vol. 1, Sam Nolutshungu Memorial Series: Human Sciences Research Council.

Mamdani, M. (1996). 'Reconciliation Without Justice.' *Southern African Review of Books*, Nov/Dec, pp. 3–5.

Marker, J. (2003). *East Timor: A Memoir of the Negotiations for Independence.* Jefferson: McFarland.

Martin, S. (2011). 'Sovereignty and the Responsibility to Protect'. *Griffith Law Review*, vol. 20, no. 1.

Massa, A.-S. (2006). 'NATO's Intervention in Kosovo and the Decision of the Prosecutor of the International Criminal Tribunal for the Former Yugoslavia

Not to Investigate: An Abusive Exercise of Prosecutorial Discretion?' *Berkeley Journal of International Law,* February 24, 2006.

Matthews, R. O.; Pratt, C. (1988) (eds). *Human Rights in Canadian Foreign Policy,* Ottawa: McGill-Queen's University Press.

Mayer-Rieckh, A., de Greiff, P. (2007). *Justice as Prevention: Vetting Public Employees in Transitional Societies.* New York: The Social Science Research Council.

Mayersen, D.; Pohlman, A. (2013) (eds). *Genocide and Mass Atrocities in Asia. Legacies and Prevention.* London, New York: Routledge.

McAuliffe, P. (2008). 'East Timor's Community Reconciliation Process as a Model for Legal Pluralism in Criminal Justice'. *Law, Social Justice and Global Development Journal,* vol. 12, issue 2.

McAuliffe, P. (2010). 'Transitional Justice and the Rule of Law: The Perfect Couple or Awkward Bedfellows?' *Hague Journal on the Rule of Law,* volume 2, issue 02, pp. 127–154.

McCloskey, S. (2000). 'Introduction: East Timor – From European to Third World Colonialism'. In: Hainsworth, P., McCloskey, S. (2000) (eds). *The East Timor Question. The Struggle for Independence from Indonesia.* New York: I. B. Taurus, pp. 3–4.

Meierhenrich, J. (2014). 'Beyond the Theater of International Justice: The Rule 98*bis* Decision in *Milošević*.' In: Waters, T. (2014) (ed). *The Milošević Trial. An Autopsy.* Oxford, New York et al: Oxford University Press, pp. 316–326.

Melvern, L. (2000). *A People Betrayed. The Role of the West in Rwanda's Genocide.* London: Zed Books.

Meron, T. (1985). 'The Meaning and the Reach of the International Convention on the Elimination of All Forms of Racial Discrimination'. *American Journal of International Law,* vol. 79.

Meron, T. (2005). 'Judicial Independence and Impartiality in International Criminal Tribunals'. *The American Journal of International Law,* vol. 99.

Moghalu, K. C. (2009). 'Prosecute or Pardon? Between Truth Commission and War Crimes Trials.' In: Sriram C. L., Pillay S. (eds). *Peace Versus Justice? The Dilemmas of Transitional Justice in Africa.* Scottsville: University of KwaZulu-Natal Press.

Mooney, E. D. (2010). 'Something Old, Something New, Something Borrowed … Something Blue? The Protection Potential of a Marriage of Concepts between R2P and IDP Protection'. *Global Responsibility to protect,* vol. 2, no. 1–2.

Moreno Ocampo, L. (2008). 'Building a Future on Peace and Justice: The International Criminal Court.' In: Ambos, K., Large J. and Wierda M. (eds). *Building a Future on Peace and Justice: Studies on Transitional Justice, Peace and Development.* Heidelberg: Springer.

Moreno Ocampo, L. (2007). 'Transitional Justice in Ongoing Conflicts.' *The International Journal of Transitional Justice,* 1, no. 1.

Ngirabatware A. (2006). *Rwanda. Le faîte du mensonge et de l'injustice.* Lille: Editions Sources du Nil.

Nhema, A., Zezela, P. T. (eds). *The Resolution of African Conflicts: The Management of Conflict Resolution and Post-Conflict Reconstruction.* Addis Ababa: Ossrea.

Nolutshungu Memorial Series: Human Sciences Research Council.

Nouwen, S., Werner, W. (2010). 'Doing Justice to the Political: The International Criminal Court in Uganda and Sudan.' *European Journal of International Law,* 21.

Nouwen, S. M. H., Werner, W. G. (2014). 'Monopolising Global Justice. International Criminal Law as Challenge to Human Diversity'. *Journal of International Criminal Justice,* vol. 12.

Nouwen, S. (2006). 'Hybrid Courts. The hybrid category of a new type of international crimes court'. *Utrecht Law Review,* vol. 2, issue 2.

Nowak, M. (1993). *UN Covenant on Civil and Political Rights: CCPR Commentary.* Kehl: Engel Publishers.

O'Neil, W. (2002). *Kosovo An Unfinished Peace.* Boulder, Co: Lynne Reinner Publisher.

OHCHR (2007). *Making Peace our Own: Victims' Perceptions of Accountability, Reconciliation and Transitional Justice in Northern Uganda.* Geneva: United Nations.

Olsen, T. D., Payne, L. A., Reiter, A. (2010). *Transitional Justice in Balance: Comparing Processes, Weighing Efficacy.* Washington DC: US Institute of Peace Press.

Olsen, T. D., Payne, L. A., Reiter, A. G. (2010). 'The Justice Balance: When Transitional Justice Improves Human Rights and Democracy.' *Human Rights Quarterly,* 32.

Oola, S. (2011). *The Coalition for Reconciliation in Uganda: Important Lessons for Proactive Civil Society Engagement in Catalysing Transitional Justice Discourse.* African Transitional Justice Research Network Workshop: Advocating Justice: Civil Society and Transitional Justice in Africa. Johannesburg.

Orford, A. (2011). *International Authority and the Responsibility to Protect.* Cambridge: Cambridge University Press.

Othman M. C. (2005). *Accountability for International Humanitarian Law Violations: The Case of Rwanda and East Timor.* Berlin: Springer.

Ottendörfer, E. (2013). 'Contesting International Norms of Transitional Justice'. *International Journal of Peace and Violence,* vol. 7.

Peskin, V. (2008). *International Justice in Rwanda and the Balkans. Virtual Trials and the Struggle for State Cooperation.* Cambridge, New York, Melbourne, Madrid, Cape Town, Singapore, São Paulo, Delhi: Cambridge University Press.

Peskin, V. (2011). *Victor's Justice Revisited. Rwandan Patriotic Front Crimes and The Prosecutorial Endgame at the ICTR.* In: Waldorf, L., Straus, S. (eds) (2011). *Remaking Rwanda. State Building and Human Rights after Mass Violence.* London, Madison: University of Wisconsin Press, pp. 173–183.

Petriello, L. T., Wierda, M. (2006). *Lessons from the Deployment of International Judges and Prosecutors in Kosovo.* New York: The International Centre for Transitional Justice'.

Pettai, E.-C., Pettai, V. (2015). *Transitional Justice and retrospective justice in the Baltic states.* Cambridge: Cambridge University Press.

Pham, P., Vinck, P., Stover, E., Moss, A., Wierda, M. & Bailey, R. (2007). *When the War Ends: A Population-Based Survey on Attitudes about Peace, Justice, and Social Reconstruction in Northern Uganda.* Berkeley: Human Rights Center University of California.

Purdey, J. (2008). 'Legal Responses to violence in post-Soeharto Indonesia.' In: Lindsey, T. (2008) (ed). *Indonesia. Law and Society.* Toronto, Singapore: Irwin Law (The Federation Press), pp. 521–523.

Ramcharan, B. (2010). *Preventive Human Rights Strategies.* London, New York: Routledge.

Reisman, M. (2007–2008). 'Acting Before Victims Become Victims: Preventing and Arresting Mass Murder'. *Case Western Reserve Journal of International Law*, vol. 40.

Reus-Smit, C. (2001). 'Human Rights and the Social Construction of Sovereignty'. *Review of International Studies*, vol. 27.

Reydams L. (2005). 'The ICTR Ten Years On. Back to the Nuremberg Paradigm?' *Journal of International Criminal Justice*, vol. 3.

Reyntjens, F. (2013). *Political Governance in Post-Genocide Rwanda.* Cambridge, New York, Melbourne, Madrid, Capetown, São Paulo, Singapore, Delhi, Tokyo, Mexico City: Cambridge University Press.

Rhodes, C. (1998) (ed). *The European Union in the World Community.* London: Lynne Rienner.

Ricoeur, P. (2006). *Memory, History, Forgetting.* Chicago: University of Chicago Press.

Risse, T., Ropp, S. C., Sikkink, K. (2002) (eds). *The power of Human Rights. International Norms and Domestic Change.* Cambridge: Cambridge University Press.

Rodriguez, C. (2009). *Tall Grass: Stories of Peace and Suffering in Northern Uganda.* Kampala: Fountain Publishers.

Romano, C. P. R., Nollkaemper, A. and Kleffner, J. K. (2004). *Internationalized Criminal Courts. Sierra Leone, East Timor, Kosovo, and Cambodia.* Oxford: Oxford University Press.

Rombouts H. (2004). *Victim Organisations and the Politics of Reparation: a case study on Rwanda.* Antwerp, Oxford: Intersentia.

Sassòli M., Bouvier A. A. (2003). *Un droit dans la guerre?* Genève: CICR.

Schabas, W. (2009–2010). 'Victor's Justice: Selecting "Situations" at the International Criminal Court'. *The John Marshall Law Review*, vol. 43.

Schabas, W. A. (2006). *The UN International Criminal Tribunals. The Former Jugoslavia, Rwanda and Sierra Leone.* Cambridge, New York, Melbourne, Madrid, Cape Town, Singapore, São Paulo, Delhi, Dubai, Tokyo: Cambridge University Press.

Schabas, W. A. (2007). *An Introduction to the International Criminal Court,* Third Edition. Cambridge: Cambridge University Press.

Schaeffer, D. (2012). *All the missing souls. A personal history of the war crimes tribunals.* Princeton, Oxford: Princeton University Press.

Serrano, M., Weiss, T. G. (2014) (eds). *The international Politics of Human Rights. Rallying to the R2P cause?* London, New York: Routledge, e-book.

Shaw, R., Waldorf, L. (eds), *Localizing Transitional Justice: Interventions and Priorities after Mass Violence.* Stanford: Stanford University Press.

Shawki, N. (2011). 'Responsibility to Protect: The Evolution of an International Norm'. *Global Responsibility to Protect*, vol. 3, no. 2.

Shetreet, S., Deschenes, J. (1985) (eds). *Judicial Independence, The Contemporary Debate.* Dordrecht, Martinus Nijhoff Publishers.

Shraga, D., Zacklin, R. (1996). 'The International Criminal Tribunal for Rwanda.' *European Journal of International Law*, vol. 7, no. 4, pp. 501–518.

Shyaka, A. (2008): 'Justice and Reconciliation in Post-Genocide Rwanda. Assessing the Impact of the International Criminal Tribunal for Rwanda.' *The Review of International Affaires* (Belgrade), vol. LIX, no. 1130–1131, April/September 2008.

Sikkink, K. (2012). *The Justice Cascade: How Human Rights Prosecutions Are Changing World Politics.* New York, London: W. W. Norton.

Sikkink, K., Lutz, E. L. (2001). 'The Justice Cascade. The Evolution and Impact of Foreign Human Rights Trials in Latin America.' *Chicago Journal of International Law* 1.

Snyder, J. & Vinjamuri, L. (2003). 'Trials and Errors: Principles and Pragmatism in Strategies of International Justice.' *International Security 28.*

Sorel, J.-M. (2007). 'La France et les juridictions internationales ou la dialectique de l'audace, des réticences et de la soumission'. In: Cahin, G., Poirat, F.

and Szurek, S.(2007) (eds). *La France et le droit international.* Paris: Pedone, pp. 279–337.

Sriram, C. L. (2008). 'Conflict Mediation and the ICC: Challenges and Options for Pursuing Peace with Justice at the Regional Level.' In: K. Ambos, J. Large, M. Wierda (eds). *Building a Future on Peace and Justice: Studies on Transitional Justice, Peace and Development.* Heidelberg: Springer.

Sriram, C. L., Pillay, S. (2009) (eds). *Peace Versus Justice? The Dilemmas of Transitional Justice in Africa.* Scottsville: University of KwaZulu-Natal Press.

Stahn, C. (2007). 'Responsibility to Protect: Political Rhetoric or Emerging Legal Norm?' *The American Journal of International Law* 101, no. 1.

Stan, L. (2008). *Transitional Justice in Eastern Europe and the former Soviet Union: Reckoning with the communist past.* London, New York: Routledge.

Stanley, E. (2009). *Torture, Truth and Justice. The case of Timor-Leste.* London, New York: Routledge.

Stromseth, J. E. (2003) (ed). *Accountability for Atrocities: National and International Responses.* New York: Transnational Publishers.

Subotić, J. (2009). *Hijacked Justice. Dealing with the Past in the Balkans.* Ithaca and London: Cornell University Press.

Subotić, J. (2009). *Hijacked Justice. Dealing with the Past in the Balkans.* Ithaca and London: Cornell University Press.

Szekely, O. (2014). 'The Costs of Avoiding Transitional Justice: Lessons from Lebanon'. In: Fisher, K. J.; Stewart, R. (2014) (eds). *Transitional Justice and the Arab Spring.* London, New York: Routledge, pp. 94–111.

Teitel, R. (2003). 'Transitional Justice Genealogy'. *Harvard Human Rights Journal,* no. 16.

Teitel, R. (2003). 'Transitional Justice in a New Era'. In: *Fordham International Law Journal,* vol. 26.

Teitel. R. (2000), *Transitional Justice.* Oxford, New York: Oxford University Press.

Thakur, R. (2006). *The United Nations, Peace and Security: From Collective Security to the Responsibility to Protect.* Cambridge: Cambridge University Press.

Thomas, O. N. T., Ron, J. & Paris, R. (2008). *The Effects of Transitional Justice Mechanisms: A Summary of Empirical Research Findings and Implications for Analysts and Practitioners.* Ottawa: University of Ottawa Center for International Policy Studies.

Thompson, L. M. (2001). *A history of South Africa.* Yale University Press.

Tladi, D. (2013), 'The ICC Decisions on Chad and Malawi. On Cooperation, Immunities, and Article 98'. *Journal of International Criminal Justice* 2013, vol. 11.

Toje, A. (2008). 'The European Union as a Small Power, or Conceptualizing Europe's Strategic Actorness'. *European Integration*, vol. 30, no. 2.

Unger, T., Wierda, M. (2008). 'Pursuing Justice in Ongoing Conflict. A Discussion of Current Practice'. In: Ambos, K.; Large, J., Wierda, M. (2008) (eds). *Building a Future on Peace and Justice. Studies on Transitional Justice, Peace and Development.* Heidelberg: Springer.

Vaisse, M. (2009). *La puissance ou l'influence? La France dans le monde depuis 1958.* Paris: Fayard.

Van Acker, F. (2004). 'Uganda and the Lord's Resistance Army, the New Order no One Ordered.' *African Affairs,* pp. 335–357.

Van den Herik, L. J. (2005). *The Contribution of the Rwanda Tribunal to the Development of International Law.* Leiden: Martinus Nijhoff.

Van Der Merwe, H., Chapman, A. R. (2009) (eds). *Assessing the Impact of Transitional Justice: Challenges for Empirical Research.* Washington DC: United States Institute of Peace Press.

Van der Merwe, H., Baxter, V., Chapman, A. R. (2009) (eds). *Assessing the impact of transitional justice.* Washington D.C.: United States Institute of Peace Press.

Waldorf, L. (2006). 'Mass Justice for Mass Atrocity: Rethinking Local Justice as Transitional Justice.' *Temple Law Review*, vol. 91, no. 1.

Waldorf, L., Straus, S. (2011) (eds). *Remaking Rwanda. State Building and Human Rights after Mass Violence.* London, Madison: University of Wisconsin Press.

Wale, K. (2013). *2013 SA Reconciliation Barometer Survey Report: Confronting Exclusition – Time for Radical Reconciliation.* Cape Town: Institute for Justice and Reconciliation.

Waters, T. (2014) (ed). *The Milošević Trial. An Autopsy.* Oxford, New York et al: Oxford University Press.

Weissman, F. (2010). '"Not In Our Name": Why Médecins Sans Frontières Does Not Support the "Responsibility to Protect"'. *Criminal Justice Ethics*, vol. 29, no 2.

Welsh, J. (2011). 'Civilian Protection in Libya: Putting Coercion and Controvercy Back into RtoP. *Ethics & International Affairs.* 25, no. 3.

Wiebes, C. (2002). *Intelligence en de oorlog in Bosnie. De rol van de inlichtingen- en veiligheidsdiensten.* Amsterdam: NIOD.

Williams, P. D. (2011). 'The Responsibility Not To Veto'. *Global Responsibility to Protect,* no. 3.

Williams, S., Sherif, L. (2009). 'The Arrest Warrant for President al-Bashir: Immunities of Incumbent Heads of State and the International Criminal Court.' *Journal of Conflict and Security Law*, 14, no. 1.

Wilson, R. (2005). 'Judging History: The Historical Record of the International Criminal Tribunal for the Former Yugoslavia'. *Human Rights Quarterly*, 27, no. 3.

Wilson, R. A. (2011). *Writing History in International Criminal Trials*. Cambridge University Press.

Wilson, R. A. (2001). T*he Politics of Truth and Reconciliation in South Africa. Legitimizing the Post-Apartheid State*. Cambridge: Cambridge University Press.

Wipman, D. (2006). 'The Costs of International Justice'. *American Journal of International Law*, vol. 100, no. 4.

Wyrzykowski, P., Kasozi, B. O. (2010). *Why Being Able to Return Home Should be Part of Transitional Justice: Urban IDPs in Kampala and their quest for a Durable Solution*. Kampala: Refugee Law Project.

The Authors

Klaus Bachmann is a professor of political science at the University of Social Sciences and Humanities in Warsaw, Poland. Previously, he worked at Wrocław University, and, as a visiting professor and research fellow, at the Universities of Vienna, Bordeaux, Renmin (China), Stellenbosch (South Africa), and Johns Hopkins in Washington D.C. His research focus is on Transitional Justice, International Criminal Law, and Modern European History. He is the author (with Aleksandar Fatić) of *The UN International Criminal Tribunals. Transition without Justice?* (New York, London: Taylor and Francis Routledge 2015).

Agnieszka Bieńczyk-Missala is an assistant professor at the Institute of International Relations, University of Warsaw (since 2004). DPhil, University of Warsaw. Vice Director for Academic Research and International Cooperation at the Institute of International Relations, University of Warsaw (2008–2012); participant in the European Project "NOHA – Network on Humanitarian Assistance" and EU Non-Proliferation Consortium; Analyst at the Polish Institute of International Affairs (2006–2008); author of books and articles on Poland's foreign policy, Human Rights, democracy, and international humanitarian law. Main works: *Human Rights in Polish Foreign Policy after 1989* (The Polish Institute of International Affairs 2006); *Rafał Lemkin – A Hero of Humankind* [coedited with S. Dębski; The Polish Institute of International Affairs 2010). Chairperson of the research project: Prevention of Massive Violations of Human Rights (financed by National Scientific Centre).

Patrycja Grzebyk, PhD, is an assistant professor in the Institute of International Relations of the University of Warsaw, Poland. She is a graduate of the departments of international relations and law at the University of Warsaw. She has published in the area of international criminal law, international humanitarian law, and international human rights law. She has authored the monograph *Criminal Responsibility for the Crime of Aggression* (Routledge 2013) and numerous other publications.

Anna Grzywacz is a Ph.D. candidate in political science at the Faculty of Journalism and Political Science of the University of Warsaw, Poland. Her research interests focus on international relations in Southeast Asia, especially in the Malay region, and on Indonesian foreign policy.

Dorota Heidrich is an assistant professor at the Institute of International Relations (IIR) at the University of Warsaw (since 2004). DPhil, University of Warsaw. Since 2011: advisor to the Chairman of the Foreign Affairs Committee of Polish parliament. Since 2010 serves as the IIR's representative in the cooperation with the International HumanDoc Film Festival "Global Development in Cinema". Her interests focus on: forced migration (with special attention to IDPs); international criminal justice; RtoP; international organizations (governmental and non-governmental). Author of *International Protection of Internally Displaced Persons. Legal Aspects and Practice* (WUW 2005) and numerous scholarly articles on topics within the aforementioned fields of interest.

Jan Hofmeyr heads the Policy and Analysis Unit at the Institute for Justice and Reconciliation (IJR), an African think-tank based in Cape Town that conducts research and offers policy advice on post-conflict peace building and state reconstruction across the continent. He has been involved in the development and implementation of both quantitative and qualitative diagnostic tools in the spheres of political and economic governance in various countries, and is currently also the Afrobarometer Survey Research Project's Core Partner Director for Southern Africa. Hofmeyr is a former principal investigator of the IJR's SA Reconciliation Barometer Survey, and editor of its Transformation Audit Publication.

Ana Ljubojević obtained her PhD in Political systems and institutional change at the Institute for Advanced Studies in Lucca, Italy. Her thesis examined the impact of war crime trials on historical narratives in Croatia and Serbia. Currently, she is conducting research within a project on *International Criminal Tribunals as actors of domestic change* at the University of Social Sciences and Humanities in Warsaw, Poland, as well as part of the *Framing the nation* project at the University of Rijeka, Croatia. From October 2015, Ana Ljubojević will be a Newfelpro postdoctoral fellow at the Faculty of Political Sciences in Zagreb, Croatia.

Gjylbehare Bella Murati, is an associated postdoctoral researcher at Human Rights Centre of Gent University in Belgium. She is also a visiting lecturer at the European Inter-University Centre for Human Rights and Democratization in Venice Lido, Italy and lecturer in international public law and human rights law at European College of Law and Governance in Prishtina in Kosovo. She worked as a research fellow at the Max Planck Institute for International Law and Comparative Studies in Heidelberg, Germany and as legal consultant for several international and national institutions, including Ombudsman Office of the Council of Europe, the United Nations Children's Fund (UNICEF), the Office for Missing

Persons and Forensic (OMPF) at the United Nations Mission in Kosovo, the Rehabilitation and Research Centre for Torture Victims in Copenhagen, and the SOROS Foundation. Her research interests include human rights and rule of law in post-conflict societies, accountability of international organizations, extraterritorial application of human rights, and law of armed conflict.

Allan Rutambo Ngari is a Researcher in the Transnational Threats and International Crime Division of the Institute for Security Studies (ISS) in Pretoria, South Africa. His professional and academic interests lie in the international criminal justice system and specifically in its impact on and correlation with national criminal justice systems. Before joining the ISS, Allan worked on a broad range of transitional justice matters at the Institute for Justice and Reconciliation in Cape Town, at Daly and Figgis Advocates in Nairobi, and the Chambers of the International Criminal Tribunal for Rwanda in Arusha, Tanzania. He is an Advocate of the High Court of Kenya and holds a Master's degree in international criminal law from Stellenbosch University, South Africa. He is currently an external PhD researcher with the International Victimology Institute (INTERVICT) at Tilburg University in The Netherlands.

Isabelle Tallec is a programme manager on international criminal justice at the Institute of High Studies on Justice (IHEJ) in Paris and a Ph.D. candidate in political science at the University of Auvergne, France. She's the co-coordinator of the IHEJ's "Forum on International Justice", a watch and exchange network for French-speaking researchers and practitioners in the field. She is currently finishing her thesis entitled "The Institutionalization of International Criminal Justice and Its Impact on State Foreign Policy: French and British Diplomacy and the Implementation of the Rome Statute of the International Criminal Court". Her research focus is on state foreign policy, human rights, and international criminal justice.

Patrick S. Wegner, DPhil, University of Tübingen (Germany). Main field of interest: impact of International Criminal Court investigations on ongoing intrastate conflicts. Author of the monograph *The International Criminal Court in Ongoing Intrastate Conflicts. Navigating the Peace-Justice Divide* (Cambridge University Press 2015).

Index of Names

Studies in Political Transition

Edited by Klaus Bachmann

Vol. 1 Klaus Bachmann: Vergeltung, Strafe Amnestie. Eine vergleichende Studie zu Kollaboration und ihrer Aufarbeitung in Belgien, Polen und den Niederlanden. 2011.

Vol. 2 Klaus Bachmann / Thomas Sparrow-Botero / Peter Lambertz: When Justice Meets Politics. Independence and Autonomy of *Ad Hoc* International Criminal Tribunals. 2013.

Vol. 3 Kim Christiaens / Idesbald Goddeeris / Magaly Rodríguez García (eds.): European Solidarity with Chile 1970s-1980s. 2014.

Vol. 4 Klaus Bachmann / Igor Lyubashenko (eds.): The Maidan Uprising, Separatism and Foreign Intervention. Ukraine´s complex transition. 2014.

Vol. 5 Klaus Bachmann / Dorota Heidrich (eds.): The Legacy of Crimes and Crises. Transitional Justice, Domestic Change and the Role of the International Community. 2016.

www.peterlang.com

www.ingramcontent.com/pod-product-compliance
Ingram Content Group UK Ltd.
Pitfield, Milton Keynes, MK11 3LW, UK
UKHW041827100926
8556IPUK00002B/53

9 783631 661727